bell hooks'
Engaged Pedagogy

Critical Studies in Education and Culture Series

Poststructuralism, Politics and Education
Michael Peters

Weaving a Tapestry of Resistance: The Places, Power, and Poetry of a Sustainable Society
Sharon Sutton

Counselor Education for the Twenty-First Century
Susan J. Brotherton

Positioning Subjects: Psychoanalysis and Critical Educational Studies
Stephen Appel

Adult Students "At-Risk": Culture Bias in Higher Education
Timothy William Quinnan

Education and the Postmodern Condition
Michael Peters, editor

Restructuring for Integrative Education: Multiple Perspectives, Multiple Contexts
Todd E. Jennings, editor

Postmodern Philosophical Critique and the Pursuit of Knowledge in Higher Education
Roger P. Mourad, Jr.

Naming the Multiple: Poststructuralism and Education
Michael Peters, editor

Literacy in the Library: Negotiating the Spaces Between Order and Desire
Mark Dressman

Thinking Again: Education After Postmodernism
Nigel Blake, Paul Smeyers, Richard Smith, and Paul Standish

Racial Categorization of Multiracial Children in Schools
Jane Ayers Chiong

bell hooks'
Engaged Pedagogy

A Transgressive Education for Critical Consciousness

Namulundah Florence

Critical Studies in Education and Culture Series
Edited by Henry A. Giroux

BERGIN & GARVEY
Westport, Connecticut • London

Library of Congress Cataloging-in-Publication Data

Florence, Namulundah, 1958–
    bell hooks' engaged pedagogy : a transgressive education for
critical consciousness / Namulundah Florence.
       p. cm.—Critical studies in education and culture, ISSN
1064–8615)
    Includes bibliographical references (p.) and index.
    ISBN 0–89789–564–9 (alk. paper).—ISBN 0–89789–565–7 (pbk.)
    1. Hooks, Bell. 2. Education—Philosophy. 3. Critical pedagogy.
4. Sexism in education. 5. Discrimination in education.
I. Series: Critical studies in education and culture series.
LB885.H626F56 1998
370′.11′5—DC21   98–11065

British Library Cataloguing in Publication Data is available.

Library of Congress Catalog Card Number: 98–11065
ISBN: 0–89789–564–9
    0–89789–565–7 (pbk.)
ISSN: 1064–8615

First published in 1998   •

Bergin & Garvey, 88 Post Road West, Westport, CT 06881
An imprint of Greenwood Publishing Group, Inc.

Printed in the United States of America

The paper used in this book complies with the
Permanent Paper Standard issued by the National
Information Standards Organization (Z39.48–1984).

10 9 8 7 6 5 4 3

Contents

PART III
Relevance of bell hooks' Educational Theory to a Third-World Context

Series Foreword

Educational reform has fallen upon hard times. The traditional assumption that schooling is fundamentally tied to the imperatives of citizenship designed to educate students to exercise civic leadership and public service has been eroded. The schools are now the key institution for producing professional, technically trained, credentialized workers for whom the demands of citizenship are subordinated to the vicissitudes of the market place and the commercial public sphere. Given the current corporate and right wing assault on public and higher education coupled with the emergence of a moral and political climate that has shifted to a new Social Darwinism, the issues that framed the democratic meaning, purpose, and use to which education might aspire have been displaced by more vocational and narrowly ideological considerations.

The war waged against the possibilities of an education wedded to the precepts of a real democracy is not merely ideological. Against the backdrop of reduced funding for public schooling, the call for privatization, vouchers, cultural uniformity, and choice, there are the often ignored larger social realities of material power and oppression. On the national level, there has been a vast resurgence of racism. This is evident in the passing of anti-immigration laws such as Proposition 187 in California, the dismantling of the welfare state, the demonization of black youth that is taking place in the popular media, and the remarkable attention provided by the media to forms of race talk that argue for the intellectual inferiority of blacks or dismiss calls for racial justice as simply a holdover from the "morally bankrupt" legacy of the 1960s.

Poverty is on the rise among children in the United States, with 20 percent of all children under the age of eighteen living below the poverty line. Unemployment is growing at an alarming rate for poor youth of color, especially in the urban centers. While black youth are policed and disciplined in and out of the nation's schools, conservative and liberal educators define education through the ethically limp discourses of privatization, national standards, and global competitiveness.

Many writers in the critical education tradition have attempted to challenge the right wing fundamentalism behind educational and social reform in both the United States and abroad while simultaneously providing ethical signposts for a public discourse about education and democracy that is both prophetic and transformative. Eschewing traditional categories, a diverse number of critical theorists and educators have successfully exposed the political and ethical implications of the cynicism and despair that has become endemic to the discourse of schooling and civic life. In its place, such educators strive to provide a language of hope that inextricably links the struggle over schooling to understanding and transforming our present social and cultural dangers.

At the risk of overgeneralizing, both cultural studies theorists and critical educators have emphasized the importance of understanding theory as the grounded basis for "intervening into contexts and power . . . in order to enable people to act more strategically in ways that may change their context for the better."[1] Moreover, theorists in both fields have argued for the primacy of the political by calling for and struggling to produce critical public spaces, regardless of how fleeting they may be, in which "popular cultural resistance is explored as a form of political resistance."[2] Such writers have analyzed the challenges that teachers will have to face in redefining a new mission for education, one that is linked to honoring the experiences, concerns, and diverse histories and languages that give expression to the multiple narratives that engage and challenge the legacy of democracy.

Equally significant is the insight of recent critical educational work that connects the politics of difference with concrete strategies for addressing the crucial relationships between schooling and the economy, and citizenship and the politics of meaning in communities of multicultural, multiracial, and multilingual schools.

Critical Studies in Education and Culture attempts to address and demonstrate how scholars working in the fields of cultural studies and critical pedagogy might join together in a radical project and practice informed by theoretically rigorous discourses that affirm the critical but refuse the cynical, and establish hope as central to a critical pedagogical and political practice but eschew a romantic utopianism. Central to such a project is the issue of how pedagogy might provide cultural studies theorists and educators with an opportunity to engage pedagogical practices that are not only transdisciplinary, transgressive, and oppositional, but also connected to a wider project designed to further racial, economic, and political democracy.[3] By taking seriously the relations between culture and power, we further the possibilities of resistance, struggle, and change.

Critical Studies in Education and Culture is committed to publishing work that opens a narrative space that affirms the contextual and the specific while simultaneously recognizing the ways in which such spaces are shot through with issues of power. The series attempts to continue an important legacy of theoretical work in cultural studies in which related debates on pedagogy are understood and addressed within the larger context of social responsibility, civic courage, and the reconstruction of democratic public life. We must keep in mind Raymond Williams's insight that the "deepest impulse (informing cultural politics) is the desire to make learning part of the process of social change itself."[4] Education as a cultural pedagogical practice takes place across multiple sites, which include not only schools and universities but also the mass media, popular culture, and other public spheres, and signals how within diverse contexts, education makes us both subjects of and subject to relations of power.

This series challenges the current return to the primacy of market values and simultaneous retreat from politics so evident in the recent work of educational theorists, legislators, and policy analysts. Professional relegitimation in a troubled time seems to be the order of the day as an increasing number of academics both refuse to recognize public and higher education as critical public spheres and offer little or no resistance to the ongoing vocationalization of schooling, the continuing evisceration of the intellectual labor force, and the current assaults on the working poor, the elderly, and women and children.[5]

Emphasizing the centrality of politics, culture, and power, *Critical Studies in Education and Culture* will deal with pedagogical issues that contribute in imaginative and transformative ways to our understanding of how critical knowledge, democratic values, and social practices can provide a basis for teachers, students, and other cultural workers to redefine their role as engaged and public intellectuals. Each volume will attempt to rethink the relationship between language and experience, pedagogy and human agency, and ethics and social responsibility as part of a larger project for engaging and deepening the prospects of democratic schooling in a multiracial and multicultural society. *Critical Studies in Education and Culture* takes on the responsibility of witnessing and addressing the most pressing problems of public schooling and civic life, and engages culture as a crucial site and strategic force for productive social change.

Henry A. Giroux

NOTES

1. Lawrence Grossberg, "Toward a Genealogy of the State of Cultural Studies," in Cary Nelson and Dilip Parameshwar Gaonkar, eds. *Disciplinarity and Dissent in Cultural Studies* (New York: Routledge, 1996), p. 143.

2. David Bailey and Stuart Hall, "The Vertigo of Displacement," *Ten 8* 2:3 (1992), p. 19.

3. My notion of transdisciplinary comes from Mas'ud Zavarzadeh and Donald Morton, "Theory, Pedagogy, Politics: The Crisis of the 'Subject' in the Humanities," in *Theory Pedagogy Politics: Texts for Change*, Mas'ud Zavarzadeh and Donald Morton, eds. (Urbana: University of Illinois Press, 1992), p. 10. At issue here is neither ignoring the boundaries of discipline-based knowledge nor simply fusing different disciplines, but creating theoretical paradigms, questions, and knowledge that cannot be taken up within the policed boundaries of the existing disciplines.

4. Raymond Williams, "Adult Education and Social Change," in *What I Came to Say* (London: Hutchinson-Radus, 1989), p. 158.

5. The term "professional legitimation" comes from a personal correspondence with Professor Jeff Williams of East Carolina University.

Acknowledgments

There is always so much to be grateful for in life, and so many people to be thankful for that in mentioning names one always risks the sin of omission. My gratitude goes to Marie C. Nelson, The Babes, Dr. John L. Elias and Dr. Clement London, whose love and support give me the courage to work for a better tomorrow. I am also indebted to Dr. Amy L. Reynolds, Dr. Barbara L. Jackson and Dr. Robert J. Starratt for their insights and support in the research process. I thank my *people*, especially my mother, Namaemba Muhindi Lyambila, and all the women on whose shoulders I stand. I thank bell hooks, *Omwana wa mayi*, for providing a springboard for my questions and aspirations. This work is dedicated to the people of my race, my gender, and my class.

Prologue

bell hooks

This section provides a brief background on the person of bell hooks. Gloria Watkins writes under the pseudonym of "bell hooks." She claimed the name bell hooks to honor a self-actualized great grandmother who withstood the racism, sexism, and classism of her time:

> a sharp tongued woman, a woman who spoke her mind, a woman who was not afraid to talk back. I claimed this legacy of defiance, of will, of courage, affirming my link to female ancestors who were bold and daring in their speech. (hooks, 1989a, p. 9)

She was born in Hopkinsville, Kentucky, in 1952 and educated at all-Black public schools—Booker T. Washington and Crispus Attucks. She received her bachelor's degree from Stanford University and attended Yale before receiving her Ph.D. from the University of California in Santa Cruz. hooks held the position of associate professor for three years in the African American Studies Department at Yale, spent a year with the African Studies program at City College of New York, worked as professor of English and Women's Studies at Oberlin College, and is currently (1998) teaching Women's and African American Studies at City College of New York in the Department of English. hooks is a prolific author. Besides the numerous articles submitted to scholarly publications and mainstream magazines, hooks has written sixteen books in the last eighteen years. She is also a popular speaker at college campuses and community forums all across the country. Her writings, articles, speeches, and interviews, in different ways and to different degrees, critique racism, sexism, and classism in American society. Building on the personal to address public/political issues, hooks draws upon her own personal experiences in the South, her involvement in the feminist movement, and currently, her position in the academy to support her critique of the social and educational system.

bell hooks proposes an engaged pedagogy to counteract the overwhelming boredom, disinterest, and apathy that so often characterize the way professors and students feel about the teaching and learning experience. hooks attributes student alienation in schools to discriminatory racist, sexist, and classist policies and practices in educational settings and the wider society. This study is a critical analysis of bell hooks' engaged pedagogy, its basis, challenge, and promise for the teaching/learning process. This study also assesses the relevance of bell hooks' critique of prevailing society and constructive strategies entailed in engaged pedagogy to a Third World context.

The analysis of hooks' writings provides a basis for her contention regarding educational policies and practices—curriculum and pedagogy—reflecting and perpetuating hierarchical social arrangements by reinforcing White supremacist, patriarchal, and capitalistic values in both the United States and the Kenyan system. bell hooks' engaged pedagogy (1994c), explicated in *Teaching to Transgress: Education as the Practice of Freedom*, goes beyond developing students to achieve a prescribed level of literacy, the development of professional skills and/or conformity to the status quo, to nurture a reflective and critical stance to social realities. The pedagogy calls for a re-conceptualization of the knowledge base, linking theory to practice, student empowerment, multiculturalism, and incorporation of passion, to make learning more engaging and meaningful. Engaged pedagogy is a "transgressive" pedagogy. The relevance of hooks' social and educational critique to the Kenyan economy is based on four primary similarities between Kenya and the United States: (a) presence of Blacks, (b) the impact of White civilization, (c) the patriarchal system, and (d) the association of social prestige to material acquisitions.

hooks' writings provide a glimpse of the kind of person she is: intellectual, direct, feminist in view, provocative, informative, passionate, and engaging. Currently a distinguished professor of English at the City of New York University, hooks is well known for her forthright social and cultural critique on racism and sexism. Breaking new ground, hooks, a Black woman from a materially underprivileged background, infiltrates the vanguard of White materially privileged males to analyze issues of race, sex, and power. hooks

questions cultural structures and the implications of social policies and practices. She brings to public debate issues typically confined to elitist circles and
scholarly journals. The personal is political. By connecting individual beliefs
and choices with structural dominations, hooks demonstrates our complicity
in structures that oppress. Similarly, hooks links efforts at self-actualization to
collective liberation struggles. Speaking boldly against a culture of lies and
domination, hooks disqualifies the association of "diplomacy" and "political
correctness" to a lack of intellectual sophistication and/or social etiquette.

Transgress is a term she proposed and one she embodies. Typically, *transgress*
has negative connotations (hooks, 1995a). *The Random House Dictionary of
the English Language* (Urdang, 1968) defines the term *transgress* as a breach of
boundary or limit, going beyond the limits imposed by a moral code, to
infringe, break, or go against. *Transgression* is not only positive but also crucial
in the development of one's self-determination and self-actualization, most
especially for members of marginalized groups. hooks (1995a) associates
transgress with moving past boundaries, the right to choice, to truth telling and
critical consciousness, the right to recognize limitations, the shift of paradigms,
and the desire to "know" beyond what is readily perceptible. Cornel West
contends:

> bell hooks's unique contribution to intellectual life, American letters and
> Black thought is that of producing a challenging corpus of work which
> proposes a singular human struggle to be candid about one's self and
> contestatory toward the dehumanizing forces in the world. Her work
> sings a polyphonic "song of the great composite democratic individual"
> yearning for a principled connectedness that promotes the distinctive
> self-development of each and everyone of us. And she sings this song in
> the antiphonal, syncopated, and rhythmic forms bequeathed to her by
> her African foremothers and forefathers who refused to be silent in a
> strange land of pharaonic treatment. Sing on, bell, sing on! (hooks &
> West, 1991, pp. 62–63)

hooks' life (1994c) is a testimony to the resilience of the human spirit, one's
ability to overcome adversaries. hooks attributes her resilience of spirit to role
models like the Latin American Liberation theologian Gustavo Gutierrez, the
Brazilian Paulo Freire, Lorraine Hansberry, Buddhist monk Thich Nhat Hanh,
James Baldwin, Malcolm X, Martin Luther King, Jr., and her great grandmother Bell Hooks. She also attributes her hope for life-giving communities
to the Christian and Buddhist religious traditions. hooks notes that her

[E]arliest models for black intellectual life were not academics; they were writers, specifically Lorraine Hansberry and James Baldwin. . . . These writers were readers, thinkers, political activists, committed to education for critical consciousness; they were individuals exuding radical openness. . . . Their openness to ideas, to engaging in critical dialogue with diverse audiences, set a powerful example. (1994b, p. 229)

hooks seems to have truly taken to heart her proposal for openness to learning. Speaking to theoretical standards in academia that perpetuate domination, elitism, and classism, hooks maintains: "Despite [their] uses as instruments of domination, [these] may also contain important ideas, thoughts, visions, that could, if used differently, serve as a healing, liberatory function" (1994c, p. 65). She distinguishes critical interrogation from the dismissal of insights from "biased" sources. hooks (1994c) comfortably draws on Freire's insights (1970/1992, 1973) in spite of the sexist language in his earlier works. In an interview with Gary Olson, hooks commends Freire's commitment to critical literacy, choosing to overlook the sexist elements in his writing, taking what is nurturing from his work:

I was like a person dying of thirst when I first came to Paulo, and the fact that there was some mud in my water was not important. I thought of his sexism as being like specks of dirt or mud because my need was so great. I was able to take what was nurturing to me and be more compassionate toward the aspect that was threatening. (Olson, 1994, p. 93)

Freire's work and her early experience of school in a Black community enables hooks to affirm her right as "subject" in spite of the oppressive forces of racism, sexism, and classism, and to articulate an educational pedagogy that seeks to develop and nurture critical consciousness in both teachers and students.

hooks' corpus of writings expresses the struggle for survival in a racist, sexist, and classist society. The pain of her marginality and oppression of spirit echoes the pain of any who has dared to claim an identity beyond cultural designations. It is a fight against hierarchical social arrangements maintained by well-meaning family members, friends, and foes. It is truly a journey through uncharted paths. It is a lonely journey. Loneliness pervades hooks' body of work. She recounts her experiences as an outsider—one who knows that what is, ought not to be. The feeling of loneliness persists in her adulthood:

Loneliness brings me to the edge of what I know. My soul is dark like
the inner world of the cave—bone black. I have been drowning in that
blackness. . . . I never tell anyone how much I want to belong. . . . At
night when everyone is silent and everything is still, I lie in the darkness
of my windowless room, the place where they exile me from the community of their heart, and search the unmoving blackness to see if I can
find my way home. (hooks, 1996a, p. 183)

It is understandable that hooks castigates the appropriation of the experience
of marginality by the privileged in writings. The pain of her marginality, the
pain her writings so clearly manifest, is truly unique. One has to have
experienced marginality to fully appreciate the significance of its negation and
the impact of subjugation.

hooks (1990; hooks & West, 1991) advocates communities of solidarity in
the struggle toward mutual growth, a recognition of differences as opposed to
the suppression of dissenting voices. Institutions can be alienating—schools,
churches, and other bureaucratic organizations. The alienation is typically
attributed to the largeness of the organization. In institutional settings, individual concerns get subordinated to the group's interests and objectives. Homes
ought to provide refuge from alienating factors in the wider society. Though
hooks (1990) primarily addresses the needs of the Black community while
Mary Leen (1995) focuses on Native American concerns, both note the
significance of "homeplace" to marginalized individuals:

It was about the construction of a safe place where black people could
affirm one another and by so doing heal many of the wounds inflicted
by racist domination. We could not learn to love or respect ourselves in
the culture of white supremacy, on the outside; it was there on the inside,
in that "homeplace," most created and kept by black women that we had
the opportunity to grow and develop, to nurture out spirits. (hooks,
1990, p. 42)

However, even in homes, the choice not to conform to cultural norms and
expectations leads hooks to a sense of alienation. hooks notes the alienation
she felt in her own home:

A dark room with no windows, cold in winter, cool in summer, it is her
place of refuge and recovery. The tensions of high school, family, friend-
ship can be released there. She can hide from the loneliness inside. She
can pretend. . . . To them she is the problem child, the source of all pain.

Everyone else gets along well. She is the one who is no fun, who makes trouble . . . . She cries about not being able to do anything right, about not fitting in, about being unfairly punished. (1996a, pp. 109–110)

Finally, hooks' invocation of religious concepts—Christian and Buddhist— is not one of cursory knowledge. She appears to be steeped in the traditions of Christian living and holistic spirituality, readily admitting to her religious convictions:

When I think of the Christian narratives that formed my own upbring- ing . . . I say to people, you know, I didn't go to thinkers like Gutierrez to learn about liberation theology because I had internalized the chapter in Matthew which said, "Unless you give to the least of these you haven't given to me," in Sunday School. (hooks & West, 1991, p. 53)

She attributes the ability of members of the Black community to survive the assault of racial discrimination to their spirituality. The religious experience sustained Black people's contact with the Divine goodness, as well as bound them to each other in love and support. Further, her vision of pedagogical orientations that promote holistic growth for culturally and materially privi- leged and marginalized individuals arises from her involvement in various religious traditions. Linking spirituality and the process of freedom to teaching, hooks contends that a broader concept of teaching

comes easiest to those of us who teach who also believe that there is an aspect of our vocation that is sacred; who believe that our work is not merely to share information but to share in the intellectual and spiritual growth of our students. (1994c, p. 13)

hooks' writings address Buddhist and Christian terminology such as: indi- vidual fulfillment, teaching as a vocation, importance of truth telling, signifi- cance of contemplation/self-reflection, conversion and self-renewal, dialogue, love, care, reconciliation, and spirituality. However, she also employs human- istic ideals such as: appreciation of self over and above culturally negating messages, call to solidarity and a respect of humanity, and communitarian over an individualistic competitive consumerism. Overall, hooks' advocacy for a communal responsibility for the underprivileged echoes the Christian "option for the poor," and invocation of notions of right living from Buddhist monk Thich Nhat Hanh. She affirms liberatory religious tradition and notes that these ideologies espouse solidarity with the poor that is expressed not simply through charity, the sharing of privilege, but in the assertion of one's power to change the world so that the poor would have their needs met, would have access to resources, would have justice and beauty in their lives. (1994b, p. 168)

One almost expects her to make the argument that all persons, irrespective of race, class, and/or sex, are equal before God!

The following discussion presents a brief analysis of her writing style.

hooks' Writing Style

In her writings, hooks makes references to the insights she has drawn from the works of Paulo Freire (1970/1992, 1973; Freire & Faundez, 1989) and her experiences with Buddhism to demonstrate the inextricable link between theory and practice, contemplation and action. hooks reiterates again and again the need for marginalized groups to acknowledge and seek to confront their marginality. Supporting hooks' contention, John Champagne (1993) advocates marginalized groups to create oppositional explanations of texts that explore different ways of being and provide alternatives to prevailing unjust social practices. hooks advocates colonized people to develop strategies for decolonizing their minds in order to fully appreciate their humanity and ability to "make" history. hooks' link of marginality in a First World to colonized peoples provides a rationale for exploring the relevance of hooks' social and educational critique, and reconstructive strategies to a Third World context.

hooks' choice of writing format (1994c; hooks & West, 1991) has limited the use of her books in higher institutes of learning. The absence of footnotes and/or page citations within a text demands of research scholars a familiarity with individual texts to facilitate follow-up on her citations. hooks (1994b, 1994c) readily admits that employing popular language causes contention with particular publishers. She contends:

Marginalized groups may lack the inclination to engage in certain ways of thinking and writing because we learn early that such work may not be recognized or valued . . . or we are told by gatekeepers, usually white, often male, that it will be better for us to write and think in a more conventional way. (1990, p. 129)

hooks maintains that her choice about footnotes was very much a choice informed by questions of class, access, and literacy levels rather than a simple devaluation of footnotes or shoddy, careless scholarship (hooks & West, 1991).

Michele Wallace, however, vehemently discounts hooks' rationale for not employing standard writing practices:

> The absence of footnotes and appropriate documentation is more annoying than usual. I don't buy hooks' "empowering the uneducated" line. The only person being empowered by her failure to use footnotes and bibliography is her. Footnotes and bibliographies take extra time to prepare and cost more money. Not only that, the reader might have a better idea of when hooks, herself, is "eating the other." (1995a, p. 8)

The poly-vocality in her writings attests to the value of employing nonjargonistic language to more adequately address an audience beyond the academy (hooks, 1992, 1994b; hooks & West, 1991). hooks (1994c) claims to have purposely used a writing style that makes her work more accessible to the general public:

> In my daily life practice as a teacher, writer, and activist, I work hard to find ways of sharing feminist thinking, black liberation struggle, with diverse groups of people, not just those who are involved in academic institutions. (1993, p. 4)

hooks' artistry in employing the many voices she speaks, "academic talk, standard English, vernacular patois, the language of the street" (hooks, 1994b, p. 7), is in itself is a commendable venture.

In raising contentious issues in schools and society, hooks typically adopts a blunt and confrontational, rather than conventional, diplomatic, or "politically correct," approach. In the violence of her criticisms, one wonders whether hooks does not alienate the very people she purports to speak for and wishes to attract, people who belong to the social, racial, and economic groups she sharply critiques. Wallace (1995a, 1995b) is relentless in her disapproval of hooks' incisive and uncharitable critiques toward members of privileged groups, ignoring the position she adopts in the process. hooks' double standards are inexcusable:

> For instance, in an essay called "Black Intellectuals" in *Killing Rage*, while she claims for herself an exemplary humility, simplicity, open-mindedness, and commitment to revolutionary struggle, she also distances herself from the rank and file of black intellectuals. (1995b, p. 21)

Notwithstanding the harshness of hooks' critiques to which she readily admits, her approach is probably the most effective way to draw attention to the urgency of issues most would rather ignore or gloss over. hooks' candid writing approach communicates the significance and urgency of the issues—racism, sexism, and classism—to marginalized groups.

Avoiding the dichotomy between the "objective" and "subjective," hooks' writings, interviews, and speeches highlight the link between the personal and the political, as she draws upon her own experiences and those of other Black women to illustrate the impact of racism, sexism, and classism. That hooks (1984, 1994b, 1994c, 1995b) typically connects the private to the public, personal experiences to the broader concerns of racism, sexism, and classism, could deflect the reader's attention from the more important and wide-reaching issues central to her essays. From Wallace's assessment, the practice antagonizes readers. Wallace maintains that the practice borders on narcistic exhibitionism.

> Constantly, citing her experiences of child abuse at the hands of her family, physical abuse by her former boyfriend, as well as the "racist" and/or "sexist" reaction of the "white feminist" and/or "black male" and/or "white supremacist patriarchal" establishment, she epitomizes the cult of victimization that Shelby Steele, Stanley Crouch, and Jerry Watts have written about so persuasively. (1995b, p. 23)

However, hooks (1994b) critiques the separation of "public" from "private" matters, associating the practice to dominations and/or dualisms in society. Living a life of "truth" avoids the necessity of unnecessary "privacy" and/or shame in one's convictions, choices, and actions. Further, the approach demonstrates the link between individual choices and collective practices. West sums it up well in his observation that hooks' books

> [H]elp us not only to decolonize our minds, souls, and bodies; on a deeper level, they touch our lives. It is difficult to read a bell hooks essay or text without enacting some form of self-examination or self-inventory. . . . She puts the flowering of Black women's possibilities and potentialities at the center of her work yet she refuses to view this flowering apart from the freedom of Black men. Her unflinching stance against patriarchal, class, imperial, and homophobic practices is rooted in a conviction that embraces the Black progressive communities. (hooks & West, 1991, p. 62)

It is understandable that Cornel West notes the response to bell hooks' writings as the call to self-examination and self-inventory. hooks continually challenges the reader to a reflective stance of day-to-day activities and choices, as opposed to perpetuating ideologies unconsciously by choices that fail to interrogate debilitating myths and dominations.

Outline of Book

The book is divided into three major parts. Part I presents bell hooks' social theory, as expressed in her critique of capitalism, patriarchy, and White supremacy in American society. The part establishes the impact of these different forms of discrimination on marginalized peoples from hooks' corpus of works to establish her social theory. hooks' writing demonstrates that commonly institutions insidiously maintain and promote particular norms, racial, sex, and class discriminatory practices. First, she maintains that both historical and contemporary factors in the United States have insidiously reinforced the superiority of White people by idealizing White people's cultural histories, and presenting their cultural traits and characteristics—manner in speech, habits of behavior, standards of beauty and success—as the norm. The process reinforces the superiority of White people over non-White cultural groups. Second, hooks, similar to feminist scholars, raises the issue of the subordination of female-related traits and characteristics by the mass media in educational settings and the wider society. She also contends that sexist discrimination is heightened in the case of Black women due to their racial identity. Third, hooks contends that middle- and/or upper-class norms and values are reinforced in educational settings through teacher/student interactions, and manner of speech and behavior sanctioned in educational settings. She notes that students from materially underprivileged backgrounds find it necessary to adopt a demeanor of privilege in order to be deemed "acceptable." The part explores the manner in which the above discriminatory factors are manifested in educational settings and the wider society.

Part II presents hooks' educational theory in its critique of the curriculum and teaching practices. The analysis of her educational theory is primarily based on her 1994 book, *Teaching to Transgress: Education as the Practice of Freedom.* Engaged pedagogy espouses a combination of anticolonial, critical, and feminist principles that enable an interrogation of biases in curricula that reinscribe systems of dominations while simultaneously providing new ways to teach diverse groups of students (hooks, 1994c). hooks terms the overall aim of this liberatory aspect of education "critical awareness and engagement," what Freire (1970/1992, 1973) calls *conscientization.* She urges educators to "transgress" the conventional approaches to the teaching/learning process by envisioning new modes of interaction in order to make education a "freeing" experience. Developing and nurturing critical consciousness in students provides them with ways of knowing that enable them to know themselves better and live in the world more fully. In sum, hooks (1994c) contends that education as the practice of freedom extends the teaching role beyond the mere sharing of information to a more holistic involvement with students. Engaged pedagogy provides the necessary forum to address this very need.

Part III establishes the relevance of bell hooks' critique of prevailing dominations in school practices and society at large, and recommendations arising from engaged pedagogy to a broader audience and to a Third World context. hooks (1994c) attributes the basis of her social theory and critique of American educational policies and practices on insights drawn from Freire's (1970/1992, 1973) analysis and critique of literacy programs in Brazil. Freire proposed a pedagogy for the oppressed to counteract pedagogies that mirrored and perpetuated the status quo. The author reverses the process yet again in seeking the relevance of a First World critique to a Third World context. Being a theoretical inquiry, the author's analysis of the relevance of hooks' social and educational critique to the Kenyan economy draws from literature on Kenya regarding race, gender, and class biases in educational settings and the wider society.

Part III is divided into an introduction and four chapters. The introductory section presents Kenya's cultural/tribal composition and related national statistics. Chapters 10 and 11 establish the relevance of bell hooks' critique of the United States to the Kenyan economy. This discussion involves a cursory exploration of the impact of colonization in promoting White supremacist values and attitudes, the effect of cultural patriarchal attitudes and practices on women, the manifestation of a capitalistic mentality, and the impact of tribal pluralism. Chapter 12 explores the relevance of the components of bell hooks' engaged pedagogy to educational policies and practices in Kenya. In Chapter 13, the author contends that in view of Kenya's colonial history, hooks' critique of an alienating curriculum and school culture can be applied to the Kenyan education context.

bell hooks'
Engaged Pedagogy

PART I

bell hooks' Social Theory

This part explores bell hooks' social theory (1981, 1984, 1989b, 1990, 1992, 1993, 1994b, 1994c, 1995b; hooks & West, 1991) to provide a basis for her educational theory. The transformational strategies in hooks' proposed educational theory, engaged pedagogy, address ideological elements embedded in a White supremacist, patriarchal, and capitalist society. These ideological elements are routinely mirrored and maintained in educational contexts (Feinberg & Soltis, 1992; McLaren, 1994; Morrow & Torres, 1995; Perkinson, 1991; Popkewitz, 1991; Starratt, 1995). hooks and the above-mentioned scholars contend that in spite of the goodwill expressed in institutional ideals, commonly insidious elements still maintain and promote particular racial, gender, and class biases. In this context, hooks critiques the work of Diana Fuss for overlooking the fact "that racism, sexism, and class elitism shape the structure of classrooms, creating a lived reality of insider versus outsider that is predetermined, often in place before any class discussion begins" (hooks, 1994c, p. 83). Given the seemingly predetermined inequalities, marginality of particular students is further exacerbated when for purposes of assimilation, students of color adopt dominant cultural attitudes and values, subordinating their primary cultural values not reflected in prevailing social structures (hooks, 1989b).

The following discussion provides a basis for hooks' view of society as racist, sexist, and classist. First, critical, feminist, and multicultural theoretical arguments to support hooks' observations and critique of American society are examined. Since hooks' corpus of writings addresses the issue of marginality with particular reference to Black people's experience in America, discussions on matters of race, class, and/or gender discrimination derive primarily from a Black person's perspective in a dominantly White cultural milieu. Second, the part explores discriminatory factors under the categories of race, gender, and class. However, as the predicament of Black women demonstrates, individuals may fall under one or more of these, which may heighten the impact of discrimination. Similarly, the degree of discrimination is lessened in Black men on the basis of class and gender and in White women on the basis of class and racial identity (hooks, 1981, 1984, 1989a). Third, hooks' basic critique of schools is included in the part essentially because schools are so intricately linked to prevailing social forces. The following part on hooks' educational theory provides a more expansive discussion on the role of schools in either perpetuating discriminatory practices or critiquing biases of race, class, and gender.

hooks (1989a, 1990) cautions against an essentialist assessment of the impact of racism on Blacks and sexism on females. It is essential to factor in status, race, and class in assessing impact of discrimination on women and Blacks. Supporting hooks' contention, John Champagne (1993) and Harvey Siegel (1995) maintain that essentialism ignores differences in degrees and forms of marginality within groupings. In a feminist context:

> Race and/or class [ought to be] seen as factors determining the
> social construction of one's gendered reality and most importantly,
> the extent to which one will suffer exploitation and domination.
> (hooks, 1989a, p. 32)

In a White supremacist society, White women experience certain privileges by virtue of their racial identity. Similarly, class determines the degree of racial and gender exploitation of individual Black women. Further, patriarchy provides Black men with privilege, however relative (hooks, 1990, 1992).

> Employing a critique of essentialism allows African-Americans to
> acknowledge the way in which class mobility has altered collective

black experience so that racism does not necessarily have the same impact on our lives. (hooks, 1990, p. 28)

As further discussions will illustrate, the interlocking nature of dominations in society add to the complexity of analyzing issues of race, gender, and class dominations as distinct categories. There is bound to be an overlap in the analysis of each discriminatory factor. The following discussion analyzes racism, sexism, and classism in this respective order to highlight elements pertaining to particular factors. The part also highlights the manner in which White supremacy is reinforced by the mass media and social norms and practices.

CHAPTER 1

Racism

bell hooks' personal experiences, shared in her writings, demonstrate the impact of White supremacy within her own family, in educational settings as well as the wider society. At a young age, hooks (1996a) was aware of the impact of White supremacy on Black people's lives despite the limited social contact between Black and White people. She recalls the lessons at school—pictures of naked Africans portrayed as savages in geography classes. Scant attention was paid to the term *race* despite its centrality to the students' lives. hooks demonstrates that as children, she, her brother, and five sisters understood without being told that the

> world is more a home for white folks than it is for anyone else, that black people who most resemble white folks will live better lives in that world. They have a grandmother who looks white who lives on a street where all the other white people are white. (1996a, p. 31)

Segregation dehumanizes by virtue of its exclusionary process. However beneficial the experience of attending all-Black schools, hooks notes the absence of choice for Black children bused past White people's schools:

> Because we were poor, because we lived in the country, we go to the country school—the little white wood-frame building where all the country kids come. They come from miles and miles away. They come

so far because they are black. As they are riding the school buses they pass school after school where children who are white can attend without being bused, without getting up in the wee hours of the morning, sometimes leaving home in the dark. (1996a, p. 5)

It was an experience hooks (1994c) was to personally experience with the school desegregation policy. hooks recalls the rage at the time. She too was forced to awaken earlier than she normally would have, to the convenience of White children in the schools.

hooks' writings highlight three main ways in which racism is expressed and perpetuated in society: mass media, White people's attitudes and discriminatory acts towards non-Whites, and the internalization and perpetuation of these attitudes and acts between and among non-White people. hooks' conceptualization and critique (1989a) of White supremacist attitudes and values is directed not only toward White people but also against Black people's complicity in upholding and maintaining racial hierarchies whether consciously or otherwise. Black people's complicity in discriminatory attitudes and practices is the subject of analysis later in the chapter.

Mass Media

In all her writings hooks highlights the role of mass media in the construction of social images.

Whether we like it or not, cinema assume a pedagogical role in the lives of many people. It may not be intent of a filmmaker to teach audiences anything, but that does not mean that lessons are not learned. (1996b, p. 2)

She further illustrates the politics of mass media

as the biggest propaganda machine for white supremacy, the socialization of everyone to subliminally absorb white supremacist attitudes and values . . . [saturating people's minds and structures] with an ideology of difference that says white is always, in every way, superior to that which is black. (1995b, pp. 116–117)

Mass media not only entertain and educate viewers but also, in the process, communicate definitions and frameworks for interpretation of social reality, social status of different roles, positions, and cultural groupings. hooks (1992) discusses the impact of mass media from two main angles. First, mass media reinforce White supremacy in presenting White people's values and traditions as mainstream norms. Second, negative imagery of non-White people reinforces their marginality in society:

> While superficially appearing to present a portrait of racial social equality, mass media actually work to reinforce assumptions that black folks should always be cast in supporting roles in relation to white characters. That subordination is made to appear "natural" because most black characters are consistently portrayed as a little less ethical and moral than whites, not given to rational reasonable action. (hooks, 1995b, pp. 114–115)

Supporting hooks' assessment on the significance of mass media in construction of social consciousness, David Trend (1994) notes that mass media shapes national identity. He ranks its influence higher than that of schools, church, and the family. Essentially, reinforced values readily translate to conventional norms in the viewer's consciousness. Modeling White people's values and attitudes to the exclusion and/or subordination of differing cultural groupings' qualities in a pluralistic society, which America is, serves a prescriptive function:

> Opening a magazine or book, turning on the TV set, watching a film, or looking at photographs in public places, we are most likely to see images of black people that reinforce and reinscribe white supremacy. (hooks 1992, p. 1)

Similar in impact to magazines and books, movies provide opportunity both to reimagine as well as to make culture. hooks points to the political implications of movies such as *Lethal Weapon* (1987), *Grand Canyon* (1991), and *Rising Sun* (1993):

> Socializing, via images by a pedagogy of white supremacy, young whites who see such "innocent" images of black males eagerly affirming white male superiority come to expect this behavior in real life. . . . The message that black males receive is that, to succeed, one must be self-effacing and consumed by a politics of envy and longing for white male power. (1996b, p. 88)

bell hooks critiques mass media reductionism in its caricature presentation of people and events. Biased representations and the oversimplification of human processes promote false consciousness. The process pacifies even as it disempowers. As Richard Ohmann surmises, the stereotypical presentation of groups ensures that their "presence is marginalized, and without reproach because impotent" (1996, p. 259). Deluded into a false consciousness and subjugated with simplistic and ready-made solutions to human dilemmas, individuals consider existing hierarchical social arrangements natural and inevitable and uncritically accept dominant cultural norms as universal standards.

Typically stereotypes of cultural groupings in mass media present caricatures rather than a comprehensive understanding of the people. The process denies the complexity in deciphering the motives, beliefs, and choices of any human being irrespective of race, gender, and/or class. Reductionism and reification of social reality oversimplifies human processes, situations or choices. In real life, privilege or misfortune are not unique to any one cultural group, at least not genetically. By the same token, human qualities such as assertiveness, affectivity, aggression, and sensitivity are not unique to any cultural grouping. The truth is, men are not always paternal or aggressive and women are not all maternal or considerate. Children may, but do not always, obey their parents. Some unruly children come from stable homes. Family tensions rarely get resolved in a half-hour, the average length of an American situation comedy.

hooks contends that it is "within the commercial realm of advertising that the drama of Otherness finds expression. Encounters with Otherness are clearly marked as more exciting, more intense, and more threatening" (1992, p. 26). Making a similar contention regarding the impact of TV on values and life-styles, Chester Mills and Rebecca Caisson argue that if

> one group is made to look superior to or better than another group, the second group would most likely emulate the first group. . . . When minority women watch TV, they see that racial identity is connected to certain ornaments, specific looks, and specific behavior that exclude them. This exclusion has a greater impact on children because children become vulnerable and are made to feel as if they do not fit the TV image (1996, p. 123).

Mark Miller's analysis of the Jamaican tourism advertisements provide a poignant illustration:

> These Jamaicans grin differentially (and with perfect teeth) at the camera, their clothes recall the slaves' wardrobe in *Gone With the Wind*—no stark rags or dreadlocks here. . . . From beginning to end, the commercial plays

brilliantly on the repressed fears and desires of white consumers, and even hints at darker, more general longings. It subtly excites those fears in order to allay them, thereby countering the viewers' misgivings before they surface into consciousness (p. 33).

However, while the Jamaican tourist advertisement exploits the semi-primitive, docile indigent, the Kenyan tourist advertisements eroticize the native and primitive—a caricature of African culture commodified and packaged for tourist consumption. The wild lions run free (never does the advertisement suggest the danger of these roaming lions). Safari mini tours drive through the National Park unharmed. The animals seem subdued in such a presence as they lie tame and enthralled by the activity. The driver would be indigenous, and therefore invisible. The focus is on the tourists, their backpacks, and surrounding wild animals (Ngugi Wa Thiong'o, 1993). The whole picture is reminiscent of the biblical creation story with Adam as master of the wild.

Mass media's frequent imaging of Blacks as social misfits, welfare dependents, and being cast in servant or subordinate roles, reinforces Black subordination to White cultural groups (hooks, 1990, 1992, 1994b, 1995b). Thus, mass media often offer debilitating imagery that fails to adequately represent Black people's identity and concerns, and subsequently undermines their ability for self-actualization and determination (hooks, 1995b). The representations of Black men as more violent and/or economical and psychological misfits and Black women as sexually available and licentious or matriarchs serve a prescriptive function in the way society perceives and treats Black people (hooks, 1981, 1990, 1992):

> Images of black men as rapists, as dangerous menaces to society have been sensational cultural agency for some time. The role it plays in the maintenance of racist domination is to convince the public that black men are a dangerous threat who must be controlled by any means necessary including annihilation. (hooks, 1990, p. 61)

Attributing lack of economic success in Blacks to genetic inferiority justifies social inequalities and the status quo in promoting the fallacy of equal opportunity and democracy (hooks, 1994b, 1995b). By implication, assimilation and/or social success for dominated cultural groups necessitates adoption of the dominant culture's traits and characteristics (hooks, 1992, 1994b, 1995b). Mass media sanction White people's values and attitudes, providing a rationale for why White people's perspective serves as normative on most matters in the American public life (hooks, 1994b, 1995b):

The message that television sends then is that the problem of racism lies with black people—that it exists in our mindset and imaginations. . . . Television does not hold white people responsible for white supremacy; it socializes them to believe that subjugation and subordination of black people by any means necessary is essential for the maintenance of law and order. Such thinking informed the vision of white folks who looked at the tape showing the brutal beating of Rodney King by a group of white men and saw a scenario where he was threatening white lives and they were merely keeping the peace. (hooks, 1995b, p. 112)

The impact of a White supremacist ideology is evident in some Black people's uncritical allegiance to White people's values and standards, and negative feelings and attitudes about Blackness (hooks, 1989a).

When black psyches are daily bombarded by mass media representations that encourage us to see white people as more caring, intelligent, liberal, etc., it makes sense that many of us internalize racist thinking. (hooks, 1995b, p. 117)

Living in a culture that devalues Blackness, Blacks are socialized into a hatred of self and fellow Black people and/or attributes (hooks, 1981, 1992, 1994b, 1995b).

Both African and Native Americans have been deeply affected by the degrading representations of red and black people that continue to be the dominant images projected by movies and television, portrayed as cowardly, cannibalistic, uncivilized, the images of "Indians" mirror screen images of Africans. . . . [M]ost people . . . do not think about the way these images cause pain and grief. (hooks, 1992, p. 186)

Reiterating hooks' observation regarding popular cultural stereotypes, Sandra McNaught (1996) cites Edward W. Said (1978), Wernick (1991), West (1991), Williams (1991), Pierterse (1992), and Culburston (1995) to illustrate the conventional link between one's moral/ethic, intellectual character to skin color and ethnicity.

The ideological nature of mass media necessitates a critical analysis and detachment to conventional cultural representations. It is hooks' contention that "Cultural criticism has historically functioned in black and white life as a force promoting critical resistance . . . that would disrupt and even deconstruct those cultural productions that were designed to promote and reinforce

domination" (1990, p. 3). She cites Malcolm X's promotion and encouragement of the "development of a critical black gaze . . . one that would be able
to move beyond passive consumption and be fiercely confronting, challenging,
interrogating" (1994b, p. 156). However, hooks (1992) also demonstrates that
movies directed by Black people, such as *School Daze* and *She's Gotta Have It*,
still reinscribe traditional White supremacist patriarchal capitalism—lighter
skinned over darker skinned actors and male over female interests. In essence,
not all movies by Black directors challenge the status quo (hooks, 1990, 1992).
To counteract the debilitating impact of mass media on marginalized groups,
especially Blacks, hooks contends:

> Everyone must break through the wall of denial that would have us
> believe a hatred of blackness emerges from troubled individual psyches
> and acknowledge that it is systematically taught through processes of
> socialization in white supremacist society. We must acknowledge, too,
> that black folks who have internalized white supremacist attitudes and
> values are as much agents of this socialization as their racist nonblack
> counterparts. (1994b, pp. 181–182)

hooks' writings highlight the ideological nature of mass media by demon-
strating the impact of mass media on social consciousness with particular
reference to cultural representation. The negative imagery of Blacks and
Black-related traits and characteristics reinforces the superiority of "Whiteness"
to which "Blackness" is usually contrasted. Further, in promoting negative
stereotypes of Black people—dependent, less ethical—mass media have had a
significant impact on the way Blacks are perceived and treated in the United
States. Notwithstanding negative representation of Black men and women in
mass media, hooks asserts that racial integration in schools did not eradicate
the assumption that "whites are somehow better, smarter, more likely to be
intellectuals, and even that they are kinder than blacks" (1992, p. 10). The
following discussion explores hooks' contention of institutionalized White
supremacy in the United States.

White Supremacy

Critical, feminist, and multicultural critics highlight the fallacy behind
mainstream norms and practices. It is argued that a pervasive false consciousness is reinforced in society due to the sanctioning of exclusive ways of being,
feeling, and knowing as the norm. Essentially, these values and traditions are
racial, gender, and class specific. Students from marginalized cultures find their

primary cultural values and traditions inadequately represented and/or denied. The subordination of one group's cultural traits and characteristics has significant impact in marginalized students' experiences of schools and/or incorporation of official curricula. In a White supremacist society, White people's values, traditions, and practices are ingrained in social policies and norms serving as basic criteria for social and economic mobility. hooks succinctly states:

> In the beginning black folks were most effectively colonized via the structure of ownership. Once slavery ended, white supremacy could be effectively maintained by the institutionalization of social apartheid and by creating a philosophy of racial inferiority that would be taught for everyone. This strategy of colonialism needed no country, for the space it sought to own and conquer was the minds of white and blacks. (1995b, p. 109)

hooks (1989a) refrains from using the term "indoctrination" in expressing the impact of "White Supremacy" and its arm, the mass media, in shaping individual attitudes, choices, and behaviors, choosing instead to use terms such as *socialization* and *colonization of the mind*. However, her persistent critique of the dominant culture and prevailing (often actualized) stereotypes of minorities, especially Black people, suggests that the process of White supremacy and class indoctrination prevails in American society. Second, her critique of traditional, authoritarian pedagogies and the role of such pedagogies in reinforcing existing hierarchically based social structures, not to mention the passivity of students in the classroom, seems to again imply such a process. hooks (1990; hooks & West, 1991) points to the sense of "powerlessness" in individuals and groups confronted by "oppressive" social structures, what she terms a seeming lack in developing a reflective stance in students and most especially marginalized peoples. bell hooks' social theory highlights the fact that a patriarchal, White supremacist, and capitalist society sanctions educational policies and practices that are sexist, racist, and classist. Patriarchy privileges the male over the female; White supremacy privileges White peoples over peoples of other races; and classism privileges the elite and economically advantaged over the disenfranchised.

White supremacy connotes a privileging of White people's traditions, values, practices, and subsequent subordination of differing cultural qualities through policy and social practice (hooks, 1981, 1984, 1990, 1992, 1994c, 1995b). The expansiveness of the discussion on White supremacy reflects hooks' contention of a pervasive and persistent reproduction of White people's values and attitudes in social norms and practices.

> Evidently it was easier for folks to see truth in referring to the economic system as capitalism and the institutionalized system of male gender domination as patriarchal than for them to consider the way white supremacy as a foundation ideology continually informs and shapes the direction of these two systems of domination. The nation's collective refusal to acknowledge institutionalized white supremacy is given deep and profound expression in the contemporary zeal to reclaim the myth of Christopher Columbus as patriotic icon. (hooks, 1994b, p. 198)

Subordinating other histories that would have provided a broader, more realistic vision of the Americas and perpetuating the "Columbus" legacy in national celebrations each year reaffirms commitment to imperialism and White supremacy (hooks, 1994b). Besides Native American accounts, hooks cites Ivan Van Sertima's *They Came Before Columbus* to demonstrate the invisibility of accounts that have emerged to debunk the "Columbus" myth.

hooks (1981, 1984, 1989a, 1990, 1993, 1994c) and hooks and West (1991) contend that the following factors express racist attitudes and contribute to disenfranchisement of Blacks in American society: (a) commodification of Black cultural experience in mass media and print and subsequent devaluation of Blackness and Black people's traits and characteristics; (b) "tendency to overvalue work by white scholars, coupled with the suggestion that such work constitutes the only relevant discourse" despite an appropriation of work by Black scholars, devalued for being too "angry," "experiential," or lacking in abstraction and critical thought (hooks, 1990, p. 55); (c) recognition of "people of color from other countries while systematically suppressing and/or censoring the radical speech of indigenous folks of color" (p. 133); (d) institution and maintenance of social structures favoring White people's interests; (e) perpetuation of a color-caste hierarchy and not unlike the slavery era, desirability of fair-skinned Black women with long straight hair; (f) paucity of non-White faculty and scholars in institutions of higher learning; and (g) curriculum monocentrism and universalization of White people's experience both of which shape perspectives of social reality and determine the social status of non-White people.

The impact of White supremacist attitudes and values is addressed from five primary angles: (a) American nationalism, (b) legitimation of Standard English, (c) racism within feminism, (d) social myths, and (e) educational biases. The following discussion traces progressive development of a system that has primarily and consistently served White people's interests (hooks, 1981, 1989a, 1992, 1994b, 1995b).

Impact of American Nationalism

In the United States, colonization of the continent led to the institution of economic, educational, and political structures that primarily served the interests of the colonizers, currently policy makers (Banks, 1988; hooks, 1992, 1994b, 1995b; McNaught, 1996). Historically, in America, Anglo-Saxon sociocultural traditions functioned as a "prerequisite to social acceptability and access to the political structure" (Banks, 1988, p. 58). However, unlike Northern and Western European immigrants, groups such as African Americans, Chinese Americans, and Mexican Americans faced greater challenges in trying to assimilate as a result of possessing differing cultural traits and characteristics from the mainstream (Banks, 1988; Nelson et al., 1996). Insisting on the primacy of racial discrimination, hooks contends:

Racism took precedence over sexual alliances in both the white world's interaction with Native Americans and African Americans, just as racism overshadowed any bonding between black women and white women on the basis of sex. (1981, p. 122)

Supporting hooks' contention regarding significance of race in America, Banks cites the works of Mary Frances Berry, John W. Blassingame and Thomas J. Archdeacon to demonstrate the societal contradictions faced by Blacks, Indians, and Mexican Americans:

Anglo-Saxons cultural characteristics and values are presented to them as ideals to attain, yet they have been denied, sometimes through legal means and castlelike institutions and practices, the opportunities to acquire the behaviors and characteristics needed to become culturally like Anglo-Americans. (1988, p. 145)

This cultural bias has persisted, reinforced though social policies and practices (New York State, cited in Nelson et al., 1996). Linking the assimilation policy to maintenance of White supremacy, hooks contends that it was not

enough for black people to enter institutions of higher education and acquire the necessary skills to effectively compete for jobs previously occupied safely by whites; the demand was that blacks become "honorary whites," that black people assimilate to succeed. (1995b, p. 189)

However, though Black people understood the necessity of accommodating White people's norms and traditions, Black children were encouraged to be cautious in spite of their dependency on White people

for evaluation, for approval. We learned not to challenge their [White supremacist] racism since they had power over us. Although we were told at home that we were not to openly challenge whites, we were also told not to learn to think like them. (hooks, 1989a, p. 99)

Besides White supremacist norms and practices in society, educational policies and practices similarly reinforce "superiority" of the White race. Assimilation rather than acculturation has been a primary goal of school policies and practices given the historical context of America (Banks, 1988). For purposes of national cohesion, all individuals and groups require socialization into a shared culture of values and norms. hooks contends that assimilation is a

strategy deeply rooted in the ideology of white supremacy and its advocates urge black people to negate blackness, to imitate racist white people so as to better absorb their values and way of life. Ironically, many changes in social policy and social attitudes that were once seen as ways to end racial domination have served to reinforce and perpetuate white supremacy. . . . Given the continued force of racism, racial integration translated into assimilation ultimately serves to reinforce and maintain white supremacy. (1995b, p. 186)

Proponents of an assimilationist approach to education fail to acknowledge that prevailing norms and values, let alone the very notion of a literacy canon, could be exclusive, racially and ethnically biased. hooks expresses reservations about the process of assimilation for Black people.

While assimilation is seen as an approach that ensures the successful entry of black people into the mainstream, at its very core it is dehumanizing. Embedded in the logic of assimilation is the white-supremacist assumption that blackness must be eradicated so that a new self, in this case, a "white" self, can come into being. Of course, since we who are black can never be white, this very effort promotes and fosters serious psychological stress and even severe mental illness. My concern about the process of assimilation has deepened as I hear black students express pain and hurt, as I observe them suffer in ways that not only inhibit their ability to perform academically, but threaten their very existence. (1989a, p. 67)

The process of assimilation begs the question of a cultural literacy canon. Sonia Nieto's research findings (1996) demonstrate the Eurocentric bias in contemporary United States' education and society. Not surprisingly, in Eric Donard Hirsch's idea of an American cultural literacy canon, "the cultures, knowledges, and values of groups that have been historically subordinated by the dominant group are notably absent from the list of 'facts' that the 'culturally literate' Americans need to know" (cited in Nieto, 1996, p. xv). Abdul R. Janmohamed (1994), too, critiques the notion of a "cultural heritage" and its implication for members of marginalized cultures and/or people whose values are not adequately represented. hooks (1994b) illustrates the impact of cultural alienation on marginalized students. Confronting her denial to speak or write on the discovery of America by Columbus, hooks makes the following confession:

> I want to forget [Columbus], to deny his importance, because those earliest childhood memories of learning about Columbus are tied to feelings of shame that "red and black" people [as I thought of us then] were victimized, degraded and exploited by those strange white discoverers. In truth, I can see my eyes and vividly call to mind those images of Columbus and his men sketched in history books. I can see the crazed and savage looks that were on the faces of shackled African slaves. I want to forget them even as they linger against my will in memory. (1994b, p. 205)

hooks' recounting accentuates the impact of racism and/or uncontested "historical" accounts that perpetuate White supremacy and the process of internalized racism on the part of non-Whites in the Americas and Third World countries that have similarly been colonized by the White race. McNaught's contention against the policy and practice of assimilation resonates with hooks' thesis: "When this belief of [white supremacy] is internalized it leads to either a malaise of nihilism, which has overtaken many minority individuals, or the anti-self, visible in those who are successful" (McNaught, 1996, p. 162). hooks (1995b) and hooks and West (1991) also recount the impact of White supremacy on Black children's as well as adults' psyches:

Returning to memories of growing up in the social circumstances created by racial apartheid, to all black spaces on the edges of town, I reinhabit a location where black folks associated whiteness with the terrible, the terrorizing. White people were regarded as terrorists, especially those who dared to enter that segregated space of blackness. . . . They terrorized by economic exploitation. (hooks, 1995b, p. 39)

Indeed, both hooks (1995b) and West (hooks & West, 1991) raise the issue of fear that plagues Blacks with respect to "Whiteness." "All black people in the United States, irrespective of their class status or politics, live with the possibility that they will be terrorized by whiteness" (hooks, 1995b, p. 46). In this context, hooks (1990, 1994b, 1994c) urges marginalized groups to claim and promote (their) individual cultural histories and traditions.

Legitimation of Standard English

hooks (1990) notes the role language plays in social definitions and classifications. She argues that language can function both as a tool for oppression and a weapon for resistance and/or re-definition. Thomas Popkewitz's (1991) observation of the dual role of language in maintenance of a social order as well as means for interpretation and redressing of social privilege resonates with hooks' contention with regard to language as a place of struggle and recovery for marginalized groups. The struggle over language in America is a case in point. Indeed, hooks (1994c) points to Black English as an oppositional strategy. In the United States, though English language emerged as a matter of practicality when citizens and immigrants alike required basic language skills to comprehend stipulations in most state laws and government documents, and to facilitate official transactions, what has developed over the years is the superiority of school English over other dialects and languages (Banks, 1988). To illustrate the indiscriminate cultural privileging of traits, Banks points to the fact that the

language of poor Blacks in the United States is often ridiculed, while the speech of White Bostonian Brahmins, which is as much a dialect as Black English, is frequently admired by Anglo-Americans. (1988, p. 88)

hooks views Standard English as a language of conquest and domination. Forced to disown their primary languages, Black slaves learned to communicate in the oppressor's language. However, though Standard English can and has been used as a shaping tool that "limits and denies . . . [and] a weapon that can shame, humiliate, colonize," hooks points to the manner in which Black English dialect was used to reclaim personal power (1994c, p. 168).

Similarly, Ngugi Wa Thiong'o vehemently critiques non-White groups' allegiance to Western languages and definitions. He links the emergence of colonial languages on the African continent to spiritual subjugation:

> [T]he biggest weapon wielded and actually daily unleashed by imperialism against [the Africans'] collective defiance is the cultural bomb. The effect of the cultural bomb is to annihilate a people's belief in their names, in their languages, in their environment, in their heritage of struggle, in their unity, in their capacities and ultimately in themselves. (1986, p. 3).

In his view the process of reclaiming one's primary language constitutes an affirmation of one's identity and cultural heritage, a decolonization of the mind. "[T]he oppressed struggle in language to recover ourselves, to reconcile, to reunite, to renew, our words are not without meaning, they are an action, a resistance" (hooks, 1990, p. 146). In this light, increasing acknowledgment of American society's pluralism in cultural languages and expression necessarily disrupts the primacy of Standard English, providing avenues for interrogating the cultural hegemony implied in American nationalism. The recent publicity regarding the State of California's legitimation of Ebonics in schools is not dissimilar to hooks' (1990) proposition for oppositional language. This however raises certain issues. On the one hand, the proposition is limited in application because of the primacy of Standard English in school textbooks, student assessment, and evaluation procedures notwithstanding corporate America's standards in the workplace. On the other hand, educational research holds to particular format and writing procedures for publication.

Racism within Feminism

Scholars (Cooper, 1994; hooks, 1981, 1984, 1989a; Scapp, 1990) note the manner in which racism is subtly maintained in feminist movements. hooks (1994c) stipulates that the interlocking impact of racist, sexist, and classist dominations heightens the oppression and exploitation of Black women. The point she reiterates is "Racism and sexism are interlocking systems of domination" (hooks, 1990, p. 62), as the discussion on sexism in chapter 2 illustrates. The following instances illustrate the manner in which a White supremacist environment privileges White women's interests and concerns because of their racial identity.

Critiquing the early feminist movement, hooks contends that while White women

> strongly advocated an end to slavery, they never advocated a change in the racial hierarchy that allowed their caste status to be higher than that of black women or men. In fact, they wanted that hierarchy to be maintained. (1981, p. 125)

hooks (1981, 1984, 1989a, 1990, 1994b, 1995b) describes feeling marginalized as a Black feminist. First, in her view the feminists who get air time and magazine coverage are all White, privileged, and pose far less of a threat to powerful White males than forthright people like her (hooks, 1990, 1994b, 1994c). hooks raises the issue of why

> work by white scholars about nonwhite people receives more attention and acclaim than similar work produced by nonwhite scholars (while at the same time, the latter's work is devalued . . . for being "too angry"— even as it is appropriated)? (1990, p. 55)

Second, hooks notes the fact that though White women have been known to receive grant money to research Black women, the opposite has yet to be the case. Further, it can be

> disheartening when new programs focusing on [racial and cultural] issues receive prestige and acclaim denied black studies. . . . Cultural studies programs are definites in this category. They are most always administered by white men and are quickly gaining a legitimacy long denied African-American and Third World studies. (pp. 124–125)

Ironically, to further the feminist cause against the exploitation and oppression of women, White women compared their experience to Black women's experiences even though liberation from sexism expressed White women's hopes and aspirations (hooks, 1981, 1984, 1995b; Scapp, 1990; Schuyler, 1990). For instance, the issue of "women" entry into the labor force ignored the fact that Black women had always worked outside their respective "homes" though with little recompense. Further, hooks reports being weary of White people's authorship of non-White experience pointing to the danger of cultural imperialism:

> Often this speech about the "Other" annihilates, erases; "No need to hear your voice when I can talk about you better than you can speak about

yourself. No need to hear your voice. . . . I want to know your story. And then I can tell it back to you in a new way. Tell it back to you in such a way that it has become mine, my own. Re-writing you, I write myself anew. I am still author, authority. I am still the colonizer, the speaking subject and you are now the center of my talk." (1990, pp. 151–152)

Third, in a "white supremacist sexist society all women's bodies are devalued, but white women's bodies are valued more than those of women of color" (hooks, 1990, p. 62). The rape of a White women attracts more attention and is seen as more significant than that of Black women (hooks, 1981, 1990; Schuyler, 1990). Fourth, in schools, colleagues, peers, and professors doubt Black females' stamina and capacity for logical and critical thought (hooks & West, 1991). hooks contends:

Racism is perpetuated when blackness is associated solely with concrete gut level experience conceived as either opposing or having no connection to abstract thinking and the production of critical theory. (1990, p. 23)

This privileging of White over Black women reflects pre–Civil Rights racism whereby Black men on the basis of gender, and White men and women on the basis of gender and race subordinated Black women's issues and concerns (hooks, 1981, 1984). hooks argues:

Even though all women are denied access to many jobs because of sexist discrimination, racism ensured that the lot of the white women would always be better than that of the black female workers. (1981, p. 147)

In the academy, publication policies mirror and reflect a White supremacist ideology (hooks, 1990, 1994c). Tied to greater recognition of White scholarship is the process of manuscript editions and rejections. hooks notes the manner in which

Black thinkers and writers in the academy, like all other marginalized groups, are constantly subjected to scrutiny. . . . If you are trying to publish anything (book, article, review, etc.), usually there is a white hierarchy determining who will edit one's work. (1990, p. 11)

Supporting hooks' contention with regard to publication politics, hooks and West allude to the forces of social control within academy, that would have it be primarily a location for the reinscription of the status quo, place a lot of pressure on people who are trying to speak to many audiences. (1991, p. 73)

The following discussion explores the manner in which social myths regarding equality and democracy lead to false consciousness in marginalized members of society. The status quo is portrayed as static and inevitable despite the biases in its operations.

Social Myths

Critical scholarship notes that communities propagate certain generalized facts that masquerade for commonly held "truths" posited as objective and neutral though such "truths" fail to reflect the interests and/or values of marginalized groups (Freire, 1970/1992, 1973; Freire & Faundez, 1989; Minnich, 1990; Shor & Freire, 1987). The propaganda effectively serves the dominant culture's need to maintain the status quo by socializing citizens into particular modes of behavior and thought by presenting its traditions as cultural norms. hooks (1990, 1994b, 1995b) collapses her discussion of social myths under the umbrella of a White supremacist ideology. She associates the impact of White supremacy on the American people to Freire's (1970/1992) assessment of economic and political oppression in Third World countries:

Despite progressive interventions in education that call for a rethinking of the way history is taught and culturally remembered, there is still little focus on the presence of Africans in the "New World" before Columbus. As long as this fact of history is ignored, it is possible to name Columbus as an imperialist, a colonizer, while still holding on to the assumption that the will to conquer is innate, natural, and that it is ludicrous to imagine that people who are different nationally, culturally, could meet each other and not have conflict be the major point of connection. (hooks, 1994b, pp. 199–200)

Reiterating hooks' observation regarding existing episteme of knowledge, McNaught (citing Knight et al.) argues that the "education of Americans is accomplished through a mixture of myths and fiction presented as facts and entertainment"(1996, p. 86).

hooks (1984, 1990, 1994b, 1995b; hooks & West, 1991) continually enjoins oppressed and exploited people to define and articulate their social reality for purposes of establishing counter-hegemonic discourse in a disenfranchising cultural milieu. In privileging its members, culturally dominating groups institute mechanisms that silence, suppress, and censor transgressive elements and/or persons in society (Shor, 1992):

> There would be no need to even speak of the oppressed and exploited coming to voice, articulating and redefining reality, if there were not oppressive mechanisms of silencing, suppressing, and censoring. (hooks, 1989a, p. 16)

Indeed, in some cultures to speak out one risks brutal punishment—imprisonment, torture, and even death (hooks, 1989a; Ngugi Wa Thiong'o, 1986, 1993; Richburg, 1997). Though hooks notes the repressive aspects of dominant groups in society and the academy toward transgressive persons by way of ostracization, censorship, or excommunication, she contends that counterhegemonic discourse in her writings "bear[s] witness to the reality that our many cultures can be remade, that this nation can be transformed, that we can resist racism and in the act of resistance recover ourselves and be renewed" (1995b, p. 7).

The issue of social myths is addressed from two main angles: racial stereotypes, and fallacy of equality and democracy in America. First, stereotypes are like fiction, substituting for the real, and often based on fantasy of the "Other" (hooks, 1992). Half truth and half myth, stereotypes impact perceptions and intergroup interactions. Exploring the impact of stereotypes, hooks' writings illustrate the manner in which stereotypical representations of non-Whites, especially Blacks, and women, especially Black women, serve a prescriptive function in interrelationships. Generally viewed as inferior, traits and characteristics of Blacks and women are marginalized in society:

> Despite so much evidence in daily life that suggests otherwise, masses of white Americans continue to believe that black people are genetically inferior—that it is natural for them to be dominated. And even though women have proved to be the equals of men in every way, masses still believe that there can be no sustained social and family order if males do not dominate females, whether by means of benevolent or brutal patriarchies. (hooks, 1994b, p. 200)

Second, hooks (1994b) attributes lack of collective effort to transform society to prevailing social myths and mass media propaganda. She associates a culture of domination to lies and denial. The following extensive reference best captures hooks' contention with regard to the interplay between social myths and personal lies.

> That lying takes the presumably innocent form of many white people [and even some black folks] suggesting that racism does not exist anymore, and that conditions of social equality are solidly in place that would enable any black person who works hard to achieve economic self-sufficiency. . . . Lying takes the form of mass media creating the myth that feminist movement has completely transformed society, so much so that the politics of patriarchal power have been inverted and that men, particularly white men, just like emasculated black men, have become victims of dominating women. . . . Add to this the widely held assumptions that blacks, other minorities, and white women are taking jobs from white men, and that people are poor because they want to be, and it becomes evident that part of our contemporary crisis is created by a lack of meaningful access to truth. That is to say, individuals are not just presented untruths, but are told them in a manner that enables most effective communication. When this collective cultural consumption of and attachment to misinformation is coupled with the layers of lying individuals do in their personal lives, our capacity to face reality is severely diminished as is our will to intervene and change unjust circumstances. (hooks, 1994c, p. 29)

hooks also castigates proponents of a return to patriarchal idealism under the guise of "family values," despite the fact that:

> Statistics on domestic violence, homicide, rape, and child abuse indicate that, in fact, the idealized patriarchal family is not a "safe" space, that those of us who experience any form of assault are more likely to be victimized by those who are like us rather than by some mysterious strange outsiders. (p. 28)

In response to prevailing social myths, hooks proposes an educational theory that interrogates, for purposes of transformation, what is taught and manner of transmission as a way of restoring "life to a corrupt and dying academy" (p. 30). hooks' educational theory is analyzed in the following part.

Social myths justify an existing order, however oppressive. Prevailing social myths privilege the elite and the dominant culture in maintaining the status quo while desensitizing the marginalized to prevailing social injustices that if "perceived" would lead to the oppressed or marginalized groups seeking a redress and, with hope, social transformation. Oppression is "domesticating." Oppression, what hooks (1990, 1994b, 1995b) terms *dominations*, not only undermines the rights of certain groups but reinforces social, political, and economic inequalities by providing a justifiable rationale for the state of affairs (Freire, 1970/1992; hooks, 1990, 1994b, 1995b). McNaught (1996) cites Richard J. Herrnstein and Charles Murray's *The Bell Curve*, as a classic illustration. Its authors link poverty to a lack of energy, thrift, farsightedness, and determination. Accordingly, diversity in intelligence quotients account for one's social and material status. However, three years after the book's debut, scholars refute its noxious claims (Weinstein, 1997).

Notwithstanding the propaganda of social equality and privilege, "cultural silencing," is reinforced by marginalized persons who internalize dominant cultural values. For instance, as a result of the cultural domination of White people's values and attitudes in society, Black and other non-White people internalize a White supremacist's devaluation of Blackness in its association of Blackness with inferiority, victimhood, and inadequacy, valuing that which is "White" and of White people, as later discussions here on internalized racism will demonstrate (hooks, 1989a, 1990, 1992, 1994b, 1995b). hooks notes that the

> university is basically a politically conservative framework which often inhibits the production of diverse perspectives, new ideas, and different styles of thinking and writing. At times individual black folks who have gained power in the academy assume the role of secret police, guarding ideas and work to make sure nothing is said to contradict the status quo. (1990, p. 7)

Indeed, hooks contends that in providing social legitimation for allegiance to White people's values and attitudes its "advocates urge black people to negate blackness, to imitate racist white people so as to better absorb their values, their way of life" (1995b, p. 186). Circumstances faced by women and minorities produce a vicious circle of discrimination and academic failure.

hooks' contention resonates with Freire's (1970/1992) view of the impact of oppression in Third World countries and maintenance of oppressive forces over the years. The oppressed or marginalized groups readily adapt to the values, standards, and goals of the dominant culture (the colonizers) which only reinforces their fear/awe of the "leader" or "authority" in school and belief in their own inefficiency. Paulo Freire even questions the beneficence of "oppressors" towards the "oppressed," arguing:

They almost always bring with them the marks of their origin; their prejudices and their deformations. . . . The generosity of the oppressors is nourished by an unjust order, which must be maintained in order to justify that generosity. (1970/1992, p. 46)

hooks' unease (1981, 1984, 1989a, 1990) with regard to efforts by White people, engaging in discourse on marginality given their location of privilege, and benevolence toward the oppressed, echoes Freire's weariness of compensatory measures towards oppressed groups by materially and culturally privileged individuals. hooks recounts Zora Neale Hurston's experience with her White patroness, Mrs. Mason, to validate her contention. To acquire financial backing for her ethnographic study, Hurston "entered" into a legal agreement making Mrs. Mason patron of her ethnographic research findings. In hooks' assessment,

Mason, though seemingly liberal because she associated with black folks, epitomized the colonizer who masks her desire to control by assuming the role of caretaker. Though [Mason] believed she behaved in a non-racist manner by working to support black writers and artists, she used their labor in the same manner as the plantation worker. (1990, p. 140)

Linking the social-cultural to the educational system, Freire (1970/1992, 1973) and hooks (1994c) maintain that a banking approach to education best suits the strategy of the dominant elites in their economic and political self-sufficiency, exploiting ignorance and emotional dependency of the masses on the system, to fill them with slogans and myths that maintain the status quo. Surprisingly, both scholars insist that freedom has to come from the margin: "[I]t is only the oppressed who, by freeing themselves, can free their oppressors" (Freire, 1970/1992, p. 42). hooks (1994c) maintains that schools mirror and perpetuate social myths in school curriculum and culture. The following part on hooks' educational theory provides a more expansive treatment of the subject of curriculum biases. However, since schools and society are so intricately linked, the manner in which social power and political dynamics are played out in schools is briefly explored.

Educational Biases

Research findings illustrate the inequalities in educational resources and pedagogical orientations between schools of predominantly White and non-White students (Banks, 1988; Kozol, 1991; Nieto, 1996). Nieto (1996) argues that similar to housing, employment, and the criminal justice institutions, schools reflect racist, classist, ethnocentric, sexist, linguistic, and anti-Semitic biases, because these forms of discrimination prevail in society. Jonathan Kozol (1991) makes a similar contention based on research findings on disparities in opportunity, expenditure, and academic success of privileged and marginalized students.

First, in addressing cultural reproduction in schools, hooks' critique (1990, 1994b, 1994c, 1995b, 1996; hooks & West, 1991) resonates with a multicultural critique of the educational system and manner in which school culture reflects and perpetuates dominant cultural attitudes and values under the umbrella of mainstream norms. hooks (1989a) notes that the study of literature within English departments consists primarily of works by White men and a few by White women. Raising a similar issue on the Eurocentrism in educational settings, Nieto notes:

> The canon as used in contemporary U.S. education assumes that the knowledge that is most worthy is already in place. According to this narrow view, the basics have in effect already been defined. Knowledge in this context, is inevitably European, male, and upper class in origin and conception, especially in the arts and social sciences. In art history, courses rarely leave France, Italy, and sometimes England in considering the "great masters." What is called "classical" music is classical only in Europe, not in Africa, Asia, or Latin America. This same ethnocentrism is found in history books, which places Europeans and European Americans as the actors and all the others as the recipients, bystanders, or bit players of history. (1996, p. 311)

Further, hooks' critique of patriarchy resonates with critical theorists' scholarship regarding political implications of educational curriculum and pedagogies. Not only are masculine traits and characteristics presented as normative but traits associated with women are typically relegated to the domestic sphere and/or labeled "supportive" roles (Martin, 1992, 1995; Minnich, 1990; Noddings, 1984; Pagano, 1995).

hooks (1994c), Pierre Bourdieu (1986; cited in Nieto, 1996), and Nieto (1996) critique the role of schools in reflecting and perpetuating both overtly and covertly the "knowledge and values of economically and culturally dominant groups in society, they validate and reinforce the cultural capital that students from such groups already bring from home" (Nieto, 1996, p. 284). It is then not surprising that students from marginalized groups are disadvantaged by the school culture. Incidents of school drop-out and other forms of delinquency are significantly represented among students from marginalized groups (Kozol, 1991; McNaught, 1996; Nieto, 1996). Reflecting upon her experience in schools, hooks recollects:

> In those days, [Black students] from marginal groups who were allowed to enter prestigious, predominantly white colleges were made to feel that we were there not to learn but to prove that we were the equal of whites. We were there to prove this, by showing how well we could become clones of our peers. As we constantly confronted biases, an undercurrent of stress diminished our learning experience. (1994c, p. 5)

Schools reify social reality in transmitting "objective" knowledge, falsely devoid of race, gender, and class politics:

> The curriculum is presented as normative, neutral and benevolent, even as it "cools you out," adjusting most students to subordinate positions in society. Inequality is presented as natural, just, and earned, given the differing "aptitudes" and "achievements" of various groups. The advantages of the elite are hidden behind a myth of "equal opportunity" while the idiom of the elites is named "correct usage," another myth of symbolic violence against colloquial speech, making the idioms of the ordinary people into inferior, outlaw languages. This social construction of inequality through schooling joins a constellation of other agencies repeating the messages and myths, in the mass media, mass advertisements, and the job market. For individual students, it becomes hard to see alternatives to the way things are and have to be. (Shor & Freire, 1987, p. 123)

Second, hooks (1994b, 1994c), similar to critical theory scholarship, attributes students' lack of interest in schooling to an alienating curriculum and an authoritative pedagogy (Banks, 1988; Freire, 1970/1992; Freire & Faundez, 1989; Shor, 1992; Shor & Freire, 1987; Starratt, 1990, 1993, 1995). The alienation is exacerbated for minority students victimized by racial and cultural biases in the school system (Banks, 1988; McNaught, 1996; Nieto, 1996). The official curriculum: (a) is heavily Eurocentric and sustains stereotypes of members of marginal groups, (b) encourages artificial distinctions between the different fields of knowledge, and (c) prioritizes "official" knowledge from knowledge acquired outside of schools and not directly related to school "subject matter" (Freire & Faundez, 1989; hooks, 1994c; Nieto, 1996).

"Official" curriculum privileges students whose cultures and values are reflected in school policies and practices (Banks, 1988; hooks, 1994c; Nieto, 1996). Thus, curriculum policies discriminate in transmitting a cultural heritage that often fails to adequately address issues of racial and cultural differences. Critiquing the "Columbus" myth, hooks contends:

> We were taught that the Indians would have conquered and dominated white folk explorers if they could have but they were simply not strong or smart enough. Embedded in all these teachings was the assumption that it was the whiteness of these explorers in the "New World" that gave them greater power. The word "whiteness" was never used. The key word, the one that was synonymous with whiteness, was "civilization." (1994b, p. 199)

A curriculum focus on Western civilization's great works and ideas and/or a patriarchal value system subordinates individuals whose traits and characteristics not reflected in mainstream values and practices are marginalized (Giroux & McLaren, 1994; hooks, 1994b, 1994c; Minnich, 1990; Noddings, 1984; Pagano, 1995).

Besides a Eurocentric curriculum focus, knowledge and values in textbooks and teachers' guides tend to reflect the backgrounds, education, and experiences of educational policy makers (Banks, 1988; Harris, 1995; hooks, 1994b, 1995b; Nieto, 1996). Nieto (1996) cites the findings of Christine Sleeter and Carl Grant from an analysis of textbooks currently used in grades one through eight to illustrate the ideological nature of textbooks. Not only are most textbooks Eurocentric but educational policies and practices also reinforce racial and ethnic stereotypes. Most textbooks continue to legitimate the status of White males by presenting European American perspectives as the norm while providing scanty coverage of the lived realities and perspectives of women and people of color (hooks, 1994b). Raising a similar contention, McNaught cites Cameron McCarthy to illustrate that

> this Eurocentric approach to history and society preserves a selected tradition through linguistic ploys that universalizes the "same" while objectifying the "other." The "same" is posited in the role of genius in their unilateral historical progression and its gestures toward the backward natives of so-called Third World countries. (1996, p. 238)

Thomas Popkewitz's assessment (1991) with regard to the political dynamics underlying official curriculum, pedagogy, school structures and role functions, and educational research supports hooks' (1994b, 1994c) and hooks and West's (1991) contention of discriminatory forces imbued in school policies and practices. In hooks' view, criteria and assessment for academic rigor and standards of excellence denote White supremacist values. The school's hidden curriculum transmits values, languages, dialects, and cultures that are invariably associated with the dominant group (hooks, 1994b, 1994c; Nelson et al., 1996; Nieto, 1996). Thus, school failure in marginalized students could justifiably be attributed to the "cultural clash" that results from the incompatibility between the experiences, values, and practices of subordinated cultures in most students' homes and the school culture (Banks, 1988; hooks, 1994c; Nieto, 1996). Besides cultural hegemony in schools, hooks raises the issue of internalized racism in some Black professors:

> One of the tragic manifestations of the pressure of black people to assimilate is expressed in the internalization of racist perspectives. I was shocked and saddened when I first heard black professors at Stanford downgrade and express contempt for black students, expecting us to do poorly, refusing to establish nurturing bonds. . . . Ideologically, the message is clear—assimilation is the way to gain acceptance and approval from those in power. (hooks, 1989a, p. 80)

In socializing youth to better fit the workings of a system that privileges a few to the disadvantage of the majority, educational policies reflect and reinforce unequal social relations (Freire, 1970/1992). Students from subordinated groups are socialized into the dominant group's values and traditions as *the* cultural norms. In school, both the manifest and hidden curriculum favor students whose home and school's cultural norms and practices are more consistent with mainstream norms. Expounding on this discrepancy between school culture and most students' lived reality, Ira Shor contends that a Eurocentric syllabus silences

> critical thought about society and ignores the culturally diverse languages and experiences of students. . . . Minority students especially face the dilemma of subordinating themselves to the language and values of White society. (1992, p. 202)

Students from marginalized cultures are confronted with the challenge of incorporating unfamiliar (culturally alienating) subject matter as well as new ways of being, feeling, and perceiving. Further, to attain social, economic, and educational mobility, marginalized groups often feel the need to "abandon" their "meaningful ethnic traits and attachments in order to attain structural inclusion into society" (Banks, 1988, p. 44).

> Schools changed utterly with racial integration. . . . Bussed to white schools, [Black students] soon learned that obedience, and not a zealous will to learn, was what was expected of [them]. Too much eagerness to learn could easily be seen as a threat to white authority. (hooks, 1994c, p. 3)

hooks (1994c) and Abdul Janmohamed (1994) concur in their assessments of the impact of cultural hegemony on the marginalized. hooks recounts her attempts at assimilation to a college-educated school culture, admitting it made her "recognize how disempowering it is for people from underprivileged backgrounds to consciously censor our speech so as to 'fit better' in settings where we were perceived as not belonging" (1990, p. 90).

The discussion on institutionalized racism illustrates the impact of inequalities in power and privilege on members of marginalized cultures. hooks (1984, 1994b, 1995b) attributes the marginalization of non-White people's cultural traits and practices to the impact of White supremacy on non-White peoples. hooks insists on the primacy of racial discrimination:

> While those feminists who argue that sexual imperialism is more endemic to all societies than racial imperialism, American society is one in which racial imperialism supersedes sexual imperialism. (1981, p. 122)

Not only have schools privileged White people's values and beliefs, and perspectives of history and social reality, but mass media in promoting negative stereotypes of non-White persons reinforced this bias coupled with the fallacy of equity and fairness in society (hooks, 1994b). The following discussion seeks to illustrate the impact of White supremacist attitudes and values on Black people's consciousness.

The previous discussion on White supremacy demonstrated the manner in which the superiority of White people, their values and attitudes, are reinforced by existing social, economic, educational, and political structures. Socially, the assimilation policy—affecting both new immigrants and non-White peoples—presented White people's traditions as a "prerequisite for acceptability and access to political structures" (Banks, 1988, p. 58). This ideology is reinforced by the hierarchical social arrangement in society. The superiority of White people has led to the negation of differing traits and characteristics. In schools, the idea of a literacy canon is based on a European, male, upper-class conception of knowledge. Again, the curriculum presents White people's perspective of history and social reality. In this context, hooks (1994b) critiques the ideology behind the "Columbus" legacy. Notwithstanding the fact that White males are portrayed as the "makers of history," the exploitation of natives and devaluation of differing traditions and perspectives further reinforce White people's "power." Further, especially in the early feminist movement, White women shied away from contact with Black women, reinforcing the racial and class distinction between the two groups. The distinction between Black and White women is further sanctioned by social structures giving recognition and consideration to White over Black women's concerns.

hooks' writings also demonstrate that social myths regarding equality and fair competition justify the prevailing status quo and reinforce marginality of minorities, especially Blacks. By implication, the harder one works the more successful the individual. Thus, social and economic failure is attributed to individual failure rather than discriminatory structural systems. Essentially, Blacks, and especially Black women who lag behind socially and economically, must not be working hard enough! Finally, hooks demonstrates the manner in which school norms and practices marginalize students whose cultural traits and characteristics are not reflected in mainstream norms. The following discussion explores the manner in which Blacks have internalized their cultural marginality and "reverence" for White people's values and attitudes.

Internalized Racism

hooks' recount (1981, 1989a, 1990, 1992, 1994c) of incidents that express internalized racist behavior include: (a) disassociation from fellow Blacks and "Black" traits, (b) "trashing" of fellow Blacks, (c) de-emphasizing the impact of racism, and (d) false belief in repaired relations between Black and White people. hooks (1989a) and Janmohamed (1994) note the impact of insidious domination from internalized hegemonic rules and regulations in marginalized peoples:

> More than ever before, educated black people internalize many of these assumptions, acting in complicity with the very forces of domination that actively oppress, exploit, and deny the vast majority of [Blacks] access to a life that is not marred by brutal poverty, dehumanization, extreme alienation, and despair. (hooks, 1989a, p. 63)

These internalized norms serve to privilege the dominant culture while simultaneously justifying the exclusion of the values and traditions of marginalized groups. Janmohamed (1994) therefore advocates Freire's pedagogy (1973) that helps nurture intellectuals who interrogate negative or often false cultural myths. A dialogic education helps unveil the basis for these hierarchical relations to counteract the domination of consciousness in learners (Freire & Faundez, 1989; hooks, 1994c; Shor & Freire, 1987).

hooks (1981, 1989a, 1990, 1993, 1995b) points to the following factors to illustrate the impact of internalized racism in Black people adopting White supremacist cultural attitudes and values: (a) negation of "blackness," (b) color-caste hierarchy, and (c) in-group factions. In addition, in learning and disseminating a monocultural history, encouraging admiration, love, and faith in a system that upholds democracy and equality of all races in the face of racial, sexual, and class distinction, and supporting a government that allows unequal distribution of resources, marginalized groups consciously and unconsciously perpetuate the very evils of a society that oppresses them (hooks, 1981, 1992, 1994b, 1995b).

Negation of Blackness

First, a negation of Black cultural traits and characteristics leads most Black people to image themselves as less worthy than Whites. hooks contends:

> Systems of domination, imperialism, colonialism, and racism actively coerce black folks to internalize negative perceptions of blackness, to be self-hating. . . . Yet blacks who imitate whites (adopting their values, speech, habits of being, etc.) continue to regard whiteness with suspicion, fear, and even hatred. (1995b, pp. 32–33)

Further, because cultural domination not only propagates degrading racial stereotypes but also fosters a reliance on the dominant cultural group's views and values, marginalized members are socialized to disavow their heritage and agency in a disenfranchising environment (hooks, 1993). hooks makes the following observation:

> [Internalized racism] is expressed in student/faculty encounters and in our encounters as professors with one another. Witness a new professor coming into an environment where there are few black women. She meets another black professor in her department who, when asked about his interests, says in an offhand manner, "I'm not into that Afro-American shit." Disassociating himself from blackness, he assumes an attitude of superiority, as though he has more accurately understood the way to succeed—assimilation, negation of the black self. (1989a, p. 69)

hooks (1990, 1992, 1994b, 1994c, 1995b) notes the effect of internalized racism on marginalized groups, especially allegiance to the dominant culture's values and knowledge. Promoting a dominant culture's norms as *the* cultural norm in society politically and socially alienates members of marginalized cultures (hooks, 1990, 1994c; McNaught, 1996; Nelson et al., 1996). In schools, students from marginalized cultures are disadvantaged in relation to their peers in environments through a failure to acknowledge contributions of marginalized group members and/or their lived realities or the provision for adequate attention and/or coverage of cultural pluralism in a society.

Speaking from her experience at Stanford University, hooks (1994c) notes how the curriculum and pedagogy reinforced racist stereotypes promoting unequal treatment of students. Black students were cast as being genetically inferior, even unable to learn and expected to conform while "exceptional" White students were often allowed to chart their own intellectual journeys. Further, hooks alludes to what she terms a more sophisticated version of assimilation in colleges when Black professors, in imitation of racist America,

act as though they believe all black students are lazy and irresponsible . . . address questions and comments in classroom settings solely to white students . . . [making] an effort not to acknowledge in any way black students so as not to be open to the critique that they have preferences, a stance which may lead them to overcompensate by being overly attentive to non-black students. (1989a, p. 68)

In their efforts at assimilation, some Black professors reify and commodify Blackness and thrash fellow Blacks with the intent of distancing themselves from "undesirable" Black traits and characteristics (hooks, 1989a).

Color-caste Hierarchy

It is hooks' contention (1981, 1984, 1989a, 1990, 1992, 1994b, 1995b) contention that a White supremacist thinking established and maintained a color-caste hierarchy during slavery that continues to plague Black communities.

All black folks, even those who know very little if anything at all about North American history, slavery, and reconstruction, know that racist white folks often treated lighter-skinned black folks better than their darker counterparts, and that this pattern was mirrored in black social relations. (hooks, 1994b, p. 174)

In Black communities, a color-caste hierarchy system prevails whereby the lightness of one's skin and/or straightness of hair enhances one's social value (hooks, 1990, 1992, 1993, 1994b, 1995b).

> Color-caste hierarchies embrace both the issue of skin color and hair. Since lighter-skinned black people are most often genetically connected to interracial pairings of both white and black people, they tend to look more like whites. Females who were offsprings of generations of interracial mixing were most likely to have long, straight hair. Light skin and long hair continue to be traits that define a female as beautiful and desirable in the racist imagination and in the colonized black mindset. . . . To this day, the images of black female bitchiness, evil temper, and treachery continue to be marked by darker skin. (hooks, 1994b, pp. 178–179)

hooks (1995b) notes with sadness the fact that some parents' first concern on the birth of a child is not so much gender as skin color. (In Kenya, parents' primary concern would be for the child's gender.) The oft-cited study of Black children's preference for White over Black images and White over Black dolls no doubt highlights this very argument of color casting (hooks, 1994b, 1995b). Black children's preference for White dolls is not unlike some Black adults' preference for White-related traits and characteristics. hooks expresses surprise at people's failure to link ethnic cleansing to racial purity and White supremacy, adding the fact that South Africa's racial apartheid—based on the "myth of white supremacy—is also being played out by black Americans when we overvalue those who are light-skinned and have straight hair, while ignoring black people" (1994b, p. 45). Indeed, both historically and in contemporary times, individuals who looked, acted, and lived in ways similar to White folk had greater access to social mobility (hooks, 1981, 1992, 1994b, 1995b, 1996a). When

> racist stereotype images were coupled with a concrete reality whereby assimilated black folks were the ones receiving greater material reward, the culture was ripe for a resurgence of color-caste hierarchy. (hooks, 1995b, p. 126)

hooks (1993, 1994b) attributes an internalized racial hatred and low self-esteem to a color-caste hierarchy and assimilation policy. In hooks' assessment: "[U]ntil black folks begin collectively to critique and question the politics of representation that systematically devalues blackness, the devastating effects of color caste will continue to inflict psychological damage on masses of black folks" (1994b, p. 181).

In-group Factions

hooks (1990, 1995b) maintains that a White racist society pits Third World scholars and African American scholars against one another in the allocation of jobs and public recognition. hooks argues that Third World nationals and intellectuals "bring to this country the same kind of contempt and disrespect for blackness that is most frequently associated with white western imperialism" (1990, p. 93). hooks (1984, 1990) attributes tensions between women of color to internalized White supremacist beliefs, expressed in feelings of self-hate, venting anger, and rage toward each other rather than economical and political oppressive forces. In-group factions between and among marginalized members arise from a squabbling over "left overs" in a disenfranchising environment:

> Often when people are suffering a legacy of deprivation, there is a sense that there are never any goodies to go around, so that we must viciously compete with one another. (hooks, 1990, p. 208)

She notes that "internalized racism and sexism make it a norm for [Black women/women of color] to treat one another harshly and with disrespect" (p. 94).

In view of an insidious perpetuation of White supremacist ideology, hooks argues that the "struggle to end white supremacy is a struggle to change a system, a structure . . . structures that reinforce and perpetuate white supremacy" (1989, p. 119). Popkewitz's (1991) view of the relation between structures and social change supports hooks' assessment regarding the structural basis of existing forms of domination. In this light, hooks' critique centers not so much on White people, but the ideology of White supremacy and its impact on both White and Black people's values and attitudes in society. hooks argues:

> It is important that everyone in the United States understand that white supremacy promotes, encourages, and condones all manner of violence against black people. Institutionalized racism allows this violence to remain unseen and/or renders it insignificant by suggesting that it is justifiable punishment for some offense. Mass media do not see it as newsworthy. (1995b, p. 22)

hooks' main thesis (1981, 1984, 1989a, 1990, 1992, 1993, 1994b, 1994c, 1995b) in her corpus of writings is the need for self-definition and self-determination for all people: those materially and culturally privileged and the marginalized. She enjoins people to a reflective stance in day-to-day choices and actions; a movement from "object" to "subject." A similar injunction is proposed by critical scholars (Freire, 1970/1992, 1973; Freire & Faundez, 1989; Giroux & McLaren, 1994; Shor, 1992; Shor & Freire, 1987). From personal experiences, hooks (1989a, 1990, 1992, 1993, 1994c, 1996a) vouches for the fact that the decolonization of one's mind for personal and political self-recovery starts with a critical interrogation of one's location, the identifications, and allegiances that inform one's life. In objectively and honestly acknowledging externally and internally imposed limitations on one's existence, one is better placed to distinguish myth from reality, one's capacity to "transgress" falsely constructed or perceived limitations. Tied to an interrogation of one's location of marginality is the process of a renewed understanding of self and an appreciation of one's agency and self-determination as one struggles toward self-actualization. In so doing, an "individual chooses to move against dominations, against oppressions . . . toward freedom, to act in ways that liberate ourselves and others" (hooks, 1994c, p. 250). Both hooks and West (1991) and Moyosore Okediji (1995) distinguish a counter-hegemonic stance from an auto-hegemonic stance that "derives authority, power, and autonomy from itself" (Okediji, p. 7). Though Okediji agrees with hooks' (1989a) view of marginality as a site of resistance, she critiques hooks' counter-hegemonic stance that pits the margin against the center. Okediji advocates establishment of a third center, independent of the center. Okediji's stance of auto-hegemony builds on the fact that "African Americans have their own traditions, their own ways—and do not need to rely on presents and props from the dominant culture" (Okediji, 1995, p. 180). She maintains that the auto-hegemonic stance is more constructive and self-empowering than a counter-hegemonic stance. Okediji's contention resonates with hooks and West's challenge to Black people to develop self-definitions beyond ones that merely react to cultural stereotypes of Black people. These two scholars cite Marcus Garvey, who

> understood the fact that Black people could only be human when they were free from the fear and failure which is imposed on them by a larger racist society, but it would not be a matter of blaming that society, it would be a matter of understanding that society and asserting themselves bodily and defiantly as human beings . . . very few Black folk ever reach that level, and more must. (1991, p. 56)

Champagne maintains that while "power 'produces' the subject, it also produces the conditions for the possibility of resistance" (1993, p. 33). In effect, the choice by some Blacks to adopt White people's values and attitudes is essentially that, a choice *for* complicity rather than resistance. However, discrimination of any form dehumanizes the victim or group. At some point, the victim internalizes the degradation, believing the "truth" in an untruth. hooks contends:

> Colonization made of us the colonized—participants in daily rituals of power where we, in strict sadomasochistic fashion, find pleasure in ways of being and thinking, ways of looking at the world that reinforce and maintain our positions as the dominated. (1990, p. 155)

Typically, expectations and economic or social standards seem to follow racial, gender, and class lines. In schools, incidents of high dropout rates and other forms of truancy are greatly represented among minority students (Kozol, 1991; Nieto, 1996). In this case, one can speak of a self-fulfilling prophecy, considering the overall cultural negation of Black traits and characteristics in both Black and White peoples. The following discussion highlights the expression and social sanctioning of sexist attitudes and practices. Some elements have been included in this chapter, such as the discussion of racism within feminism. In the next chapter, therefore, the manifestation and impact of sexism on women, especially Black women who are discriminated against on the basis of race, gender, and often class is highlighted.

CHAPTER 2

Sexism

Mary Belenky, Blythe Clinchy, Nancy Goldberger, and Jill Tarule (1986) in their ground breaking book, *Women's Ways of Knowing: The Development of Self, Voice, and Mind,* illustrate the "silence" that characterizes most women's lives. bell hooks (1994c) attributes the "silence" in women to the pressures of living in a patriarchal society. She makes a distinction between an appeasing and the "freeing" speech of self-actualized people. Self-actualized individuals comfortably claim their identities, and express their fears and hopes despite the social pressure to conform. Supporting hooks' distinction, Ronald Scapp maintains that the "liberatory voice necessarily confronts, disturbs, demands, that listeners alter their ways of hearing and being" (1990, p. 293). hooks contends that in majority Black communities, women switch from an appeasing to a "freeing" speech based on the audience:

[hooks] could not tell her mother how [the mother] became a different person as soon as the husband left the house in the morning, how she became energetic, noisy, silly, funny, fussy, strong, capable, tender, everything that she was not when he was around. When he was around she became silent. She reminded her daughter of a dog sitting, standing obediently until the master, the head of the house, gave her orders to move, to do this or to do that, to cook his food just so, to make sure the house was clean just so. (1996a, p. 98)

hooks (1990, 1994c, 1995b) attributes dominations in social arrangements to the ideology of distinctions and hierarchy of elements in Western metaphysical dualism. In hooks' view,

> Even though western metaphysical dualism as a paradigmatic philosophical approach provides the "logical" framework for structures of domination in this society (race, gender, class exploitation), individuals from oppressed and exploited groups internalize this way of thinking, inverting it. (1990, p. 8)

Thus, racial, gender, and class biases reflect a metaphysical dualism of distinctions and hierarchies of elements. Patriarchy privileges males over females, capitalism the economically privileged over the underclass, and White supremacy White people over non-White peoples. Employing similar dualistic hierarchical thought patterns, earliest advocates of feminism, more so than its recent advocates, posited men as the enemy of all women. On the other hand, some Black people wish to replace Black with White supremacy (hooks, 1981, 1990, 1994b, 1995b). The following discussion addresses the issue of sexism and sexual exploitation from three main angles: (a) the impact of socialization patterns on gender roles, (b) sexist attitudes and practices in society, and (c) the expression of internalized sexism.

Socialization

hooks' critique (1981, 1990, 1993, 1995b; hooks & West, 1991) of socialization patterns and subsequent perpetuation of sexism and sexist attitudes resonates with Wendy Kohli's (1995a) analysis of the impact of discriminatory practices on marginalized groups. hooks maintains: "Family is a significant site of socialization and politicization precisely because it is there that most of us learn our ideas about race, gender, and class" (1995b, p. 72). Kohli (1995a) cites Franz Fanon, Paulo Freire, and contemporary feminists such as bell hooks, Audre Lorde, and Toni Morrison who critique prevailing institutionalized oppressive forces as well as the perpetuation of domination by the complicity of marginalized groups. To address this phenomenon, one needs to appreciate the degree to which socialization impacts a marginalized group's view of self and social reality. Socialized into structures that present a supposedly unified cultural heritage (despite the partiality of its basis), marginalized groups still use such norms (typically the dominant culture's—race, class, or gender) as criteria for assessing what is considered "successful," "good," "right," "proper," etc. (hooks, 1984, 1989a, 1992, 1994b, 1995b, 1996b; Martin, 1992, 1995; Minnich, 1990; Noddings, 1984, 1995a, 1995b).

Socialization impacts the manner in which women and men understand their respective roles in society (hooks, 1995b).

> In our Southern black Baptist patriarchal home, being a boy meant to be tough, to mask one's feelings, to stand one's ground and to fight . . . being a girl meant to obey, to clean, to recognize that you had no ground to stand on. (hooks, 1992, p. 87)

At a young age, children are socialized into rigid stereotypes and male children are socialized to regard females as an enemy and a threat to their masculine status and power (hooks, 1981, 1995b). In Black communities, male privilege is extended to adulthood:

> Many [Blacks] were raised in homes where black mothers excused and explained male anger, irritability, and violence by calling attention to the pressures black men face in a racist society where they are collectively denied full access to economic power. (hooks, 1990, p. 75)

(Ironically no such concessions are made for women's "irrational" behaviors.) On a wider scale, hooks and Cornel West note the threat posed by "talented women . . . to men in general and black men in particular" (1991, p. 120).

Reflecting upon her own childhood, hooks distinguishes the atmosphere in the presence and absence of (Black) males:

> One was a world without the father . . . that world was full of speech . . . we could express ourselves loudly, passionately, outrageously. The other was male-dominated social space where sound and silence were dictated by his [the father's] presence . . . we would turn our volumes down, lower our voices; we would, if need be, remain silent . . . we feared speech. We feared the words of a woman who could hold her own in any discussion or an argument with a man. (1989a, p. 128)

Further, socialization patterns, what hooks (1981, 1990, 1993) attributes to patriarchy, relegates females to the childbearing roles and the task of creating and sustaining a home, leading to the virtuous commendation of the self-sac-rificing Black mother in Black autobiographies, fiction, and poetry. hooks (1981) roots current sexist practices to past trends that legitimated sexual exploitation of Black females:

Coming home from a hard day of work at a low-paying job, or after a day of searching for work or feeling the burden of unemployment, an individual black man demanding in a coercive or aggressive way, that his wife serve him may not see his actions as sexist or involving the use of power. This "not seeing" can be, and often is, a process of denial that helps maintain patriarchal structures. (hooks, 1990, p. 74)

Sexist Attitudes and Practices

hooks (1981, 1984, 1989a, 1990, 1992, 1993, 1994b, 1995b) provides extensive references to incidents in Black communities and wider society to illustrate the manner in which sexism leads to the exploitation of all women, and Black women in particular:

While institutionalized sexism was a social system that protected black male sexuality, it [socially] legitimized sexual exploitation of black females. The female slave lived in constant awareness of her sexual vulnerability and in perpetual fear that any male, white or black, might single her out to assault and victimize. (hooks, 1981, p. 24)

The following factors drawn from hooks' writings cited previously provide a clear indication of sexism and sexist behavior: (a) socio-cultural sanctioning of the superiority of males, (b) relegation of female and female related traits and characteristics to secondary status, (c) tolerance of violence against women, (d) economic and political structures that limit the advancement of women, (e) sexual exploitation of women, (f) negative representation of women and most especially Black women in mass media, (g) male domination and control of women and children in patriarchal systems, (h) objectification of women as sex objects, (i) poor remuneration toward women, (j) high illiteracy rates among women especially the underclass, (k) denigration of women's talk and concerns, and (l) sexist propaganda in mass media and popular culture. hooks links the sexist, misogynist, patriarchal ways of behaving glorified in gangsta rap music to "values, created and sustained by white supremacist capitalistic patriarchy" (1994b, p. 116). The rationale for condoning violence against women derives from a similar bias. As objects of desire and sex, women are viewed either as property, symbol, or ornament and extensions of the male ego with neither value nor individual worth.

In our cultural retelling of history we must connect the Columbus legacy with the institutionalization of patriarchy and the culture of sexist masculinity that upholds male domination of females in daily life. The cultural romanticization of Columbus's imperialistic legacy includes a romanticization of rape. White colonizers who raped and physically brutalized native women yet who recorded these deeds as the perks of victory acted as though women of color were objects, not subjects of history. If there was conflict it was between men. Females were perceived as though they and their bodies existed apart from the struggle between males for land and territory. From that moment on, women of color have had to grapple with a legacy of stereotypes that suggest we are betrayers, all too willing to consent when the colonizer demands our bodies. (1994b, p. 203)

Besides social cultural sexist factors, the Christian portrayal of woman as "evil sexual temptress, the bringer of sin into the world" has further exacerbated the denigration of women in society (hooks, 1981, p. 29). In a racist, classist, and sexist society, Black women feel the weight of any form of domination. During slavery,

> white men could justify their de-humanization and sexual exploitation of black women by arguing that they possessed inherent evil demonic qualities. Black men could claim that they could not get along with black women because they were so evil. And white women could use the image of the evil black woman to emphasize their own innocence and purity. (p. 85)

hooks (1981, 1990, 1992) takes issue with mass media's sexist imagery from two primary angles. One the one hand, hooks (1981, 1992) argues that this very imagery has sanctioned sexism and sexist exploitation in Black communities. Not only has the sexual metaphor equating freedom to manhood resulted in an equation of Black liberation to Black men's acquisition of economic and political rights, but in so doing contributed to the exclusion of Black women's concerns and therefore their subsequent invisibility in national concerns. hooks (1981) contends that granting Black men suffrage before White women indicated the depth of sexism in White males. In this case, sexism took precedence over racism. The patriarchal bonding between White and Black males was based on belief in the inherent inferiority of women. Despite racist oppression, patriarchy provides Black men with power over women, however relative. It comes as no surprise that

Many black nationalists will eagerly embrace critical theory and thought as a necessary weapon in the struggle against white supremacy, but suddenly lose the insight . . . when it comes to . . . analyzing sexism and sexist oppression in particular and specific ways it is manifest in black experience. (hooks, 1994c, p. 69)

Equating liberation to gaining full participation in the existing order, Black men fought for the elimination of racism, not capitalism or patriarchy. hooks argues:

By allowing white men to dictate the terms by which they would define black liberation, black men chose to endorse sexist exploitation and oppression of black women. And in so doing they were compromised. They were not liberated from the system but liberated to serve the system. The movement (1960s Black liberation) ended and the system had not changed; it was no less racist or sexist. (1981, p. 181)

hooks' contention (1981, 1984, 1989a, 1990, 1992, 1994b) regarding the impact of sexism, the subordination of women's concerns and related traits and characteristics to Black men, resonates with feminist scholarship with regard to the subordination of most women (Lorde, 1984; Martin, 1992, 1995; Noddings, 1984, 1992, 1995a, 1995b; Pagano, 1995, Stone, 1995). Jane Roland Martin's research findings (1984, 1995), based on a study of women in educational thought, illustrates that women have traditionally been excluded from the standard texts and anthologies in the history of educational thought, education of girls and women not perceived to be a relevant topic of interest, and the existence of female educational thinkers scarcely acknowledged. Works by great education thinkers such as Plato, Socrates, and Rousseau illustrate that traditional models of education were originally designed for men and methods of assessing the effectiveness of learning process based on male standards (Martin, 1995; Minnich, 1990; Noddings, 1984, 1992).

hooks "warns against sexualization of black liberation in ways that support sexism, phallocentrism, and male domination" (1990, p. 60):

Sexuality has always provided gendered metaphors for colonization. Free countries equated with free men, domination with castration, the loss of manhood, and rape—the terrorist act re-enacting the drama of conquest, as men of the dominating group sexually violate the bodies of women who are among the dominated. . . . Dominated men are made powerless [i.e., impotent] over and over again as women they would have a right to possess, to control, to assert power over, to dominate . . . are [possessed] by the dominating victorious male group. (p. 57)

The sexual metaphor for liberation privileges male interests, subordinates women's concerns, and thus provides social legitimation for sexism and sexist behavior. First, hooks (1990, 1992) observes that equating the Black liberation struggle to Black male "freedom" subsumes the concerns of Black women under that of Black men even as it subordinates their contribution to the struggle for racial equality in American society. The invisibility of Black women provided impetus for her first book (hooks, 1981), *Ain't I a Woman: Black Women and Feminism*: "I was compelled to confront Black women's reality, our denied and buried history, our present circumstances" (hooks, 1989a, p. 30). Second, not only does institutionalized sexism privilege men over women but in Black communities Black men's concerns are pitted against the Black women's; financial and economic inadequacy of Black men are often blamed on Black women (hooks, 1981, 1990, 1993, 1995b; hooks & West, 1991):

Contemporary equation of black liberation struggle with subordination of black women has damaged collective black solidarity. It has served the interests of white supremacy to promote the assumption that wounds of racist domination would be less severe were black women conforming to sexist role patterns. (hooks, 1990, p. 48)

Education practices that treat women-related responsibilities and concerns as secondary reflect the value society places on women in general (Martin, 1984, 1995). Not surprisingly, affective and "service-oriented" activities such as caring and nurturance to which women are traditionally associated are typically relegated to the domestic sphere and termed "supportive" roles; qualities of detachment and rationality are reinforced while interdependency and passion traditionally associated with women are relegated to nonacademic spheres and posited as something to be outgrown (Martin, 1984, 1995).

Paul McGhee and Terry Freuh (1980), Stephen Craig (1992), and Mary Mwangi (1996) raise the issue of mass media's reflection and reinforcement of sex-role stereotypes in society. Richard Ohmann critiques the portrayal of women in their "vocation of domesticity, domestic subordination, bourgeois family ideal of motherhood (1996, p. 267). Stephen Craig's (1992) study illustrates the gender bias in program timing and characters. Even though men may not be portrayed as central characters, men still exude the aura of authority and patriarchal dominance. Craig further notes that men's roles are more expansive than women who are normally portrayed in domestic and family roles. Men are modeled as celebrity spokesman, husband, professional, and often shown in a wide variety of social roles and activities. Characteristics typically associated with males such as independence, aggressiveness, competitiveness, and physical strength are portrayed in a more positive and attractive light than related female qualities such as sensitivity or affectivity. Masculine traits and characteristics are portrayed as laudatory standards by which female portrayals are measured and to which impressionable children aspire.

Subordinating women's roles and concerns in the public sphere is heightened in the case of Black women on the basis of interlocking dominations (race, gender, and class). hooks (1981, 1984, 1994c, 1995b) defines Black women in both the academy and society as an invisible group, appropriated under the categories of "female" and "Black," and yet whose experiences are not legitimated by either group. Notice how

> [w]hen women were talked about, the experience of white women was universalized to stand for all female experience and that when black people were talked about, the experience of black men was the point of reference. (hooks, 1994c, p. 121)

Exclusion of women as objects and subjects of educational thought ignores women's contribution in history and by virtue of omission, indirectly undermines responsibilities traditionally associated with women. In the process not only are the tasks, duties, and traits and institutions society traditionally associates with women excluded but so are contributions of women in and to history (Martin, cited in Martin, 1984, p. 344). hooks (1981, 1984, 1989a) points to the public acclaim surrounding Martin Luther King, Malcolm X, A. Phillip Randolph, Marcus Garvey, Amiri Baraka, and Roy Wilkins over women's contribution such as Sojourner Truth, Ann Cooper, Mary Church Terrell, Harriet Tubman, Rosa Parks, Daisy Bates, and Septima Clark, in Black communities. In schools, pedagogical orientations reflect a similar gender bias. Sonia Nieto (1996) illustrates the manner in which sexism is played out in schools. Expecting girls to be submissive and passive, teachers reinforce this gender bias in interactions with female students. Nieto (1996) points to Myra Sadker and David Sadker's research findings documenting sexism in educational practices, the manner in which even

> [w]ell intentioned teachers [often] treat their female students far differently from their male students, interacting with them less frequently, asking them fewer questions, and giving them less feedback than they give male students. (Nieto, 1996, p. 36)

hooks (1981) identifies three primary expressions of sexism within the Black community: (a) the exclusive acclaim awarded Black male leaders despite joint efforts of men and women for racial equality, (b) sexist role patterning and resentment of women who fail to assume traditional passive roles (hooks, 1981), (c) extensive scholarly attention given to de-masculinization of men during slavery but not to its impact on Black women, and (d) the sexism propagated in *The Colored Museum* play, and Spike Lee's *She's Gotta Have It* and *School Daze*, among others (hooks, 1990).

In view of the previous arguments, feminist and critical theory scholars point to the partiality of claims, the bias in narratives, and disfiguring portraits in Western culture's theories to illustrate the need for a more adequate representation of what passes for "cultural literacy" and/or "cultural norms" (Giroux & McLaren, 1994, hooks, 1994b; Martin, 1984, 1995; Minnich, 1990; Nieto, 1996; Noddings, 1992, 1995b). Further, hooks (1981, 1990, 1992) notes the implications of a sexist (masculinized) metaphor of liberation and civilization in promoting sexist attitudes and practices. Thus, inclusion and/or exclusion of elements in a "canon" both determine and reinforce its worth. Omission of texts pertaining to women and other minorities reinforces marginality of these groups' interests and values. To counteract this "absence" of marginalized groups in traditional curriculum, feminists call for an inclusive curriculum that helps "promote both the desired recognition of difference and connection . . . crucial to social change" (Leach, 1995, p. 359). Similar to the manner in which Blacks often internalize the negation of Black traits and characteristics in readily adopting White people's standards, women often internalize society's devaluation of their personhood as the following discussion demonstrates.

Internalized Sexism

hooks (1995b) attributes the focus of Black women on looks, clothing, and relationships with men to what this author terms "internalized sexism." hooks contends:

> Male supremacist ideology encourages women to believe we are valueless and obtain value only by relating to or bonding with men. We are taught that our relationships with one another diminish rather than enrich our experience. (1984, p. 43)

In a patriarchal society, women are socialized to relate to each other as competitors for men's attention, in dressing and dating (hooks, 1994b). Most

Black women's primary focus is on "how we look, what we will wear, and how well we will submit to male authority" (hooks, 1995b, p. 70). Further, patriarchal allegiance is expressed in the manner in which Black women often police one another to maintain positions of power and authority, especially in professional settings (hooks, 1990):

> Between women and men, sexism is most often expressed in the form of male domination which leads to discrimination, exploitation, or oppression. Between women, male supremacist values are expressed through suspicious, defensive, competitive behavior. It is sexism that leads women to feel threatened by one another without cause. While sexism teaches women to be sex objects for men, it is also manifest when women who have repudiated this role feel contemptuous and superior in relation to those women who have not. Sexism leads women to devalue parenting work while inflating the value of jobs and careers. . . . Sexism teaches women woman-hating, and both consciously and unconsciously we act out this hatred in our daily contact with one another. (hooks, 1984, p. 47)

Black women are socialized into linking their self-esteem to their capacity to serve others (hooks, 1993). On the other hand, "many black females learn early to objectify themselves, their bodies, and use their sexuality as a commodity that can be exchanged in the sexual market place" (hooks, 1993, p. 115). Schooled into a sexist ideology that values women as objects of male desire and service, Black women respond accordingly.

In *Breaking Bread: Insurgent Black Intellectual Life*, hooks and West address the issue of relationships between Black women and men. These scholars point to the hindrances to Black female and male partnerships as a result of unacknowledged sexism, and the jostling for positions and acclaim in a disenfranchising milieu:

> In the past few years, especially among black critical thinkers and writers, there's been a great deal of jockeying for positions between black women and men. There has been a kind of proliferation of the false notion that if black women are being heard, black men's voices are necessarily silenced, and if black men's voices are heard, black women must assume a voiceless position. (1991, p. 3)

In this context, hooks (1981, 1984, 1989a) notes the allegations regarding Black women's hindrance to Black men's progress:

When white women enter the work force today it is seen as a positive step . . . while more than ever before in our history black women who enter the work force are encouraged to feel that they are taking jobs from black men or de-masculinizing them. For fear of undermining the self-confidence of black men, many young college-educated black women repress their own career aspirations. . . . most black women . . . believed men are superior to women and that a degree of submission to male authority was a necessary part of woman's role. (hooks, 1981, p. 83)

Besides impact of socialization patterns on women, patriarchal sanctioning of works such as Shahrazad Ali's (cited in hooks, 1994c) *The Blackman's Guide to Understanding the Blackwoman* promotes sexism in rationalizing domination of men by women as a "natural" and sanctioning subordination of Black women to Black men. By implication the success of Black men is pitted against that of Black women. This reasoning follows a trend. Indeed, hooks contends that in the early

[s]eventies individual black women decided they could repair the damages done to black men within this racist society by repressing their advancement and assuming a secondary, supportive role; they found themselves in relationships where black males exercised power in ways that were dominating and coercive. (1990, p. 76)

Ironically, despite the economic, sexist, and racist victimization of Black women there prevails the conventional stereotype of Black women as matriarchs (hooks, 1981, 1993). In hooks' contention:

The term matriarch implies the existence of a social order in which women exercise social and political power, a state which in no way resembles the condition of Black women or all women in American society. (1981, p. 72)

In the academy, "[i]t seems as though a racialized gendered hierarchy is established . . . wherein the writing on 'race' by black men is deemed worthier of in-depth study than the work of black women critics" (hooks, 1994c, p. 79). Both hooks (1981, 1984, 1994c, 1995b) and Audre Lorde (cited in hooks, 1994c) illustrate how Black women's criticisms were initially discounted in mainstream feminist circles on the basis of race and class, and their involvement in the feminist movement rooted in sexism, seen as a betrayal of the struggle for the rights of Black people. Employing Mary Belenky et al.'s metaphor

(1986) of "voice," hooks (1981) associates silence in Black women during and after slavery to a resignation and acceptance of the interlocking racist and sexist dominations. As an aside, while hooks (1990) attributes the "silence" in Black men to the slaughter and loss of rebels during the Black liberation struggle, hooks and West (1991) attribute it to a poor leadership vision and quality, and the fear and failure that plagues Black people from living in a racist society.

While hooks (1994c) addresses the interplay of race, gender, and class biases in education, most feminist scholars (Martin, 1995; Minnich, 1990; Noddings, 1992; Pagano, 1995) focus their critique on patriarchy, illustrating the manner in which society's valuing of women is reinforced in school curriculum and pedagogy, both of which are modeled after masculine modes of thought and behavior. Thus, in a White supremacist society, the "white male symbolizes power and privilege while women of all races and ethnicities, and men of color [are] viewed as marginalized groups" (hooks, 1994c, p. 130). hooks also explains the triad scorn of Black women in terms of socio-historical factors:

> As far back as slavery, white people established a social hierarchy based on race and sex that ranked white men first, white women second, though sometimes equal to black minorities, who are ranked third, and black women last. (1981, pp. 52–53)

The previous discussion analyzed the manifestation and perpetuation of sexism in society. First, hooks (1981, 1984, 1989a, 1990) contends that socialization patterns within family units lay the foundation for sexism in privileging male over female children. Second, society reinforces this gender bias in presenting male traits and characteristics as the norm while presenting female-related traits and characteristics—including dependency on others, and association to the home—as something to be outgrown. A sexist (masculinized) metaphor for liberation and civilization underscores the primacy of male interests and objectifies women, reducing females to pawns on a chessboard. Third, the Christian account associating women with evil provides further justification for the marginality of women in society. Fourth, mass media have for the most part portrayed women in subordinate roles and in need of male support and guidance. Mass media also reinforce the primacy of White, male, middle-class values. Fifth, the racial and class differences between Black and White women hindered effective solidarity between the two groups. To reiterate the interlocking nature of dominations, hooks (1981, 1984, 1989a, 1990) illustrates the difference in the impact of racial bias on Black men and women and the difference in the impact of gender bias on White as opposed to Black women. The following discussion illustrates the manner in which a capitalist consumer society equates success and social status to acquisition of wealth and fame and by implication promotes a particular value system within society. hooks sees a link between class and White supremacy insofar as White people constitute a larger percentage of people in the middle and upper classes.

CHAPTER 3

Classism

bell hooks' writings reiterate the interlocking nature of dominations. The disproportional racial representation in different economic classes supports hooks' claim with regard to the interlocking nature of dominations. Further, hooks suggests that the "absence [of minorities in the academy] is no doubt related to the way class politics and class struggle shapes who will receive doctorates" (1994c, p. 189). The discussion on classism is divided into five main sections: (a) composition of policy makers, (b) bourgeois norms, (c) classism among Blacks, (d) classism in schools, and (e) classism within feminism.

Composition of Policy Makers

hooks illustrates the manner in which racial discrimination continues to manifest itself in contemporary America:

Despite civil rights struggle, the many reforms that have made it possible for [Blacks] to study and teach at universities throughout the United States, we continue to live in a white-supremacist country. While [Blacks] no longer live within the rigid structures of racial apartheid that characterized earlier moments in our history, we live within a culture of domination, surrounded by institutions—religious, educational, etc.—

which reinforce the values, beliefs, and underlying assumptions of white supremacy. (1989a, p. 63)

According to Joel Spring, most "boards of education in the United States tend to be more composed of white male professional or business persons" (1978, p. 94). This cultural composition of policy makers impacts policy and practice in schools and society (Banks, 1988; Goodlad, 1984; Kozol, 1991; Nieto, 1996; Spring, 1978). It could be argued that this composition of policy makers represents qualified personnel interested in education. However, correlation between a particular composition of policy makers' economic and political values and school policy makes representation significant (Banks, 1988; hooks, 1995b; Nieto, 1996; Spring, 1978). Individual biases easily translate into institutional biases, biases of race, class, and gender. Mainstream norms and practices typically reflect the backgrounds, education, and experiences of the groups with access to economic and political resources, in this particular case, European Americans. hooks (1990) argues that subjugation of Black people globally has been maintained by perpetual construction of economic and social structures that serve the interests of White people:

> Placed in the position of authority in educational structures and on the job, white people could oversee and eradicate organized resistance. The neo-colonial environment gave white folks even greater access and control over the African American mind. Integrated educational structures were locations where whites could best colonize the minds and imaginations of black folks. Television and mass media were the other great neo-colonial weapons. (hooks, 1995b, p. 110)

Social inequalities in power and privilege easily translate to reproduction of policy and practice that favor a particular ideology concerning social reality, criteria for assessing standards of knowledge and its acquisition, and definition of what constitutes "proper" life-style (Banks, 1988; hooks, 1989a).

> While it is true that the nature of racist oppression and exploitation has changed as slavery has ended and the apartheid structure of Jim Crow has legally changed, white supremacy continues to shape perspectives on reality and to inform the social status of black people and of all people of color. (hooks, 1995b, p. 187)

Supporting hooks' assertion (1989a) regarding institutionalized racism, Banks makes the following observation concerning power and privilege in society:

The basis for the unequal distribution of rewards is determined by elitist groups in which power is centered. Powerful groups decide which traits and characteristics are necessary for full societal participation. They determine traits on the basis of the similarity of such traits to their own values, physical characteristics, life-styles, and behavior. (1988, p. 181)

As a corrective to the cultural bias in policy maker representation and student body, Richter (1994) advocates a faculty and student composition that reflects a nation's cultural plurality.

Bourgeois Norms

hooks' writings critique the materialistic mentality manifested even in materially underprivileged Black communities. hooks advocates a nonmaterialistic value system in contending that aesthetics is more than a philosophy or theory of art and beauty. She associates aesthetics to one's manner of inhabiting space, an appreciation of the immediate and natural, both of which she contrasts with the materialistic mentality in society:

I understood that advanced capitalism was affecting our capacity to seek, that consumerism began to take the place of that prediction of heart that called us to yearn for beauty. Now many of us are only yearning for things. (1990, p. 104)

Raising a similar caution against consumerism, Sandra McNaught asserts:

Social and political passivity is the logical outcome of consumerism, and endless consumption engenders a sense of futility. Consumer society also produces a sense of nihilism and hopelessness because it articulates an ideology of change that leaves reality unchanged and individuals unfulfilled. (1996, p. 202)

hooks (1993) cautions Black women against the addiction to overspending to ease the pain of negation and oppression. She notes the ease with which one slips into (over)spending patterns.

Paulo Freire (1970/1992) attributed "cultural silence" to oppressive economic and political conditions in most Third World countries, maintained by social myths that justify existence of the status quo. Recent scholarship on similar issues in First World countries (Harris, 1995; hooks, 1990, 1992, 1994b; McNaught, 1996) illustrate that social myths in education and citizenship in liberal states also result in a "cultural silence." The primary aim of social myths is to maintain an existing social order with its social inequalities in power and privilege.

In the minds of most Blacks, "White" continues to be associated with privilege and power while "Black" conjures images of inferiority and a general "lack" in various aspects of life (Fordham, 1996; Ngugi Wa Thiong'o, 1986, 1993). hooks contends that there is systemic reinforcement of White racist norms and practices in the United States:

> While the Eurocentric biases taught to blacks in the educational system were meant to socialize us to believe in our inherent inferiority, it was ultimately the longing to have access to material rewards granted whites (the luxury and comfort represented in advertising and television) that was the greatest seduction. Aping whites, assimilating their values (i.e., white supremacist attitudes and assumptions) was clearly the way to achieve material success. And white supremacist values were projected into our living rooms, into the most intimate spaces of our lives by mass media. . . . Even though most black communities were and remain segregated, mass media bring white supremacy into our lives, constantly reminding us of our marginalized status. (1995b, p. 110)

First, this materialistic thinking leads to individualism, competitiveness, and an obsession with material gain and consumer goods over and above a sense of ethics and self-appreciation (hooks, 1990, 1993, 1994b, 1995b).

> Many privileged black folks obsessed with living out a bourgeois dream of liberal individualistic success no longer feel as though they have an accountability in relation to the black poor and underclass. (hooks & West, 1991, p. 15)

Second, in promoting values and beliefs of privileged White people, mass media create a yearning in the underprivileged for material possessions, equating materialism to freedom.

> The public figures who speak the most to us about a return to old-fashioned values embody the evils [Martin Luther] King describes [materialism, militarism]. They are most committed to maintaining systems of domination—racism, sexism, class exploitation, and imperialism. They promote a perverse vision of freedom that makes it synonymous with materialism. (hooks, 1994c, p. 27–28)

Classism Within Schools

Third, hooks (1989a, 1994c) contends that in the academy, focus on jargonistic, abstract writing is classist, divorcing theory from practice, the public from academic elites. Theoretical standards set up by academia

> set up unnecessary and competing hierarchies of thought which rein-scribe the politics of domination by designating work [of minorities] as either inferior, superior, or more or less worthy of attention . . . [result-ing] in the production of an intellectual class hierarchy where the only work deemed truly theoretical is work that is highly abstract, jargonistic, difficult to read, and containing obscure references. (hooks, 1994c, p. 64)

Ronald Scapp (1990) contends that most communities of the world today have built in mechanisms of censoring dissenting voices. hooks (1995b) notes that among marginalized groups, like African Americans, the most open-minded individuals are more likely to be isolated, and that isolation is likely to be intensified if their intellectual work is linked to progressive politics. Scapp's observation resonates with hooks' writings with regard to marginalization of non-Whites, women, especially Black women, and the underclass. Speaking from her experi-ence at Stanford University, hooks notes how school culture disenfranchised students from low-income backgrounds, usually non-White:

> There is little or no discussion of the way in which attitudes and values of those materially privileged classes are imposed upon everyone via pedagogical strategies. Reflected in the choice of subject matter and the manner in which ideas are shared, these biases need never be overtly stated. . . . Silencing enforced by bourgeois values is sanctioned in the classroom by everyone. (1994c, p. 180)

Invariably, schools promote middle- and upper-class values, tastes, language, and dialects, while classroom discussions invoke bourgeois experiences and ideals.

> Assimilation makes it very easy for those of us from working class backgrounds to acquire all the trappings that make us seem like we come from privilege, especially if we are college educated and talk the right kinda talk (every time I try to get clever and throw some vernacular black speech into my essays, they are perceived as errors and "corrected"). (hooks, 1990, p. 90)

In class, middle-class norms shape pedagogical practices. Typically, silence and obedience to authority are rewarded while loudness, anger, emotional outbursts normally associated with low-class members are deemed unacceptable (McNaught, 1996). In addition, the university curricula's constant evocation of materially privileged class experience subtly promotes middle-class values as a universal norm to the exclusion of other perspectives. hooks (1994c) notes the pressure Black folks coming from poor, underclass communities who enter the universities or privileged settings experience: "It was assumed that any student coming from a poor or working-class background would willingly surrender all values and habits of being associated with this background" (1994c, p. 182). Further analyzing the experiences of Black students at Yale University who grapple with their Black identity, hooks makes the following observation:

> Uncertain about the value of racial solidarity, today's black students have been encouraged to believe that assimilation (to make similar, to be absorbed) is the way to succeed. They rarely critique the insistence on conformity to a white, privileged class norm but rather work to adapt this mode of being. (1989a, pp. 66–67)

hooks (1994c) and Scapp's (1990) observations demonstrate the manner in which conflict between classes, rich and poor, the powerful and powerless continues to be reenacted in classrooms (Feinberg & Soltis, 1992; hooks, 1994c). In Black communities, consumerism

> creates a market culture where one's communal and political identity is shaped by the adoration and cultivation of images, celebrityhood, and visibility, as opposed to character, discipline, substantive struggle. (hooks & West, 1991, p. 95)

On the other hand, school culture sanctions upper-class values and ideals through school culture, privileging groups with similar cultural norms while requiring other students to conform for assimilation and/or social mobility (Banks, 1988; hooks, 1994c). From her experience at Stanford University, hooks contends:

> If one was not from a privileged class group, adopting a demeanor similar to that of the group could help one advance. It is still necessary for students to assimilate bourgeois values in order to be deemed acceptable. (1994c, p. 178)

Expounding on Plato's *Republic*, Scapp (1990) illustrates the manner in which communities exclude and include persons or ideas through a process of legitimation. The separation of academia and theory from common language usage denies the liberatory function of education as a tool for the development of critical consciousness, setting a dichotomy between intellectuals and the masses (Beyer, 1995; Freire & Faundez, 1989; hooks, 1994c; Shor, 1992). As the following part illustrates, critical, feminist, and multicultural scholarship argue for a closer link between theory and practice, the academics and students' lived reality.

Classism Among Blacks

The impact of the American people's allegiance to the middle-class norms is evident in the manner in which

> [m]ost black academics, irrespective of their politics, whether they iden-
> tify as conservative, liberals, or radical, religiously uphold privileged-class
> values in their manner and style in which they teach, when it comes to
> habits of being, to mundane matters like dress, language, decorum.
> (hooks, 1995b, p. 174)

Materially privileged, upper- and middle-class Blacks often feel the need to disassociate themselves from "poorer" Blacks to avoid the stigma of Blacks as an underclass race (hooks, 1994b, 1995b):

> It grieves me to observe the contempt and utter disinterest black indi-
> viduals from privileged classes often show in their interactions with
> disadvantaged black folks . . . particularly those of us whose background
> are poor and working class. (hooks, 1995b, p. 182)

hooks contrasts a White supremacist capitalistic mentality with traditional community values wherein an individual's "[V]alue was connected to integrity, to being honest and hardworking" (1994b, p. 167). Notwithstanding propaganda on ethical values, most people participate wholeheartedly in consumer capitalism, the attachment to material possessions, individualistic competitiveness, and power in both the economically privileged and underprivileged in the American society (hooks, 1993, 1994b, 1995b; hooks & West, 1991). Further reinforcing a materialistic value system, the mass media praises minorities "who have made their way out of the ghetto, barrio, or reservation" (Ogbu, 1992, p. 3). Not only do Blacks who have "made" it economically and socially feel privileged by their association to the dominant culture but even Black people living in "poverty or situations of economic stress and deprivation . . . are all socialized by television to identify with the values and attitudes of the bourgeois and ruling class" (hooks, 1995b, p. 255).

Classism Within Feminism

The issue of *class* also arises in feminist discourse. hooks (1981, 1984) critiques a vision of sisterhood within feminism, rooted in shared victimization, especially when White women had little desire to associate with Black women and were more privileged economically and politically.

> [White women] wanted to project an image of themselves as victims and that could not be done by drawing attention to class. As a group, white participants did not denounce capitalism. They chose to define liberation using the terms of white capitalist patriarchy, equating liberation with gaining economic status and money power. (hooks, 1981, p. 145)

Further, noting the absence of Black women's experiences in Betty Friedan's *The Feminine Mystique* and Caroline Bird's *Born Female*, hooks (1994c) contends that inadequate coverage is given to impact of class in the United States.

> [W]e do not talk enough about the way in which class shapes our perspectives on reality. Since so many of the early feminist books really reflected a certain type of white bourgeois sensibility, this work did not touch many black women deeply; not because we did not recognize the common experiences women shared, but because those commonalities were mediated by profound differences in our realities created by the politics of race and class. (1994c, pp. 51–52)

Aware of the interlocking nature of dominations, hooks (1984, 1989a, 1990, 1994b; hooks & West, 1991) cautions minorities and activists not to repudiate domination in one form while supporting it in another. hooks notes the way "race and class determine the degree to which one can assert male domination and privilege and most importantly the ways racism and sexism are interlocking systems of domination which uphold and sustain one another" (1990, p. 59). (Not surprisingly, the image of the White colonizing male is superior on all counts.) In Black men, this takes the form of decrying the ills of racism while upholding sexist patterns, in White men and White women taking sexism seriously while upholding racist patterns. In hooks' assessment,

> if we are only committed to an improvement in that politic of domination that we feel leads directly to our individual exploitation or oppression, we not only remain attached to the status quo but act in complicity with it, nurturing and maintaining those very systems of domination. Until we are all able to accept the interlocking, interdependent nature of systems of domination and recognize specific ways each system is maintained, we will continue to act in ways that undermine our individual quest for freedom and collective liberation struggle. (1994b, p. 244)

The previous discussion has analyzed the manifestation and perpetuation of bourgeois values within schools and the wider society. By portraying attractive images of material privilege, the mass media present material success as the criteria for one's social status. This creates a yearning for materialistic gain and consumer goods, most especially in the underclass. In schools, students from low-income families feel pressured to adopt middle-class traits and characteristics to facilitate their assimilation in educational settings. The credit card saga—manner in which most people in the United States spend well beyond their financial means—best expresses the association of material acquisition to social status and one's self-esteem. hooks argues:

> Two addictions affecting black women, which may not be as evident as alcohol and drug abuse, are food addiction and compulsive shopping. Since constant consumerism is such an encouraged societal norm, it is easy for black women to mask addictive, compulsive consumerism that threatens well-being, that leads to us to lie, cheat, and steal to be able to "buy" all that we desire. (1993, p. 71)

The following discussion provides the author's analysis of bell hooks' social theory and critique of schools.

CHAPTER 4

Reflections on hooks' Social Theory

bell hooks demonstrates a thorough understanding of racial, gender, and class bias in schools and the wider society. What is commendable is her choice and manner of raising issues that are normally glossed over for lack of reflection on the part of individuals and in keeping with conventional promotion of "political correctness." The insights drawn from her books raise the author's consciousness to the impact of race, gender, and class on interrelationships besides one's understanding of self and the "Other." This chapter is divided into three subparts: (a) issues on which hooks and the author are in agreement, (b) issues raised by hooks with which the author agrees though with reservation, and (c) issues raised by hooks and which the author believes requires further clarity.

Issues hooks and the Author Agree Upon

Negation of Blackness

There are few among White and Black folk who view *Blackness* in a positive light. From the analysis of hooks' body of works as well as the author's personal experiences, there appears to be a profound hatred for *Blackness* in the United States. This is an insight drawn by both. Incidentally, though this fact is heightened in the case of the United States (the publicized impact of slavery may partly account for this), a similar phenomenon is evident in other countries, including those with a majority of Black citizens. hooks challenges Africans everywhere to critically analyze the nature of White supremacy and Black people's complicity in perpetuating White supremacist attitudes and values.

The negation of *Blackness* is an issue that keeps coming up in hooks' corpus of writing as well as other works pertaining to African peoples. Sadly, as elements of the stereotype of Africans (Blacks)—intellectually inferior to White people, incapable of self-governance (on a smaller scale, self-determination), exceptionally difficult to deal with, prone to irrationality, lazy, lustful, uncultured, and with undesirable features—are insidiously promoted in most cultures and deeply ingrained in the psyches of most Black people. (Ironically, patriarchy associates similar elements with femaleness.) The love/hate relationship between the dominant and the dominated explored by Paulo Freire and James Baldwin aptly expresses the impact of internalized self-negation in the dominated. Despite "talk" of hating the oppressor, the oppressed yearn to attain the very values that the social group sanctions and exalts—civilization, success, freedom, standards of beauty, elegance—as defined by traditional frameworks. To "make it" translates to material acquisition, political and economic leverage. The criteria for assessing one's social prestige appear to be based on White people's manner and style of social interactions, from ways of being to mundane matters such as dress, speech, and language. Not surprisingly, those who have made it feel the need to disassociate themselves from negated (non-White) traits and characteristics. The Black, honorary Whites are rewarded for successfully adopting dominant cultural values and traditions.

Terms such as *passing for White*, *acting White*, *internalized racism*, and *Uncle Tom* are but the tip of issues that plague Black communities. Of note is the limited discourse on the need for Black folks to identify with *Whiteness*. Stereotypes aside, the mass media publicize middle-class people's lives, privileges, and opportunities that marginalized groups desire for assimilation and equality. One may wonder what White supremacy has to do with mainstream norms and practices. Think for a minute. Whose cultural norms and values are reflected in school norms and practices? Who excels in standardized tests? Which form of English is utilized in schools, or official papers, or social interactions? Whose experiences are invoked in schools? Which school would you want to teach in, or send your children to—majority Black or majority White schools? Clearly, "White" is more than a color category. Come to think of it, since "White" is about opportunity, privilege, and power, would not non-White people desire to be White?

In Kenya, the fact that beauty pageant judges select contestants who are most similar to White people in skin texture, coloring, and manner of speech is sad but revealing in itself. Signithia Fordham raised a disturbing observation in noting that a significant number of high-achieving Black ninth- and eleventh-grade students in majority Black schools identified themselves as male, rather than "Black" while underachieving male and female students readily identified themselves as "Black." The implicit denigration of what is Black and association of "White" with superiority in so young a population is overwhelming to say the least. This author finds the continued negation of Blackness extremely disturbing. The students' choice to identify with the White race resonates with one of hooks' insights regarding the yearning in non-White peoples for White people's traits and characteristics. This author anticipates resistance in non-White people to entertain such a thought. On the other hand, the thought that there are people out there who love Blackness (not as an opposing element to Whiteness!) is both joyous and hopeful. Few do. Many must. bell hooks is one such person!

A year ago, this author would easily have overlooked the political message of the following illustrations: (a) stereotypes in movies and the mass media, (b) Black women's preference for straight hair and/or lighter skin, (c) the recognition for speaking "proper" English, (d) the disassociation of upper-class Blacks from the Black underclass and related traits and characteristics, and (e) the cultural biases in school curriculum and pedagogical orientations. Over and above the cited expressions of most Black people's preference for White people's cultural traits and characteristics, the imaging of virtuous characters and advertisements of professional occupations by White people definitely reinforces White supremacy. The negation of *Blackness* is also evident in majority Black countries. Keith Richburg's (1997) *Out of America: A Black Man Confronts Africa* recounts his experience in Kenya as a darker skinned African American. In Kenya, preferential treatment to White people hardly raises eyebrows (Richburg, 1997). In fact, a Kenyan Black would be shocked were one to treat a fellow Black man/woman with the reverence given to White expatriates. Not surprisingly, Black-skinned foreigners mistaken for local people do not receive preferential treatment.

Denial of Subjectivity

One wonders whether hooks' idealism with regard to individual "subjectivity" does not compromise the practicality of her arguments and propositions for social transformation. To what extent do social structures account for individual choices? Specifically, to what extent are Black people responsible for their marginality? This author too retains feelings of ambiguity regarding subjectivity and/or the degree to which social institutions account for individual subjugation.

hooks argues: "[W]hite folks promote black victimization, encourage passivity by rewarding folks who whine, grovel, beg, and obey" (1995b, p. 18). She further maintains that some Blacks feel embracing victimhood mediates relations with Whites, providing a cause for sympathy on the part of Whites rather than a redress or reparation for the ills of racism. One could also argue that Blacks as subjective beings have responsibility to choose, however difficult this may be, what enhances their humanity even when and if not supported by the surrounding environment. For if power is rightly understood as the ability to control or determine one's actions however limited the scope, Blacks are (to a degree) accountable for acceding to their "objectivity." In fact, on this score, John Champagne maintains that while "power 'produces' the subject, it also provides the conditions for possibility of resistance" (1993, p. 33).

Indeed, hooks (1989a, 1994c), similar to Freire (1970/1992, 1973), contends that one cannot enter the struggle as "object" with the intention of emerging as "subject." The lives of historically prominent Black political leaders such as Sojourner Truth, Malcolm X, Septima Clark, Martin Luther King, Jr., Charles Houston, James Baldwin, and other civil rights heroes testify to both the possibility and prize of self-actualization in a White supremacist, patriarchal, capitalist environment. Similarly, Black scholars such as hooks, Cornel West, Michele Wallace, Henry Louis Gates, and Toni Morrison critique in print and speech existing forms of racism, sexism, and classism in contemporary America. Though hooks cites some of these personalities, she fails to provide an adequate rationale for their resilience of spirit as Black folks daily confronted with negating messages. This author argues that either an illustration of strategies to self-actualization or the love for *Blackness* would be of greater benefit to other Black folk than mere injunctions.

Though discriminatory social forces belie individual efforts at social transformation, individuals as subjects of history can claim and actualize their imprint on history. Chanta Haywood's research findings on the resilience of Black women preachers in the nineteenth century validate this argument. In her study the lives of Black women preachers and writers demonstrate that it is "[s]ocial constructs that limit women, not divine ones" (1995, p. 73). The women did not view their marginality in bell hooks' (1984) terms, as *sites of deprivation*, but used their religious convictions as a basis for constructing counter-hegemonic discourse by employing the Word of God to deconstruct oppressive race, class, and gender ideologies. However limiting, marginality can also function as a site for resistance (Champagne, 1993; hooks, 1990). This author commends John Champagne's acknowledgment of both the limits and potential of marginality. Often, however great the desire of subjectivity and/or self-definition in marginalized people, circumstances beyond their control significantly impact their choices and/or actions. Champagne (1993) illustrates the oversimplicity in aspirations to subjectivity in marginalized members of society. He critiques hooks' notion of agency, pointing out that the West has often either denied marginalized peoples subjectivity, or granted a specific subjectivity that limits both expression and critique of prevailing cultural norms and practices. Champagne further argues that an emphasis on marginality as a site of resistance underscores the process of exorcising both the oppressor within and without. Since marginalized peoples are part and parcel of the "system," the difficulty comes in one's capacity to distance oneself enough to allow for objectivity and self-reflection.

Separatism

There are two sides to hooks' advocacy (1984, 1989a, 1990, 1994b, 1994c) for writing "from the margins." The articulation of marginality serves two functions: expression and audience (Scapp, 1990). hooks urges marginalized groups to "speak out." Speaking out, however, goes beyond the ability to express oneself. It is crucial that one's voice be heard, acknowledged, and one's position incorporated within the mainstream. hooks (1989a, 1994c) reiterates the necessity of marginalized groups to define the "location" of marginality as a process of reclaiming their identity and making history in a culturally alienating environment milieu. She terms the process a "coming to voice." Both Kathleen Donovan (1994) and hooks call for an alternative representation of social reality, one that presents an inclusive view of reality and credible views of marginalized people. Second, both advocate literacy as a strategy of resisting the appropriation of "voice" in a phallocentric culture. Donovan and hooks note how the reclamation of "women's agency and language from a patriarchal culture and its imperialistic polarities through their writing brings healing" (Donovan, 1994, p. 231). Similarly, Ronald Scapp (1990) and Chanta Haywood (1995) maintain that hooks' critique of White middle-class, feminist, and patriarchal sexism offers a way to see the full force of the significance of "voice" both within feminism and beyond. Scapp contends that a critical analysis of the "politics of voice" presents a valuable tool in attempting to dismantle the mechanisms of oppression brought about by the desire for homogeneity, the forces of appropriation, and the hostility toward difference. Interestingly, though Stotts commends hooks' call to "talk back" from the margins, she maintains that silence can also be a "subtle" form of resistance—

"an active non-response from a subject which itself carries nuances and implications that can be read or interpreted" (1993, p. 24).

In a culture that sanctions and promotes a particular group's values and traditions as the West has done through a White supremacist patriarchal capitalism value system, the disenfranchised group's traits and characteristics get subordinated to marginal status. Articulating one's experience of marginality affirms one's identity, confronting and deconstructing prevailing cultural hegemony and definitions by the "Other." In this context, hooks (1994c) expresses gratitude to those who in creating theory from personal pain and struggle provide experience to "teach and guide, as a means to chart new theoretical journey" (1994c, p. 74). hooks (1984, 1989a, 1990, 1994b, 1994c) critiques authors who theorize on marginality without interrogating their location of privilege, arguing that the practice smirks of cultural imperialism. On the one hand, Nel Noddings (1995b) supports hooks' advocacy of writings by marginalized individuals as opposed to "White" or privileged perspectives for an "objective" social reality. Noddings contends:

> Women and other oppressed groups are in a privileged position with respect to their oppression. Feminist "standpoint epistemologists claim that knowledge of women's condition constructed from the standpoint of women has an authenticity that so called objective knowledge can never achieve." (1995b, p. 110)

There is value to personal and direct expression. hooks (1990) points to the political implications of "having" one's experience defined by a privileged "Other." Implied in such a process is a form of marginality—in being spoken for and about to the exclusion of one's own "Voice." This resonates with Belenky et al.'s studies (1986) on need for "coming to voice" in women. Notwithstanding the value personal experience adds to theoretical discourse, to speak for oneself, to claim one's voice amounts to "claiming" one's identity or in Freire's (1970/1992) and hooks' (1990, 1994c) conceptualization, the process of a movement from "object" to "subject" of one's history.

Scholars are divided on this particular issue of "exclusive" writings primarily by or for marginalized groups. It is argued that marginalized groups require a re-articulate of their primary experiences. However, Champagne (1993) and Noddings (1995b) discourage this exclusionary practice in authorship, the fact that marginality is best addressed by marginalized people. Noddings (1995b) cautions against the danger of such exclusivity because objectivity comes from incorporating views from the "Other." Rebutting hooks' (1984, 1990, 1992) contention, Champagne (1993) argues that such a practice devalues the contributions from members outside particular groups. Though hooks (1992) critiques "pseudo-progressive whites" who would "eat the other" in their perpetual attempt to appropriate the transgressive energies of artists, writers, and theorists of color, her current status as distinguished university professor drawing a significant enough salary does raise the issue of her authority on matters of marginality, and her self-proclaimed status of spokesperson for the marginalized. Further, her failure to give credit to other artists of color in her work implies a "deliberate attempt on hooks' part to obliterate the vast and subversive history of black feminist thought" (Wallace, 1995b, p. 21). Creating an Insider-Outsider classification limits engagement that ought to typify intellectual discourses. Upon further reflection, the suggestion could easily lead to an intellectual bigotry, putting unnecessary limits on a discourse. Tied to the issue of authorship by and for marginalized groups is the contention over social interactions between Black and White people.

Allan Bloom (1987) and Dinesh D'Souza (1992) blame White and Black student separatism (exclusive social groupings of White and Black students) on Black students. However, hooks (1990, 1993, 1995b) argues that such reasoning fails to take into account the need for Black students living in a racial apartheid to create "separate places, the times apart from whiteness . . . for sanctuary, for reimagining and remembering" (hooks, 1995b, p. 6). This need for recovery of "space" for marginalized groups resonates with Mary Leen's notion of a need for "homeplace" in American Indian communities. Leen maintains that in a "hostile environment, a boundaried homeplace provides a retreat in which one may think, work, rest, and accumulate stories to help people remember" (1995, p. 23).

hooks attributes the subjugation of Black folk to the "perpetual construction of economic and social structures that deprive many folks of the means to make a homeplace" (1990, p. 46). Living in a cultural milieu that typically negates Blackness and/or related traits and characteristics, homeplace—an affirming forum, individuals, family, or community—provides a location that affirms one's being, color, and love for the other; a place one can return to for self-renewal and recovery (hooks, 1990, 1993, 1994b, 1994c, 1996a). This author agrees with hooks' suggestion on the significance of "homeplace" for self-recovery. Ironically, while hooks (1992, 1993, 1994b, 1994c, 1995b) focuses her critique on the ills of White supremacy and its impact on margi-nalized cultural groups, D'Souza (1992) and Bloom (1987) attribute, particu-larly in schools' contexts, maintenance of "separatism" to culturally marginalized groups. Bloom contends:

> There is now a large black presence in major universities frequently equivalent to their proportion in the general public. But they have, by and large, proved indigestible. Most keep to themselves. . . . [White] students have made the adjustment, without missing a beat, to a variety of religions and nationalities, the integration of Orientals and the change in women's aspirations and roles. . . . There is nothing more that White students can do to make great changes in their relations with blacks. (1987, pp. 91–92)

In this author's opinion, such "blanket" allegations smirk of racial bigotry. Putting the blame solely on Black students promotes the very separatist attitude that prevails in communities, and promotes the racist stereotypes associating White with purity and goodness and Black with evil. Such allegations fuel racial animosity rather than build racial harmony. Allegations that attribute strained interracial relations to either group fail to do justice, underestimating the complexity of the issue. This author argues that individuals are capable of justice but are also prone to injustice.

Issues Raised by hooks with Which the Author Agrees Though with Reservation

Opportunism

Freire (1970/1992, 1973) continually warns against what this author terms an "oppressed turned oppressor" syndrome. hooks' critique (1992, 1994b) of White supremacist values and attitudes of both White and Black people resonates with Freire's caution regarding complicity of the oppressed. hooks acknowledges the manner in which "power as dominations reproduces itself in different locations, employing similar apparatus, strategies, and mechanisms of control" (1992, p. 115). (Anti-White propaganda in Black radicals is no less appropriate as is anti-Black propaganda.)

hooks (1992, 1994b) raises two aspects of domination in her critique of White supremacy: the impact of White people's attitudes and treatments of Blacks and the complicity of Blacks in perpetuating White supremacist values and attitudes. In addition, hooks' writings reiterate the interlocking nature of dominations in her critique of Black male sexism and White female racism and classism though she fails to underscore that the elimination of dominations in society is typically compromised by individual self interests. This author argues that there is no guarantee that transformation would not involve the substitution of dominations and/or extremism in critique of either Whites instead of

Blacks and/or females instead of males. It often appears easier and more probable for individuals to exploit situations that promise some form of personal control, however unhealthy (drugs, violence, and/or domination of others), given objectifying and dehumanizing social forces. Indeed, hooks notes: "Though critical of white cultural imperialism, nationalist black males see no contradiction between that analysis and their support of hierarchical models of social organization that affirm coercive control and domination of others" (1995b, p. 246). In subscribing to patriarchal norms and equating Black liberation to male empowerment, Black men fail to critique a self-serving system of domination (hooks, 1990, 1992, 1993, 1994b, 1995b; hooks & West, 1991). In fact, hooks (1994b) argues that the eradication of sexism would lessen the animosity and competitiveness between sexes to create solidarity between Black men and women in a White supremacist society.

Champagne (1993) emphasizes the possibility of complicity in dehumanizing practices by marginalized individuals. In his view, the idea of marginality as a site of resistance underscores the pressure of exorcising the oppressor within and without. Marginalized persons are part and parcel of a system, a fact that compromises individuals' objectivity and self-reflection. This is, no doubt, further heightened in instances whereby one's self interest is served in one or more ways by prevailing systems. While heralded as a champion of the marginalized (hooks & West, 1991; McNaught, 1996), Michele Wallace (1995a, 1995b) presents hooks as a charlatan of sorts.

> *Art on my Mind* consists of hooks' usual formula of recycled pieces— catalogue essays and reviews . . . as well as new or re-published interviews. . . . But a substantial portion of the book is devoted to the autobiographical reveries/critical musings for which hooks is well known. Her consistently self indulgent writing has at least two distinct registers, the disarmingly playful and the correctly political. (Wallace, 1995a, p. 8)

> Much like her previous work, *Killing Rage: Ending Racism* consists of collection of unconnected essays, some of them recycled from earlier books. As usual, the writing is leftist, dogmatic, repetitive, and dated. (Wallace, 1995b, p. 19)

> Hooks has made herself queen of P.C. rhetoric. Without the unlovely code phrases, "white supremacist," "patriarchal domination," "self-recovery," hooks couldn't write a sentence. (Wallace, 1995b, p. 23)

Further, in the vignette at the introduction of *Killing Rage: Ending Racism*, hooks complains of the racist treatment her friends received from an airline representative. At no point in the event does hooks consider sacrificing her first class airline seat to join her friend who has been forced to travel coach. Wallace (1995b) terms this a case of "celebrity-tis."

Issues Raised by hooks That Require Further Clarification

Interrogating Ideologies

D. C. Phillips (1995) critiques Greene's position (1995), which is not unlike hooks' (1990, 1994c, 1995b), for attributing repressive aspects in education to the phallocentrism and colonialism in Western philosophy. Phillips points to the history of Christianity and atrocities committed in tribal communities all over the world to illustrate the widespread nature of repressive practices. Attributing repressive elements in education solely to Western philosophy amounts to an unfair apportionment of blame. To what degree do the ills of society hinge on "White supremacy"? Take the different forms of oppression in most of the Third World countries. Can these be wholly attributed to White supremacy? Were there perhaps existing oppressive structures before Western intervention? Was patriarchy the basis of such dominations? Should one perhaps push beyond "White supremacy" to patriarchy, or even beyond that? Karl Marx would attribute the "dominations" to capitalism.

Systems and/or ideologies are maintained by those whose interests are served—patriarchy benefits most men; capitalism, those with wealth; and White supremacy, White more than Black people. Though hooks (1981, 1984, 1989a) acknowledges complicity in individuals privileged by a particular social arrangement, in feminist circles (race/class over gender considerations), in her critique and proposed strategies for educational change, hardly any mention is made of the process the dominant culture has to go through in order to desire a change that would mean loss of existing privileges. Ideals of humanity, justice, peace, and harmony are often just that, ideals. Ideals by nature imply impracticality of attainment in failing to provide concrete and immediate strategies for individual and/or social transformation.

Harvey Siegel (1995) contends that the essentialism employed to define the "condition" of women ought to be nuanced just as should feminists in "male-epistemology." Otherwise, such critiques fall into a similar he very Western thought bias that most feminists critique (Min- This echoes Champagne's (1993) critique of hooks' definition of '89a, 1990). What both Champagne (1993) and Siegel (1995) ntialism ignores differences in degrees and forms of marginality within groupings. Countering positions such as hooks' (1981, 1984, 1989a) in her focus on Black and women's issues, Siegel contends that in the final analysis: "There are sameness and differences across women, across people, and across theories" (1995, p. 193). In this context, though hooks (1981, 1984, 1989a) critiques essentialism in early feminist writings, she readily offers personal experiences of marginality to express racist, sexist, and classist discriminatory practices in society, which however one looks at it, amounts to essentialism. Her personal experiences may, but do not necessarily, represent the experiences of Blacks, women, and/or materially underprivileged members of society. Further, Meriwether (1993) maintains that hooks seems to fall prey to what she opposes in her use of entities and subentities to make her case regarding the different levels of "oppression." hooks raises the issue of cultural domination and its impact on marginalized cultures. However, in most of her literature, hooks' writings focus on the impact of White supremacy primarily on Black folks. Though the exclusive focus on Black folks' experience could be intentional on hooks' part, it is at variance to hooks' proposition for cultural pluralism in society and educational settings. Meriwether's critique of hooks highlights the fact that (a) the level of oppression can be circumstantial, (b) all marginalized peoples warrant attention, and finally (c) membership in any one category does not absolve one of moral responsibility in perpetuating other forms of oppression. On a similar score, despite the charges of school as racist, sexist, and bureaucratic, a number of minority youths manage to escape poverty and experience social class and economic mobility (Banks, 1988).

This author is in agreement with hooks with regard to the following issues: (a) the negation of Blackness and its impact on Black people, (b) the possibility of complicity of marginalized persons in the maintenance and perpetuation of White supremacist values and attitudes, (c) the need for articulation and recognition of marginalized cultural histories, and (d) the need for "homeplace" in a culturally alienating environment. However, this author reservedly agrees with hooks on the elimination of dominations in schools and society, and seeks further clarification on the degree to which "dominations" account for an individual's lack of self-determination and self-actualization. To what degree, it can be argued, is the inability of one to attain self-actualization to be ascribed to her or his racial, gender, and/or class identity. Overall, this author is in agreement with hooks' analysis of race, gender, and class biases in schools and society.

In sum, hooks' views and oppositional arguments resonate with critical, feminist, and multicultural scholarship assessment regarding the often insidious cultural (sexist, classist, racist) reproduction within the schooling system (Feinberg & Soltis, 1992; Giroux, 1983; Giroux & McLaren, 1994; Martin,

1992, 1995; McLaren, 1989; Morrow & Torres, 1995; Noddings, 1995a, 1995b; Starratt, 1995). hooks contends: "Biases that uphold and maintain white supremacy, imperialism, sexism, and racism have distorted education so that it is no longer about the practice of freedom" (1994c, p. 29). Corrective measures to a discriminatory education system ought to involve an acknowledgment of how class shapes social values, attitudes, and relations, and the biases that inform the way knowledge is given and received. Critical interrogation of White supremacist, patriarchal, and capitalist ideologies embedded in schools' practices ought to be an effective starting point for transformation of official curriculum and pedagogies. hooks' educational theory (1994c) offers strategies for interrogating racial, gender, and class biases embedded in educational policies and practices, which is the theme of the following part.

PART II

bell hooks' Educational Theory

The preceding part presented bell hooks' social theory based on her writings. It advanced arguments to support hooks' contention regarding racist, sexist, and classist biases in educational settings and the wider society. This part analyzes the transformational strategies of bell hooks' educational theory, engaged pedagogy. Since hooks' libertarian education (1994c) addresses the issue of cultural reproduction of dominant and discriminatory elements in educational settings and in society, the manner in which the different components of engaged pedagogy address the issues raised in hooks' social theory is explored. The part is divided into five major sections: (a) theories related to bell hooks' engaged pedagogy, (b) components of engaged pedagogy, (c) the role of teachers, (d) limitations of hooks' educational theory, and (e) a closing discussion.

The analysis of bell hooks' educational theory is based on her 1994 book, *Teaching to Transgress: Education as the Practice of Freedom*. The educational theory, engaged pedagogy, espouses a combination of "anticolonial, critical, and feminist pedagogies . . . for interrogating biases in curricula that reinscribe systems of domination . . . while simultaneously providing new ways to teach diverse groups of students" (hooks, 1994c, p. 10). Since hooks bases her pedagogy on anticolonial, critical, and feminist pedagogies, the section on related theories explores similarities between bell hooks' engaged pedagogy, and critical, multicultural, and feminist scholarship. The part also includes a discussion of teachers' role and the limitations of hooks' transformative pedagogy.

bell hooks' education theory arises from the context of her past experiences as a Black and marginalized student and her present experiences as an educator in what she terms a racist, sexist, and classist society. Her critique and proposals for educational transformational strategies are drawn primarily from personal experiences. Indeed, hooks (1989a) devises strategies to reflect her politics of inclusion as a response to her experience of oppressively authoritarian professors and the pleasure and joy she derived from teaching. Her objective is to

> emphasize that the pleasure of teaching is an act of resistance countering the overwhelming boredom, uninterest, and apathy that so often characterize the way professors and students feel about teaching and learning, about the classroom experience. (hooks, 1994c, p. 10)

hooks (1994c) acknowledges the fact that though her initial audience for *Teaching to Transgress: Education as the Practice of Freedom* was teachers, the inability to make one of her classes an "exciting, learning community" made her realize the crucial role students play in creating a conducive learning environment. Indeed, the transformational strategies proposed by hooks presume a degree of commitment in both students and teachers to make the learning process interactive and relevant to students' lived realities.

First, engaged pedagogy seeks to counteract hierarchical relations in social arrangements and the often insidious cultural reproduction in schools. hooks (1981, 1984, 1989a, 1990, 1992, 1994b, 1994c, 1995b) cautions against an uncritical allegiance to educational and cultural norms and practices in society. She argues that social myths suggesting that power and privilege are earned through fair competition camouflage the impact of race, gender, and class discriminatory practices in educational settings and the wider society. Specifically, hooks (1994b, 1994c), similar to critical theory scholars, contends that a monocentric curriculum privileges students whose cultural norms are reflected within school culture, granting them "authority" in classroom settings and discussions while simultaneously alienating students whose cultural histories and traditions are subordinated and/or excluded. hooks, similar to critical theory scholars, associates the focus on White people's ways of being, feeling, and knowing to monocentrism. In effect, social/cultural inequalities easily translate to inequalities in educational settings. Second, engaged pedagogy critiques the "prescribed roles" of teachers as privileged voices, learners as passive recipients of "established truths." Looking back to her college years, hooks recalls that the primary lesson reinforced was "obedience to authority" (1994c, p. 4). In contrast, engaged pedagogy promises greater teacher/student interaction and empowers students to assume responsibility for creating conducive learning environments in conjunction with teachers.

To fully appreciate the significance of bell hooks' educational theory, one needs to understand her view of the goals of education. In stressing the link between theory and practice, engaged pedagogy avoids reification of knowledge from issues faced by most students, both within and outside of educational settings. Engaged pedagogy provides students with multiple perspectives that enable them to know themselves better and to live in the world more fully. In contrast to engaged pedagogy is the idea of the university "as a haven for those who are smart in book knowledge but who might be otherwise unfit for social interaction" (hooks, 1994c, p. 16). hooks terms the overall aim of this liberatory aspect of education "critical awareness and engagement," what Freire (1970/1992, 1973) calls "conscientization."

hooks (1989a, 1990, 1994b, 1994c) critiques the following elements in traditional educational practices: (a) the metaphysical notion of knowledge as universal, neutral, and objective; (b) the authoritative, hierarchical, dominating, and privileged status of professors; (c) the passive image of students as recipients of compartmentalized bits of knowledge, which limits student engagement in the learning process by not considering them as whole human beings with complex lives and experiences; (d) the traditional notion that the sole responsibility for classroom dynamics rests on teachers; and (e) the Western metaphysical denial of the dignity of passion and the subordination of human affectivity to the rationality. She further argues that reification of official knowledge from the implications stated above reinforces White supremacist, patriarchal, and capitalist ideologies. hooks' main critique (1989a) of racial integration in educational settings is that schools have failed to provide a means to resist White supremacist oppression. To counteract these biases in educational practices, hooks advocates: (a) re-conceptualization of the knowledge base; (b) relating of theory to practice to make education more relevant and meaningful, (c) empowerment of students to assume responsibility in conjunction with teachers, for creating a conducive learning environment; (d) encouragement of teachers' pedagogical emphasis on learner participation and engagement; and (e) understanding of teaching beyond "compartmentalized" schooling, a longer term involvement, development of critical consciousness, and teacher/student self-actualization. In sum, in addressing issues that impact students' day-to-day lives, engaged pedagogy "restores to education and the classroom excitement about ideas and the will to learn," while simultaneously nurturing critical consciousness in students (hooks, 1994c, p. 12). The following section explores critical, feminist, and multicultural educational strategies that resonate with various components of hooks' engaged pedagogy.

CHAPTER 5

Related Theories

Critical Theory

bell hooks (1994c) advocates an engaged pedagogy to counteract student passivity and authoritarian pedagogical orientations. Her desire to address the reasons and implication of student passivity and authoritative pedagogies resonates with critical theory scholarship. To illustrate the politics in schooling, a critically based approach and a traditional transfer-of-knowledge approach to education are contrasted. The terms *transforming education, education as the practice of freedom, critically based education, question-posing education, dialogic approach to education* are employed interchangeably. Though posited by different critical theorists, the main intent of each of these pedagogical orientations is to counteract the traditional transfer-of-knowledge pedagogy characterized by learner passivity rather than the development of critical consciousness.

The following section on critical theory makes extensive references to Paulo Freire (1970/1992, 1973) because hooks (1994c) attributes and relates insights of her social and educational theory to him. hooks credits the Brazilian thinker Freire with introducing her to critical pedagogy:

I found a mentor and a guide, someone who understood that learning could be liberatory. With his teaching and my growing understanding of the ways in which the education I had received in all-black Southern schools had been empowering, I began to develop a blueprint for my pedagogical practice. (1994c, p. 6)

hooks disputes the fallacy of a value-free knowledge, and critiques the image of passive students, the privileged voice of professors, hierarchy of knowledge fields, and the cultural reproduction in schools and norms and practices. She also critiques the notion of static knowledge and standardized pedagogical orientations. The following discussion illustrates the overlap between hooks' engaged pedagogy (1994c) and a critically based or transformative pedagogy.

In the academy, hierarchical conceptions determine the academic status of knowledge fields and defines the model for the teacher-student relationship. hooks' critique of the hierarchical principle in Western metaphysics stems from two perspectives. On the one hand, academic subjects—scientific and techni- cal—receive greater recognition than the humanities and social science sub- jects. On the other hand, the hierarchical principle contributes to the image of teachers as dispensers of established "truths" to "unknowing" students. The implications of the teacher-student relationship mirrors hierarchical relations in the wider society between dominant and marginalized group members. hooks notes Freire's critique of an "authoritarian, dominating model where knowledge is transferred from a powerful professor to a powerless student" (1989a, p. 101). Similarly, contrasting a transforming education and a traditional "transfer-of- knowledge" pedagogy, Shor and Freire (1987) note: (a) "knowledge" is pro- duced by education experts outside of school, reducing the act of learning to a mechanical study and memorization of established facts; (b) knowledge is presented as value free though essentially from an establishment point of view; (c) a political hierarchy of knowledge exists whereby the technical and scientific knowledge are privileged over the humanities; and (d) school culture reinforces rather than critiques the reproduction of dominant cultural norms.

As an educator, hooks is aware of the implications of teaching strategies on teacher-student relations. She views the detachment of teachers from engage- ment in a learning environment in terms of the

reproduction of a privileged class of values, of elitism. . . . That's exactly what's threatening to conservative academics—the possibility that [such] critiques will dismantle the bourgeois idea of a "professor" . . . [drastically changing the] significance of [their] role as teachers in the classroom. (1994c, p. 140)

hooks also notes the manner in which some teachers discount students' contributions to classroom discourse. She links the mentality to a reinforcement of "dominations" as opposed to a "freeing" education. hooks' discussion of a "banking" approach to education is similar to Freire's critique of traditional education and the manner in which hierarchical relationships between the educators and students mirror hierarchical social arrangements in privileging one group (teachers/elites) over other groups (students/the masses):

a. the teacher teaches and the students are taught;

b. the teacher knows everything and the students know nothing;

c. the teacher thinks and the students are thought about;

d. the teacher talks and the students listen—meekly;

e. the teacher disciplines and the students are disciplined;

f. the teacher chooses and enforces his choice, and the students comply;

g. the teacher acts and the students have the illusion of acting through the action of the teacher;

h. the teacher chooses the program content, and the students [who are not consulted] adapt to it;

i. the teacher confuses the authority of knowledge with his own professional authority, which he sets in opposition to the freedom of students;

j. the teacher is the subject of the learning process, while the pupils are mere objects. (Freire, 1970/1992, p. 59)

Based on these elements in teacher-student interactions, Freire (1970/1992, 1973) associated hierarchical relations in schools to social relations between Third World (dominant) elites and the economically and politically disadvantaged masses. hooks (1990, 1994b, 1994c) makes a similar association to circumstances in the First World. Indeed, hooks recollects that most of her professors, "seemed enthralled by the exercise of power and authority within their mini-kingdom, the classroom" (1994c, p. 17). In a classroom teachers, as the privileged source of information and authority, regulate the content and manner of transmission of official knowledge (hooks, 1994c). Finkelstein's (cited in Popkewitz, 1991) assessment of teaching and pedagogy in the eighteenth and nineteenth centuries resonates with Freire's (1973) and hooks' contention with regard to hierarchical relations in more contemporary times.

A "banking" approach to education extols the role of an educator while limiting learner involvement to receptivity and memorization of handed down facts (hooks, 1994c). hooks recalls having taught in institutions where the "prevailing pedagogical model [is] authoritarian, hierarchical in a coercive and often dominating way, and certainly one where the voice of the professor is the 'privileged' transmitter of knowledge" (1994c, p. 85). Most students learn early to adapt to the workings of the system without critically analyzing their situation and/or challenging its mechanics. Freire termed this a dehumanizing system insofar as it denies students the "vocation of becoming more fully human" (1970/1992, p. 28). In Freire's opinion, in the name of the "preserva-tion of culture and knowledge" we have a system that achieves neither true knowledge nor true culture (p. 68).

There is significant overlap between components of a critically based education and hooks' engaged pedagogy (1994c). It is then not surprising that both Freire (1970/1992, 1973) and hooks (1994c) accentuate "freedom" as one of the primary aims of education. Contrasting a "banking" approach from a "transfer-of-knowledge" pedagogy that sanctions inequalities in social ar-rangements, both note that a critically based education desocializes students from traditional relationships and norms of being and knowing by: (a) encour-aging students to be self-directing; (b) linking social contexts to the academics and honoring scholarship both within and outside the academy; (c) seeking to transform interrelations between students, teacher, school, and society; and (d) incorporating students' critical thought with the formal subject matter to avoid the focus on mere techniques for gaining literacy or gaining professional skills.

hooks critiques White supremacist patriarchal and capitalistic ideologies and the manner in which the ideologies shape and define social reality and social consciousness. Her recount of her experiences at Stanford aptly expresses the experiences of marginalized students:

> It was disheartening for me and other non-white students to face the extent which education in the university was not the site of openness and intellectual challenge we had longed for. We hated the racism, the sexism, the domination. (1989a, p. 100)

She illustrates the link between education and political freedom in maintaining:

> Education is a political issue for exploited and oppressed people . . . without the capacity to read and write, to think critically and analytically, the liberated [slave] would remain forever bound, dependent on the will of the oppressors. (p. 98)

hooks (1994c) commends Paulo Freire's commitment (1970/1992, 1973) to adult literacy programs that sought to counteract the false consciousness prevalent in members of marginalized groups. hooks identifies the real dilemma in teaching as one of striking a balance between empowering and equipping students for what makes for success in the "world." hooks' engaged pedagogy (1994c) highlights the "freeing" aspect of education. The title of her book, *Teaching to Transgress: Education as the Practice of Freedom*, echoes Freire's whole aim (1973) of a transformative education. The slogan "Education as the Practice of Freedom" grew out of Paulo Freire's work with adult literacy programs in Brazil before his exile in 1964, and thereafter in various Third World countries. It was Freire's contention that history making is the responsibility of an entire populace and not the creation and maintenance of an elite and/or dominant group. To counteract the perpetuation of dominations, Freire advocated an education that incorporates a literacy component whereby the masses are taught how to read and write and a political component whereby the oppressed experience the power to seek ways to transform social reality through critical analysis of prevailing conditions in society. Thus, the slogan "Education as the Practice of Freedom" goes beyond the mere transfer of information or the act of depositing established facts in the students, beyond the "perpetuation of the values of a given culture," beyond "an attempt to adapt the students to the milieu" to a dynamic interaction whereby educator and students as subjects in their own right, seek to create a more effective and meaningful education process and ultimately a more humane society (Freire, 1973, p. 149).

hooks' educational theory (1994c) advocates mutuality between teacher and students as opposed to the traditional hierarchical relationships. She argues that it is only through a process of praxis, the reciprocal arrangement between those helping and those being helped that the act of "helping" is freed from manipulative and domineering motivations. hooks' writings express her weariness of the beneficence of "oppressors" toward the oppressed, the powerful to the powerless. Undergirding the beneficence of the powerful toward the powerless is the issue of subjectivity and subordination. The interaction between a superior and inferior subject reinforces the domination of one over the other, the subordination of one's subjectivity toward the advantaged party in the interaction. However well intentioned the interaction (Is it not true that all teachers want to "help" their students!), there is an element of the giver and the given. hooks' assessment of teacher/student reciprocity echoes Freire's stipulated role (1973) of a successful educator in its accentuation of a mode of reciprocity over a focus on teachers' persuasive skills. Freire (1970/1992) advocated humility, an educator's openness to learners and their views as opposed to the feeling of self-sufficiency.

To educate as the practice of freedom has significant implications for the teaching and learning process. It impacts an educator's choice of content and mode of transmission. hooks (1994b) advocates a multicentric curriculum that reflects the cultural plurality of a student body and/or national history to avoid the exclusivity implied in a monocentric curriculum. In the American context, a Western-oriented curriculum based on White people's cultural histories and traditions reinforces and exalts the groups' cultural experiences. hooks terms the process an induction into White supremacy. hooks (1989a, 1994c) contends that authoritarian pedagogical orientations reinforce the hierarchical principle of superiority and subordination. She maintains that often teachers may offer an inclusive curriculum experience while reinforcing the politics of domination in their interactions with students.

Similar to critical theorists, hooks (1994c), contending for a libertarian education, advocates an inclusive curriculum and highlights the responsibility that teachers and students have for re-creating "official knowledge" to more adequately reflect prevailing conditions: cultural pluralism and emerging ways of being and knowing. The process gives greater meaning to school processes and ultimately students' lives. It is through a liberatory pedagogy that learners develop a critique of ideological elements in schools and society. In this context, developing critical consciousness in students involves teaching students, "so that they do not perpetuate domination . . . [or] support colonialism and imperialism, but [do] understand the meaning of resistance" (hooks, 1990, p. 132). In contrast to students' passive reception of knowledge in traditional pedagogies, hooks and West associate the acquisition of "knowledge" to the development of critical consciousness:

> [I]ntellectual life enables one to make sense of reality, to confront and comprehend the concrete . . . intellectual life is a necessary part of liberation struggle, central to the efforts of all oppressed and/or exploited people who would move from object to subject, who would decolonize and liberate their minds. (1991, p. 150)

hooks (1994c) acknowledges that changing from the traditional transfer-of-knowledge pedagogy to a more participative and engaging pedagogy is a gradual process. Critical theory scholars support hooks' critique of discriminatory policies and practices that subordinate and/or exclude the contributions of marginalized groups (Freire, 1970/1992, 1973; Shor, 1992; Shor & Freire, 1987). Freire and Antonio Faundez's (1989) and Elizabeth Minnich's (1990) discussions on communal responsibility expound on hooks' concept of collective involvement (and an inclusive recognition!) in the making of knowledge and history. Freire and Faundez maintain that the task for transforming education and society belongs not only to designated leaders but to every individual because by "recreating ourselves, individually and socially, we [shall] change society" (1989, p. 82). It is no surprise that critical theory scholars commend a multicultural curriculum given its persistent critique of exclusivity in the Western curriculum and its impact on marginalized groups. Shor contends:

> Existing canons cannot be delivered to students as universal standards of excellence because they are products of undemocratic knowledge making in an unequal academy and society. . . . This exclusive canon and discourse need multicultural, nonsexist reinventions to become democratic and representative. (1992, p. 256)

In sum, critical theory interrogates the underlying biases of institutional ideologies such as the "banking approach" to education, hierarchical social arrangements, and an exclusive curriculum canon. The elements imbue in individuals a particular view of social reality. The process denies students a freedom that would involve a critical interrogation of social myths that legitimate institutions that serve the interests of the status quo (hooks, 1990, 1994b, 1994c). In advocating the slogan "Education as the Practice of Freedom," Freire (1973) and hooks (1994c) highlight the importance of an educational system that counteracts the propagation of ideological elements in a racist, sexist, and classist society by interrogating the political implications of an "externally" imposed curriculum content and hierarchical arrangements within educational settings. In effect, an authoritative curriculum, hierarchically based social arrangements, and standardized pedagogical orientations reinforce the marginality of students in encouraging passivity in learning as opposed to developing a more active engagement and critical interrogation. The former focus reinscribes White supremacist, patriarchal, and capitalistic value ideologies. The following discussion explores the link between multicultural scholarship and hooks' engaged pedagogy (1994c).

Multicultural Theory

To counteract a growing "return to narrow nationalism, isolationism, and xenophobia," hooks calls for a "recognition of cultural diversity, a rethinking of ways of knowing, a deconstruction of old epistemologies" (1994c, pp. 28–29). In contrast to perpetuating forms of knowledge in ways that reinscribe colonialism and dominations, hooks (1990, 1994c) envisions the academy as a place where differences can be acknowledged and integrated in mainstream norms. hooks' emphasis on the significance of accommodating differences and an openness to the "Other" is reflected in a multicultural critique and strategies for educational change. Nieto contends:

> The curriculum has been sanitized to such a point that opportunities for critical reflection on personal and collective identity and on issues of social justice are minimized. (1996, p. xxvii)

The following discussion presents multicultural education strategies to address issues of cultural alienation, resistance to school learning, and subsequently low academic performance in minority students. hooks' engaged pedagogy addresses the alienation of students whose cultural histories are subordinated and/or excluded from mainstream norms, advocating for pedagogical orientations that acknowledge the students' experiences. She contends:

> To hear each other (the sound of different voices), to listen to one another, is an exercise in recognition. It also ensures that no student remains invisible in the classroom. (1994c, p. 41)

In contrast to a privileging of White supremacist values and attitudes, a multicultural approach to education encompasses inclusive pedagogical orientations in offering multiple perspectives to ways of being, feeling, and knowing.

First, accommodating linguistic and cultural differences makes education more consistent with diverse ethnic realities in most societies, a process that reduces the degree of victimization of minority students (hooks, 1990, 1994c). Second, empowering minority students by legitimating cultures and experiences other than those reflected in mainstream cultural norms counteracts a negative self-concept and attitude toward marginalized cultures. The process leads to greater student "engagement" in a learning process and subsequently academic improvement in students formerly marginalized in educational settings (hooks, 1994c). In this context, Cultural Studies provide a necessary forum for accommodation of cultural pluralism and critical interrogation of cultural dominance (hooks, 1990). Providing venues to honor instead of subordinate "difference" for a falsely based cultural hegemony is an issue that hooks reiterates:

> Working with a critical pedagogy based on my understanding of Freire's teaching, I enter the classroom with the assumption that we must build "community" in order to create a climate of openness and intellectual rigor. . . . What we ideally share is the desire to learn—to receive actively

knowledge that enhances our intellectual development and our capacity to live more fully in the world. (1994c, p. 40)

An empowering and/or inclusive education, what hooks (1994c) terms *engaged pedagogy*, desocializes students away from traditional pedagogy and curriculum, a patriarchal and Eurocentric bias that excludes feminist and multicultural perspectives in educational discourses. hooks maintains:

> as we educate one another to acquire critical consciousness, we have the chance to see how important airing diverse perspectives can be for any progressive political struggle that is serious about transformation. Engaging in intellectual exchange where people hear a diversity of viewpoints enables them to witness first hand solidarity that grows stronger in a context of productive critical exchange and confrontation. (1990, p. 6)

Incorporating the "voices" of students in classroom discourse is one way of acknowledging and integrating traditionally marginalized cultures and varied forms of expression in a culture. The process of including marginalized cultural histories interrogates White supremacy, patriarchy, and capitalism. Making a similar argument, Lawrence Grossberg (1994) links the ability of envisioning alternatives to the acknowledgment of social, cultural, economic, and political plurality. Henry Giroux contends that Cultural Studies provide a necessary interrogation of what he, similar to hooks (1984, 1989a, 1990, 1992, 1994b, 1995b), terms White supremacy. It is his view that Cultural Studies help to "identify, challenge, and rewrite such representations . . . for purposes of producing, reinforcing, or resisting the dominant cultural representation and self-definition (Giroux, 1994a, p. 49). On a similar note, Nancy Fraser commends the emerging trend of "discursive arenas where members of subordinated social groups invent and circulate counter-discourses, which in turn permit them to formulate oppositional interpretations of their identities, interests, and needs" (Fraser, 1994, p. 84).

A multicultural approach to education affirms differences by recognizing multiple perspectives and challenging a monocultural view of social reality (hooks, 1994b, 1994c). hooks contends: "Multiculturalism compels educators to recognize the narrow boundaries that have shaped the way knowledge is shared in the classroom . . . [encouraging learners] to surrender to the wonder of re-learning and learning ways of knowing that go against the grain" (1994c, 44). hooks contrasts a multi-centric curriculum from a mono-centric curriculum that reflects dominant cultural values and traditions. A monocentric curriculum indirectly socializes students into existing social (hierarchical) relations. In contrast, a multicultural (multicentric) approach acknowledges differences in ways of being, feeling, and knowing, presents a view of social reality that is open to interpretation and therefore change (hooks, 1994c). Similar to hooks' contention regarding integrating subordinated cultural and/or cultural histories, Banks maintains that a

> curriculum that includes the experiences of different ethnic groups *and* presents these experiences from diverse perspectives and points of view is needed to help students understand the complexity of the human experience and how a nation's various groups have strongly influenced each other culturally and interacted within the social structure. (1988, p. 161; emphasis in original)

hooks' engaged pedagogy (1994c) addresses this need for inclusivity in advocating for respect for difference and providing avenues whereby each student's presence is acknowledged and contribution encouraged. Linking a multicultural approach to critical consciousness, hooks argues that multiculturalism

> forces us all to recognize our complicity in accepting and perpetuating biases of any kind . . . [thus] educators . . . can give students the education they desire and deserve . . . [and] teach in ways that transform consciousness, creating a climate of free expression that is the essence of a truly liberatory liberal arts education. (1994c, p. 44)

hooks recounts her early childhood memories of learning about Columbus's discovery of America, and the subsequent feelings of shame that "Red and Black" people were victimized, degraded, and exploited by White explorers:

> When I recall the shame I felt seeing those images, of the Indian and the "great" white men, I recognize that there is also rage there. I was not only angry at these images: which did not feel right in my heart, I felt that being forced to look at them was, like being forced to witness the symbolic reenactment of a colonizing ritual, a drama of white supremacy. The shame was feeling powerless to protest and intervene. (1994b, p. 205)

She further maintains that the "Columbus legacy is clearly one that silences and eradicates the voices—the lives—of women" (p. 204). hooks' critique of the "Columbus" legacy and the manner in which the ideology reinforces marginality of "colonized" groups echoes Banks' critique of the presentation of non-Western cultural heroes as an addition or appendage to the regular curriculum, and the practice of limiting multicultural exposure to particular months and/or events. He notes:

> Blacks often dominate lessons during Black History Week or on Martin Luther King's birthday but are largely invisible in the curriculum during the rest of the year. . . . The infusion of bits and pieces of ethnic content into the curriculum not only reinforces the idea that ethnic minority groups are not integral parts of US society, it also results in the triviali- zation of ethnic cultures. (1988, p. 158)

By addressing racial and cultural pluralism a multiethnic education challenges stereotypical attitudes toward students from dominated cultures (hooks, 1990, 1994b, 1994c). In this context, similar to Molefi Kete Asante's rationale (cited in Marriott, 1991) for an Afrocentric curriculum, Banks advocates that the

> curriculum for marginalized ethnic groups should recognize their feelings toward self, help them to clarify their racial attitudes, liberate them from psychological captivity, and convince them of their humanness, since the dominant society often makes them believe they are less than human. (1988, p. 186)

Critics of an ethnocentric focus such as Afrocentrism point to the manner in which it tends to replace old myths with the new while simultaneously segregating students by race and gender (D'Souza, 1992). In the process of offering an alternative curriculum to a Eurocentric bias in official curriculum, some Cultural Studies programs often fall into a similar bias in propagating rigid, nationalistic, exclusionary, and ideological curricula as opposed to being open and self-critical (Alston, 1995; D'Souza, 1992; Marriott, 1991). No doubt what belies attempts at developing a multicultural curriculum is the seeming lack of texts. Dinesh D'Souza (1992), Elizabeth Minnich (1990), and Nel Noddings (1995b) argue that the official curriculum is often diluted by use of texts based on unfounded "truths" and/or discarded theories. D'Souza (1992) critiques the "Afrocentric" curriculum taught in some Black colleges in the United States. The "compensatory" strategy of offering a falsely based knowledge body raises the issue of intellectual honesty over the need to affirm marginal people after years of misrepresentation and exclusion in dominant cultural histories. However, arguing for an Afrocentric curriculum, Molefi Kete Asante calls for a curriculum that highlights the "African" experience over the frequent representation of Africans as victims of history (Marriott, 1991).

Critics point to the fact that not unlike the previous Eurocentric bias in educational settings, such intentions often border on ideology (Bloom, 1987; D'Souza, 1992). Kal Alston contends that such studies often repeat the "errors of 'Eurocentric curricula' in refusing to submit to self-criticism and emphasizing the 'centric' rather than Asante's [envisioned] 'contextual' perspective" (1995, p. 285).

As opposed to a Eurocentric curriculum and standardized teaching strategies, a multicultural approach to education, as the above discussion illustrates, offers an avenue for interrogating cultural monocentricism (White supremacy) through an accommodation of differing cultural values and traditions in a learning environment. The process involves an acknowledgment of originally subordinated cultural histories to provide alternative ways of being, feeling, and knowing. This process both affirms formerly marginalized students and promises greater student participation in a learning process. Renée Vincente Arcilla argues that such an approach to education helps "prevent the seeds of monocultural domination from taking root in our diverse youth" (1995, p. 165).

It could be argued that the objective of feminism is similar to multiculturalism in that it calls for an acknowledgment of the "Other." In critiquing exclusionary practices in traditional curriculum, feminist scholarship aims at exposing and critiquing traditional norms and practices that stunt the possibility of any particular group's self-definition. The following discussion presents a feminist critique and advocacy for a curriculum that honors female-related traits and other marginalized groups in society (hooks, 1994c). Indeed, hooks claims that "feminist classrooms were, on the whole, one location where [students] witnessed professors striving to create participatory spaces for the sharing of knowledge" (1994c, p. 15).

Feminist Theory

hooks (1981, 1984, 1989a, 1990) raises three issues that resonate with a feminist critique of classical education: (a) voice and representation, (b) relational versus hierarchical models, and (c) focus on effectivity versus rationality. The issue of "voice"—marginality, privileging, silencing, and censorship—is central to bell hooks' analyses (1984, 1989a, 1990, 1994c) of the impact of White supremacy, patriarchy, and capitalism in schools and society. Mary Belenky et al. illustrate the centrality of the "metaphor of voice" to "depict [women's] intellectual and ethical development; and [that] the development of a sense of voice, mind, and self [as being] intricately intertwined" (1986, p. 18). hooks (1984, 1989a, 1990, 1994c) extends the need for "coming to voice" to all marginalized people in contending that White supremacy, patriarchy, and capitalism are typically privileged voices of White, male, and materially privileged students. The process of "coming to voice" goes beyond the mere telling of one's experience. In classrooms, "coming to voice" involves allowing different perspectives to illuminate and counteract the cultural hegemony characteristic of many school environments (hooks, 1994c). Drawing from personal teaching strategies, hooks recognizes:

> Students from marginalized groups enter classrooms where their values have been neither heard nor welcomed, whether these students discuss facts—those which any of us might know—or personal experience. (1994c, p. 84)

She maintains that honoring students' voices deconstructs the concept of "privileged" voice.

hooks critiques exclusivity in educational ideals where focus is on thoughts, attitudes, and experiences of White and materially privileged people to the exclusion of a working class perspective. She argues that students "who enter the academy unwilling to accept without question the assumptions and values held by privileged classes tend to be silenced, deemed troublemakers" (1994c, p. 179). This practice reinforces the "superiority" of students who fall under these categories while disempowering other students on the basis of race, gender, and/or class. Feminist scholars raise a similar contention in critiquing conventional understandings of knowledge and certainty in traditional "modernist" epistemology (Kohli, 1995a; Minnich, 1990; Noddings, 1995a; Siegel, 1995). The following extensive reference from Minnich aptly captures a feminist critique of classical "knowledge."

> The *root problem* . . . is, simply that while the majority of humankind was excluded from education and the making of what has been called knowledge, *the dominant few not only defined themselves as the inclusive kind of human but also as the norm and the ideal.* A few privileged men defined themselves as constituting mankind/humankind and simultaneously saw themselves as akin to what mankind/humankind ought to be in fundamental ways and distinguished themselves from others. Thus, at the same time they removed women and nonprivileged men within their culture and other cultures from "mankind," they justified that exclusion on the grounds that the excluded were by nature "lesser" people [if they even thought of the others as having "cultures"]. Their notion of who was properly human was *both* exclusive *and* hierarchical with regard to those they took to be properly subject to them—women in all roles; men

who worked with their hands; male servants and slaves; women and men of many other cultures. (1990, pp. 37–38; emphasis in original)

hooks (1994a, 1994c) and other feminist scholarship (Martin, 1995; Noddings, 1995a, 1995b; Jo Anne Pagano, 1995; Sarah Schuyler, 1990) illustrate the potential bias in a dualistic thought process of Western metaphysics in traditional pedagogies. Dualisms provide a basis for body/mind, rationality/emotionality, subjective/objective, nature/nurture, and private/public distinctions. Indeed, hooks contends:

Trained in the philosophical context of Western metaphysics dualism, many of us have accepted the notion that there is a split between the body and mind. Believing this, individuals enter the classroom to teach as though only the mind is present, not the body. (1994c, p. 191)

Critiquing dualisms, hooks contends that the

desire to simplify one's critical response, to contain it within a dualistic model of good and bad, accepted and rejected, is an approach to ways of knowing that liberatory pedagogy seeks to alter. (1990, p. 8)

Similarly, Wendy Kohli (1995a) and Mary Leach (1995) maintain that dualisms lend themselves to a "reductive vision of human thought, which devalues the imagination in favor of the pursuit of scientific truth, defined as objective, detached" (Leach, 1995, p. 362). Further, Jane Roland Martin (1992, 1995), Sonia Nieto (1996), and Nel Noddings (1992) critique the artificial

division of knowledge into separate and discrete "subject matter" such as math, science, social studies and language. . . . Students learn to see the world as disconnected bits of information that belong in preordained compartments. (Nieto, 1996, p. 96)

In this context, despite the practicality of employing divisions such as Math, Science, and Social Studies, for learning purposes, subject matter thus presented loses its interconnectedness. Lived experience testifies to interrelatedness of subject matter and need for different forms of "knowledge" in one's day-to-day interactions. Not only does this academic "separatism" promote a dualistic thought pattern in student's view of social reality, it also leads to lower prioritization of courses not defined as "core curriculum" (Nieto, 1996).

A dualistic view of entities and nature also impacts teachers' conception of students, and shapes student/teacher interactions. Notwithstanding the significance of respect for the "Other," hooks advocates a more holistic conceptualization of learners: embodied beings as opposed to exalting the technical and rational over the affective in students' lives. She argues that to "teach in a manner that respects and cares for the souls of our students is essential if we are to provide the necessary conditions where learning can most deeply and intimately begin" (1994c, p. 13). The recognition of biases in a traditional conceptualization of knowledge raises the issue of incorporating formerly subordinated cultural traits and characteristics such as effectivity and interdependence. Similar to hooks' emphasis (1994c; Olson, 1994) on the incorporation of passion (love) for subject matter and students, feminist scholars advocate a knowledge of connection and dependence, one that incorporates the three Cs of care, concern, and connection, a valuing of domesticity both in the public and private spheres, by men as well as women (Leach, 1995; Martin, 1992, 1995; Noddings, 1995a, 1995b; Pagano, 1995). hooks (1994b, 1994c) argues that the official knowledge base primarily reflects a White male middle- and/or upper-class way of being, feeling, and knowing.

The previous discussion highlighted three main areas of contention raised by hooks (1994c) that resonate with a feminist critique of educational systems. In privileging the experiences and/or "voices" and cultural traits and characteristics of dominant groups, the either/or dualist pattern reinforces the marginality of most students by sanctioning White supremacy, patriarchy, and a capitalistic value system. The subordination and/or exclusion of a particular group's traits and characteristics indirectly reinforces and exalts the superiority of cultural traits and characteristics that are presented as normative. Thus, presenting White, male, and/or privileged groups' experiences and traditions as normative grants the groups higher status relative to other groups in society. Overall, dualism leads to unnecessary distinctions within schools and the wider society, subordinates female related traits and characteristics, and results in a hierarchy in fields of knowledge within educational settings. Most, like Harvey Siegel, acknowledge that the

feminist, postmodernist, and multiculturalist streams in feminists' thoughts promise to replenish and energize the too frequently stagnant waters of Philosophy of Education. All such movements are forcing society and philosophers as part of it, to clarify and justify the aims of education, and establish moral and ethical considerations to guide and constrain educational activities, obligations of educators and educational institutions, how curriculum is best understood and designed, etc. (1995, p. 199)

In the following chapter the different components of engaged pedagogy as a means for addressing issues of monocentrism, hierarchical social arrangements, and a dualistic thought pattern raised by critical, multicultural, and feminist critique of learning institutions and the manner in which these institutions reflect social discriminatory practices are analyzed.

CHAPTER 6

Major Components of Engaged Pedagogy

The following aspects of engaged pedagogy are proposed by bell hooks (1994c) and highlighted by various critical, feminist, and multicultural scholarship: (a) re-conceptualization of knowledge, (b) linking of theory and practice, (c) student empowerment, (d) multiculturalism, and (e) incorporation of passion. The discussion explores the manner in which these components of engaged pedagogy address issues of race, gender, and class biases, as raised in the previous part on bell hooks' social theory. The discussion presents arguments advanced to support each of the elements by different theorists but mostly by hooks.

Conceptualization of Knowledge

There are two primary forms in which power is manifested in classrooms: through the conceptualization of "knowledge" and the manner of transmission. An educator's view of "knowledge" significantly impacts his/her method of instruction. A transfer-of-knowledge approach is appropriate for educators who view "knowledge" as established facts and/or technical skills to be mastered. Acknowledging the temporary nature of knowledge (as a social construct) emphasizes student-teacher discourse as opposed to a lecture method that gives "authority" to subject matter and the transmitter over the recipients and process of learning (hooks, 1994c). Thus, underlying the incorporation and promotion of learner participation is the issue of power redistribution. The following discussion illustrates the manner in which an official knowledge base and curriculum content reinscribe a White supremacist, patriarchal, and capitalist value system.

Knowledge Base

hooks' writings illustrate the implications of equating White middle/upper-class male experiences and cultural histories to a national cultural heritage and/or national standards of academic performance. She notes that an exclusive recognition of works by White men and women subordinates other cultural expressions while simultaneously legitimating White hegemonic authorial canonicity (hooks, 1990). hooks (1994b) contends that the "Columbus" legacy perpetuates White supremacist values and attitudes in reinforcing the superiority of White people. Endorsing White people's perspective of civilization of the American continent as the norm to historical events has led to a persistent subordination and resistance to incorporation of marginalized cultural histories into official curriculum. Supporting hooks' (1994c) contention regarding the politics of curriculum content and pedagogy, David Richter (1994) points to the 1988 furor over Stanford University's debate on the content of the required Western Civilization course to illustrate the fact that universities often serve as "Ideological State Apparatus," perpetuating self-serving myths as opposed to being discursive venues of varied ideologies and practices. hooks also illustrates the fallacy of employing White women's and bourgeois values as norms for women and universal aspirations, respectively. In a similar vein, Minnich (1990) illustrates the inadequacy and political implications of portraying masculine traits and characteristics as normative for all humanity.

Contesting the Columbus legacy, hooks maintains that society is called to "choose between a memory that justifies and privileges domination, oppression, and exploitation and one that exalts and affirms reciprocity, community, and mutuality" (1994b, p. 202). She maintains that the Columbus myth sanctions White supremacy and patriarchy in devaluing the experiences of African Americans, Native Indians, and women in general. Supporting hooks' contention, Jane Roland Martin maintains that a static and ideal imagery of a cultural heritage leads to two major handicaps. The imagery

> relieves us of moral and social responsibility, [but] the truth is that every society must pick and choose just what elements of its past—what knowledge, traditions, values, worldviews—constitute the capital it wants to transmit to the next generation. . . . As the world changes, either

a culture's choices change or the education it extends to its young will begin to be dysfunctional. (1992, p. 202)

In schools, the notion of a curriculum canon translates to a presumption of an "established" knowledge body (hooks, 1994b; Nieto, 1996). Supporting hooks' observation regarding the resistance to incorporate marginalized cultural histories, Martin notes that proponents of classical traditions display the selfsame exclusionary bent as

> realtors once did about the racial and religious purity of the people to whom they sold property. . . . [Education conservatives] equate giving curriculum space to research by and about women and nonwhite men with a lowering of quality and a diminution of content. (1992, p. 68)

hooks (1994c) critiques Allan Bloom's (1987) and Dinesh D'Souza's (1992) focus on the neutrality and objectivity of official knowledge, associating the stand to a denial of people's subjectivity and a perpetuation of dominations in society. The notion of knowledge as universal, neutral, and objective, equates learning to memorizing deposited "truths." In contrast, a multicultural or feminist approach recognizes multiple ways and multiple references to teaching and/or knowledge. The view promotes active student engagement in the construction of knowledge. hooks argues:

> We are all subjects of history. . . . By recognizing subjectivity and the limits of identity, we disrupt that objectification that is so necessary in a culture of domination. That is why the efforts to acknowledge our subjectivity and that of our students has generated both a fierce critique and backlash. (1994c, p. 139)

Supporting hooks' critique of education conservatives, Henry Giroux maintains that the view of literacy espoused in works such as Allan Bloom's *The Closing of the American Mind* reduces literacy to mastery of technical skills with an emphasis on "individual mastery and the passive consumption of knowledge" (Giroux, 1994b, p. 65). Ironically, while critical and feminist theorists point to the bias and partiality of claims in official knowledge, education conservatives such as Eric D. Hirsch hold that there is a

> specifiable body of cultural knowledge which can be identified by the culturally educated which everyone must know to be literate, and that it

is the primary purpose of public schools, their civic aim, to transmit this information through direct instruction. (Giarelli, 1995, pp. 207–208)

Bloom (1987) and D'Souza (1992) argue that books and ideas of Western civilization have and do provide an adequate basis for assessing a cultural heritage and literacy base.

Curriculum

hooks links the interrogation of existing forms of knowledge to a transgressive resistance:

> Progressive professors working to transform the curriculum so that it does not reflect biases or reinforce systems of domination are most often individuals willing to take the risks that engaged pedagogy requires and to make their teaching practices a site of resistance. (1994c, p. 21)

On the one hand, the idea of a standardized canon and curriculum suggests a static and idealized view of culture and knowledge (hooks, 1994b). On the other hand, a curriculum focus on technical skills and/or abstracted concepts in different fields fails to nurture critical consciousness in students in reifying classroom knowledge. Similar to hooks, Giroux's premise (1994a, 1994b) is that developing critical consciousness is preferable to a "transfer-of-knowledge" approach to education in that the latter socializes students into existing power relations while undermining creativity and a reflective stance.

hooks critiques the notion of abstracted knowledge and by implication, the view of knowledge as objective and neutral. The conceptualization of knowledge fails to acknowledge and address issues of racial, gender, and/or class biases imbedded in schools' norms and practices. To illustrate the abstraction of official knowledge, hooks maintains:

> In philosophy classes today, work on race, ethnicity, and gender is used, but not in a subversive way. It is simply used to update the curriculum superficially. This clinging to the past is mandated by the profound belief in the legitimacy of all that has come before . . . [and] the classroom to be the way it has always been. (1994c, p. 142)

Similar to hooks' contention, critical and feminist theorists critique the fallacy of basing the official curriculum on a supposedly "common" cultural heritage when in reality the "said" cultural heritage manifests a racial, gender, and class bias (Beyer, 1995; Minnich, 1990; Shor, 1992; Shor & Freire, 1987). Henry Giroux and Peter McLaren (1994) and David Richter (1994) point to the political implications of official school curriculum. The issue of what eventually constitutes a school's official curriculum typically hinges on whether focusing on an inclusive curriculum by accommodating cultural pluralism outweighs the benefits of a more structured curriculum based on classical works in view of established educational policies. Underlying hooks' contention is that what passes for "commonly" established values is racially and culturally biased. Arguments advanced in favor of a more inclusive curriculum will be further explored.

hooks (1994b) calls for a reevaluation of the official curriculum to reflect cultural plurality and feminist values. Similarly, critiquing the classic view of education, feminist scholarship advocate the three Cs of care, concern, and connection to counteract an exclusive focus of the three Rs (Martin, 1992, 1995; Noddings, 1992, 1995a, 1995b). An ethic of care (encompassed in the three Cs) provides an alternative philosophy of education based on the web of social connectedness, communication, and community to alleviate the alienation that results from an emphasis on an abstracted curriculum and the lecture method of instruction (Martin, 1995; Noddings, 1992, 1995b):

> [T]he ethic of care binds carers and cared-fors in relationships of mutual responsibility. . . . It recognizes that we are dependent upon one another. . . . Thus a major aim of the ethic of care is to prevent the very separation that induces the dualisms exploiter/exploited, oppressors/oppressed, moral agent/object, and so on. (Noddings, 1995b, p. 190)

However, Bloom (1987), D'Souza (1992), and Hirsch (1987, cited in Giarelli, 1995) commend the traditional curriculum. In their view, the classical curriculum provided structure, content, and the high academic standards in contrast to the current ambiguity that surrounds the demands for an inclusive curriculum and a pedagogy directed by students' interests and speech.

hooks' engaged pedagogy (1994c), in line with critical, feminist, and multicultural scholarship, interrogates White supremacist, patriarchal, capitalist ideologies reflected in the notion of standardized curriculum, pedagogical orientations, and a static view of social reality. She maintains that a banking system of education is based on the "assumption that memorizing information and regurgitating it represented gaining knowledge that could be deposited, stored and used at a later date" (hooks, 1994c, p. 5). An elitist view of knowledge easily translates into an alienating curriculum (hooks, 1994c). To counteract this process of learner passivity, Paulo Freire (1970/1992) and, in agreement, hooks (1994c) advocate a problem-solving educational theory as opposed to the traditional deposit-making approach, whereby through dialogue, students and teachers in interacting with subject matter experience mutual growth. Engaged pedagogy challenges teachers to maintain a healthy balance between content and process, subject matter, and subjects.

In *Teaching to Transgress: Education as the Practice of Freedom*, hooks (1994c) urges educators to "transgress" conventional educational norms and practices, and to create strategies for making the teaching/learning process more dynamic, exciting, and meaningful to students. Acknowledging the nature of knowledge as a process, opens up existing knowledge to discourse and review and accommodates alternative perspectives to ways of being, feeling, and knowing. The recognition and validation of "differences" in mainstream values is an aspect that is typically subordinated when educational institutions focus on curriculum, cultural literacy canons, and standardized methods of teaching (hooks, 1994c). In transmitting a culturally biased curriculum, teachers reinforce inherent misconceptions regarding social reality, stereotypes of members of marginalized groups and other social myths that maintain the status quo (hooks, 1994b). Supporting hooks' call to "transgress" conventional pedagogical orientations, McLaren adjoins educators to get

> outside the admixtures and remains of languages—the multiplicity of stereotypical voices that already populate their vocabulary and fill up all the available linguistic spaces—in order to find different ways of appropriating or mediating the real. (1994, p. 212)

The previous discussion on the manner in which the conceptualization of knowledge reinforces racial, gender, and class biases in schools and society highlighted the fact that perpetuation of the Columbus legacy, despite evidence of prior occupancy of the continent, reinforces the superiority of the Aryan race and patriarchy while simultaneously marginalizing members from subordinated cultural histories. Similarly, an elitist conceptualization of knowledge that focuses on abstraction of concepts and use of sophisticated language that bears little resemblance to most students' lived realities creates a class barrier between the world of the academy and the masses (hooks, 1994b, 1994c). Further, subordination of female traits and characteristics in educational settings and the wider society has contributed to the marginality of women (hooks, 1984, 1989a, 1990, 1994b). The following discussion analyzes the process of linking theory to practice in learning environments to counteract student alienation in educational settings.

Linking Theory to Practice

The separation of theory from practice leads to reification and promotion of an uncritical reflection of social reality. bell hooks argues that the process perpetuates class elitism by reinforcing the separation between theory and practice, the academy, and most students' lived realities. Subsequently, both members of the dominant and the dominated groups "deny the power of liberatory education for critical consciousness, thereby perpetuating conditions that reinforce our collective exploitation and repression" (1994c, p. 69). She maintains that linking theory to practice integrates two aspects of an issue and allows for interrogation of one based on the other, a process that educates learners on contentious issues in society. Linking theory to practice affirms the intricate relationship between theory and practice, while avoiding a reification of the teaching/learning process from contentious issues of racial, gender, and class biases in schools and society. hooks recounts one of her student's confession with regard to the transformational implications of an engaged pedagogy:

"We take your class. We learn to look at the world from a critical standpoint, one that considers race, sex, and class. And we can't enjoy life anymore." Looking out over the class, across race, sexual preference, and ethnicity, I saw students nodding their heads . . . white students learning how to think more critically about questions of race and racism may go home for the holidays and suddenly see their parents in a different light. (1994c, p. 43)

hooks contends that the reification of official knowledge relieves teachers of handling otherwise controversial issues of racial, gender, and class biases. Because of the classroom discussion "aura" of political neutrality,

[s]cholars become disturbed when classroom discussions take on an overtly political tone even though they may not be disturbed by course syllabi which promote and perpetuate white supremacy. . . . The issue is especially relevant to black scholars. We too have been seduced by the false assumption that the goal of academic freedom is best served by postures of political neutrality, by teaching methods that belie the reality that our very choice of subject matter, manner, and style of presentation embodies ideological and political signifiers. (1989a, pp. 64–65)

hooks (1994c) highlights the manner in which abstracted official knowledge privileges students from dominant cultural groups and reinforces unequal social relations. Engaged pedagogy provides venue for acquiring established knowledge but also discourse of contentious issues faced by most students both in and outside of educational settings. It is hooks' contention that students find it hard to retain abstract information that bears little if any relevance to their day-to-day lives. hooks maintains:

> [T]he most important learning experience that could happen in [a] classroom was that students would learn to think critically and analytically, not just about books, but about the world they live in. . . . Education for critical consciousness . . . invites critique of conventional expectations and desires. (1989a, p. 102)

Similarly, Paulo Freire and Antonio Faundez (1989) commend linking "formal" and "commonsense" knowledge and insist on the fact that concepts mediate reality and not vice versa. hooks illustrates the manner in which subject material is presented in a "politically" neutral manner:

> Anyone witnessing the current cultural and academic focus on race has to note the new way race is being talked about, as though it were in no way linked to cultural practices that reinforce and perpetuate racism, creating a gap between attitudes and actions. (1990, p. 51)

Raising a similar contention, Freire and Faundez (1989) maintain that the notion of "scientific," "objective" knowledge as an intellectual's prerogative gives teachers power over the masses who do not possess "knowledge" and therefore lack "power." This arises from the conception of knowledge as separate from practice, what Freire and Faundez (1989) term the separation between the world of *episteme* and the world of *doxa*. hooks (1994c) stresses the significance of linking theory to practice so that academic knowledge and information more adequately address students' lived realities. Landon Beyer (1995) argues that the school curriculum's dichotomy of academic from most students' lived realities fails to accommodate students' experiences and, therefore, issues students are daily immersed in and discourses in academic settings. Similar to hooks' assessment, critical scholarship note that typically most academic training focuses more on the understanding of concepts than its application (i.e., linking concepts to concrete reality) (Freire, 1970/1992, 1973; Freire & Faundez, 1989).

hooks insists on an intrinsic link between theory and practice. Theory provides venue for analyzing experience (practice). However, practice is just as significant. Through practice, theories are used to assess their applicability and effectiveness. Through theory, marginalized groups articulate their experience and explore strategies for addressing matters of concern to most students. hooks associates the process of theorizing the location of one's marginality to healing. She contends:

> Where our lived experience of theorizing is fundamentally linked to processes of self-recovery, of collective liberation, no gap exists between theory and practice. Indeed, what such experience makes more evident is the bond between the two—that ultimately reciprocal process wherein one enables the other. (1994c, p. 61)

The process of linking theory to practice provides an avenue for interrogation of discriminatory factors in White supremacist, patriarchal, capitalist social structures. hooks maintains:

> Within academic and intellectual climates that are striving to respond to the reality of cultural pluralism, there should be room for discussions of racism that promote and encourage critical interrogation. It should be possible for scholars, especially those who are members of groups who dominate, exploit, and oppress others, to explore the political implications of their work without fear or guilt. (1990, p. 124)

Indeed, hooks' major premise (1994c) of linking theory to practice is for purposes of making learning more relevant, involving, and enjoyable to students. Supporting hooks' contention regarding the incorporation of students' lived realities to make the learning process more interactive and meaningful, Elizabeth Minnich maintains that incorporating contemporary human experiences adds to the richness of "official" knowledge by exploring a

> richer range of materials, lives, voices, visions, and achievements, to learn the stories and modes of thought and creation of others . . . working with [students] to approach an education that might be . . . liberatory, compatible with freedom. (1990, pp. 181–182)

hooks (1994c) illustrates that linking formal subject matter to social reality acknowledges learners as source and bearer of knowledge. First, an elitist education alienates students who feel the need to subordinate their primary cultural traits and characteristics in order to assimilate prevailing modes of knowledge and feeling. The process "silences" students whose ways of being, feeling, and knowing differ from prevailing modes. An exclusive focus on dominant cultural experiences and histories in classroom discussions and the elitism in academic disciplines result in an image of schools and school experiences as separate from students' lived realities. hooks contends:

> Students are much more engaged when they are learning how to think critically and analytically by exploring concrete aspects of their reality, particularly their experience of popular culture. Teaching theory, I find that students may understand a particular paradigm in the abstract but are unable to see how to apply it to their lives. Focusing on popular culture has been one of the main ways to bridge this gap. (1990, p. 6)

This author argues that it is easy for one to get caught up in an abstract and scholastic focus whereby concepts are viewed as separate entities, a prerogative of scholastic circles. However, as Ira Shor and Freire maintain, the issue is not to deny abstraction and academic concepts

> but rather how to use them in such a way that they are put next to concreteness. . . . How to diminish the distance between academic context and the reality from which the students come, the reality which I must know better to the extent that I am engaged in some way with a process of changing it. (1987, p. 148)

hooks raises another aspect to incorporating lived theory with practice. Education ought to allow a place for languages and cultures that have been traditionally marginalized. To illustrate the impact of promoting a particular language in educational settings to the exclusion of other languages, hooks contends:

> Standard English is not the speech of exile. It is the language of conquest and domination; in the United States, it is the mark which hides the loss of so many tongues, all those sounds of diverse, native communities we will never hear, the speech of Gullah, Yiddish, and so many other unremembered tongues. (1994c, p. 168)

Though hooks views the teaching of Standard English as a form of "cultural imperialism," the issue has become extremely complex in countries such as the United States where English has been "adopted" as the official and primary language of communication. Indeed, Ira Shor and Freire (1987) strongly urge marginalized students to acquire the skill of Standard English, in view of the fact that one's ability to function effectively and/or critique social practices hinges on command of the English language (this applies to the United States and most British colonies such as Kenya). However, Shor and Freire enjoin teachers to go beyond teaching the rules of English to an exploration of its political implications.

The previous discussion based on hooks and critical, feminist, and multicultural scholars demonstrates that linking theory to practice serves various functions: (a) avoids the elitism behind separating academic from the public; (b) integrates contemporary human experience to "official" knowledge and invokes social reality as a means to understanding technical concepts, a process that avoids the reification of school knowledge; (c) enhances integration of subject matter in building on most students' realities and making in class discussions relevant to life outside the classrooms; (d) provides an avenue for interrogating contentious issues of race, gender, and class biases in educational settings and the wider society; (e) allows for an interrogation and reconstruction of old epistemologies through an accommodation of multiple perspectives on ways of being, feeling, and knowing; and thus (f) makes learning more meaningful and relevant to most students' lived realities. Commending hooks' approach to linking theory to practice, Tom Fox maintains that "bell hooks' insistence on the connection between activism and literacy reconnects the academy with the political work that we have a responsibility to take up" (1994, p. 111). In classroom discussions, linking theory (established knowledge) to practice involves embracing experience, confessions, and testimony as vital dimensions of the learning process (hooks, 1994c). The pedagogy calls teachers to take the first risk in linking confessional narratives to academic discussions illustrating the interplay between theory and practice. hooks cautions:

> Professors who expect students to share confessional narratives but who are themselves unwilling to share are exercising power in a manner that could be coercive . . . when professors bring narratives to their experiences into classroom discussions it eliminates the possibility that we can function as all-knowing, silent interrogators. (1994c, p. 21)

The following discussion on student empowerment highlights the implications of the metaphor of schools as learning communities, the process of student engagement, and the significance of incorporating students' experiences in a learning process.

Student Empowerment

Community Image

Even though hooks recognizes that teachers' ability to empower students is limited by standardized school policies and practices, she notes the manner in which individual teachers employ traditional pedagogical models for "security" purposes:

> Fear of losing control in the classroom often leads individual professors to fall into a conventional teaching pattern wherein power is used destructively. It is this fear that leads to collective professorial investment in bourgeois decorum as a means of maintaining a fixed order, of ensuring that the teacher will have absolute control. (1994c, p. 188)

Learning communities offer a different model to traditionally orchestrated power relations in the classroom. In the latter model, difference is suppressed and hierarchical relations reinforced in social arrangements. The image of schools as learning communities avoids the trap of coercive hierarchies in empowering and respecting the contribution of both students and teachers while honoring individual differences. hooks contends:

> As a classroom community, our capacity to generate excitement is deeply affected by our interest in one another, in hearing one another's voices, in recognizing one another's presence. . . . There must be an ongoing recognition that everyone influences the classroom dynamic, that every-one contributes. . . . Seeing the classroom always as a learning communal place enhances the likelihood of collective effort in creating and sustaining a learning community. (1994c, p. 8)

Supporting hooks' image of school (1994c) as a mutual learning community, Nel Noddings maintains that the

> contributions of teachers and students are necessarily unequal, but they are nonetheless mutual; the relationship is marked by reciprocity. Students cannot be expected to teach their teachers, but they can be expected to respond to growing sensitivity to attempts to promote their own growth. (1992, p. 108)

hooks argues that unlike traditional concepts of the teaching/learning process, students and teachers are mutually responsible for creating a conducive learning atmosphere. It is

> rare that any professor, no matter how eloquent a lecturer, can generate through his or her actions enough excitement to create an exciting

classroom. Excitement is generated through a collective effort. (1994c, p. 8)

The fact that class members acknowledge each other's presence and entertain multiple perspectives to issues both enriches and enhances students' integration of subject matter. In contrast to bureaucratic school arrangements, hooks' image of school as a learning community suggests collective and active engagement of teachers and students in the pursuit of knowledge. She contends: "Sharing experiences and confessional narratives in the classroom helps establish communal commitment to learning" (1994c, p. 186). Both teachers and students are responsible for creating the necessary climate of openness and intellectual rigor. Further, hooks maintains that the

> exciting aspect of creating a classroom community where there is respect for individual voices is that there is infinitely more feedback because students do feel free to talk—and talk back. And, yes, often this feedback is critical. (1994c, p. 42)

In accommodating "differences," hooks maintains that solidarity and connection are possible even with those one feels no ready sense of connection. Empowering students by modeling schools on a community image and promoting mutuality and dialogue in classroom environments addresses the issue of marginality of non-White, female, and materially underprivileged students:

> What those of us . . . now know, that the generations before us did not grasp, was that *beloved community* is formed not by the eradication of differences but by its affirmation, by each of us claiming the identities, and cultural legacies that shape who we are and how we live in the world. (hooks, 1995b, p. 265; emphasis in original)

Affirming community in diversity enriches classroom discourse by eliciting greater interaction among students and between students and teachers. Students "recognize" each other and most important, appreciate "difference" as opposed to the xenophobia manifested in interactions with those different from us. Further, the denial and subordination of those who are in any way different, typically translates to an "I against them" attitude and the superior/inferior syndrome.

hooks recognizes:

Students from marginalized groups enter classrooms within institutions where their voices have been neither heard nor welcomed, whether these students discuss facts—those which any of us might know—or personal experience. [Engaged] pedagogy has been shaped to respond to this reality. . . . I circumvent this possible misuse of power by bringing to the classroom pedagogical strategies that affirm their presence, their right to speak, in multiple ways on diverse topics. . . . If experience is already invoked in the classroom as a way of knowing that coexists in a nonhierarchical way with other ways of knowing, then it lessens the possibility that it can be used to silence. (1994c, pp. 83–84)

She links the recognition and celebration of "difference" to a community experience. The process of dialogue between students and teachers avoids the imposition of one individual's ideas on the other by creating an environment in which "truth" is explored and arrived at through an interaction that honors each party's contribution to a discourse. hooks' proposition, similar to that of feminist scholars Nicholas Burbules, 1995; Elizabeth Minnich, 1990; Nel Noddings, 1992; Jo Anne Pagano, 1995, advocates discursive venues that acknowledge and nurture consideration of a plurality of "facts" and/or "intentions" in discourses.

hooks' metaphor of schools addresses the resistance of students of color and White women to classroom participation. She recalls White professors' comments regarding poor participation of non-White students in classrooms:

White professors have often voiced concern to me about nonwhite students who do not talk. As the classroom becomes more diverse, teachers are faced with the way the politics of domination are reproduced in the education setting. For example, white male students continue to be the most vocal in our classes. Students of color and some white women express fear that they will be judged as intellectually inadequate by these peers. (1994c, p. 39)

She, therefore, advocates nurturing learning communities whereby teachers encourage active participation of students and recognition of each student's presence and contribution to a learning process. In schools, a shared commitment between teachers and students would be characterized by the "desire to learn—to receive actively knowledge that enhances [our] intellectual development and [our] capacity to live more fully in the world" (p. 40). hooks notes that engaged pedagogy requires teachers to genuinely *value* everyone's presence. There must be an ongoing recognition that everyone influences the classroom dynamic, that everyone contributes. These contributions are resources. Used constructively they enhance the capacity of any class to create a learning community. (p. 8)

hooks' metaphor of school as a learning community resonates with Jane Roland Martin's image of a schoolhome. A schoolhome combines the traditional emphasis on the three Rs—reading, writing, and arithmetic—with an ethic of care (Martin, 1992). Martin argues that schools ought to design "environments in which boys and girls can do some things together and others separately without slipping into those ill-fitting mantles of manhood" (1992, p. 118).

hooks' writings reiterate the issue of marginality of students whose cultural traits and characteristics are not adequately reflected in mainstream values and attitudes. She notes:

All too often, students from nonmaterially privileged backgrounds assume a position of passivity—they behave as victims, as though they can only be acted upon against their will. Ultimately, they end up feeling they can only reject or accept the norms imposed on them . . . [which] sets them up for disappointment and failure. (hooks, 1994c, p. 183)

Some teachers may consciously sidestep posing questions to "nonparticipative" students to avoid putting undue pressure on them and/or embarrass the students by exposing their ignorance. However, hooks argues that educators can help students overcome their resistance to "talking" in classrooms by eliciting their contributions, promoting dialogue, and developing an atmosphere that acknowledges and honors "difference." To circumvent the idea of thinking in a foreign language, hooks encourages non-White students to write out their essays in their primary language and translate the work to Standard English. The process addresses the issue of marginality of non-White, female, and materially underprivileged students. hooks advocates incorporating differing cultural values from the mainstream norms and specifically accommodating different patois of English. She maintains that both educators and students:

learn from spaces of silence as well as spaces of speech, that in the patient act of listening to another tongue we may subvert that culture of capitalist frenzy and consumption that demands all desire must be satisfied immediately, or we may disrupt that cultural imperialism that suggests one is worthy of being heard only if one speaks in Standard English. (1994c, p. 174) hooks maintains that making the classroom a democratic setting where every-one feels responsibility to contribute is a central goal of a transformative pedagogy. Similar to hooks' contention regarding learner involvement, critical theory scholarship advocates student empowerment and a question-posing pedagogy to subvert traditional classroom dynamics that privilege teachers over students and "academics" over lived reality (hooks, 1994c). hooks (1994c) and Chandra Mohanty (1994) maintain that social power and politics are re-enacted in school norms and practices. To counteract the cultural privilege of particular students, Elsa Brown advocates interrogation of the "normative" by incorporating "a variety of experiences, a variety of ways of understanding the world, a variety of frameworks of operation, without imposing consciously or unconsciously a notion of the norm" (Mohanty, 1994, p. 152). Mohanty advocates a pedagogy that addresses the "questions of audience, voice, power, and evaluation, while retaining a focus on the material being taught" (p. 153).

Dialogue is central to a transformative pedagogy. Dialogue not only enables the deconstruction of teachers' image as privileged source of information, but also empowers students, creating space for reconstruction of "knowledge" and the learning process. hooks (1994c), similar to critical theory scholars, main-tains that greater participation between students and teachers empowers students, drawing focus away from teachers as privileged sources of informa-tion. Incorporating learner experience communicates to students that their contributions matter, and that responsibility for the "success" of the learning encounter rests on them as well as teachers. In offering an alternative model to hierarchical social arrangements, the discussion on imaging of schools as learning communities highlights the conjoint responsibility of teachers and students for creating a conducive learning environment. hooks contends that one of the joys of education for the practice of freedom is that it "allows students to assume responsibility for their choices" (1994c, p. 19). The following discussion analyzes the significance of learner engagement.

Learner Engagement

According to hooks, education as the practice of freedom extends the teaching role beyond the mere sharing of information to a more holistic involvement with students:

> To embrace the performative aspect of teaching we are compelled to engage "audiences," to consider issues of reciprocity . . . [teaching] is meant to serve as a catalyst that calls everyone to become more engaged, to become active participants in learning. (1994c, p. 11)

She, however, recognizes the impact of teachers' expectations on the learning environment, stating that many

> professors have conveyed to [her] their feeling that the classroom should be a "safe" place; that usually translates to mean that the professor lectures to a group of students who respond only when called on. (p. 9)

The focus on "security" promotes prolonged silence or lack of student engagement. In contrast, incorporating students' experiences in classroom discussions serves various functions: (a) students are seen as individuals and interacted with according to their needs, (b) classrooms become democratic settings where everyone feels a responsibility to contribute, and (c) the exchange of ideas contributes to stimulation of serious intellectual and/or academic engagement insofar as the concept of a privileged voice of authority is deconstructed by collective critical dialogue (hooks, 1994c). Indeed, experiential knowledge can enhance the learning experience and inform how and what students know.

hooks, similar to Freire (1973), contends that a dialogical approach to education benefits teachers as well as students. She maintains that to

> engage in dialogue is one of the simplest ways we can begin as teachers, scholars, and critical thinkers to cross boundaries, the barriers that may or may not be erected by race, gender, and class, professional standing, and a host of other differences. (1994c, p. 130)

The dialogical exchange in classrooms ultimately leads to feedback and greater classroom interaction. Supporting hooks' contention, Henry Giroux (cited in hooks, 1994c) and Raymond Morrow and Carlos Torres (1995) recognize the significance of accommodating differing values, voices, and intention of learners in classroom discussions. Similarly, dialogue and critical thinking are two crucial elements in Freire's pedagogy. Freire defined dialogue as the "encounter between men, mediated by the world, in order to name the world" (1970/1992, p. 76). His notion of critical thinking was based on the premise that reality is a process and as such open to discourse, and requiring reevaluation and re-definition.

Recollecting her experience as a student at Stanford, hooks raises the issue of estrangement as a result of her working-class background. Besides the stigma of being on tuition scholarship, hooks illustrates the impact of class biases:

> It was the constant invocation of materially privileged class experience (usually that of the middle class) as a universal norm that not only set

those of us from working-class backgrounds apart but effectively excluded those who were not privileged from discussions, from social
activities. (1994c, p. 181)

She contends that a banking approach to education best serves the interest of
those wishing to maintain the status quo. Official "knowledge" reinforces the
supremacy of White, middle-class males whose cultural experiences are reflected in mainstream norms. And yet, as she observes, there is

[l]ittle or no discussion of the way in which the attitudes and values of
those from materially privileged classes are imposed upon everyone via
biased pedagogies. Reflected in the choice of subject matter and the
manner in which ideas are shared, these biases need never be overtly
stated. (pp. 179–180)

To counteract the cultural alienation, hooks advocates an interrogation of
biases in educational settings and an acknowledgment of different ways of
being, feeling, and knowing. Similarly, Shor and Freire propose a dialogical
method of instruction that "contradicts the logic of domination, contradicts
the dichotomized curriculum, and challenges the social relations of learning
which inhibit democracy and critical thought" (1987, p. 138).

hooks argues that engaging in "intellectual exchange where people hear a
diversity of viewpoints enables them to witness firsthand solidarity that grows
stronger in a context of productive critical exchange and confrontation" (1990,
p. 6). A greater interaction among teacher, students, and subject matter makes
education more relevant and meaningful whereas an authoritarian classroom
setting has a dampening effect on students' participation and curiosity (hooks,
1994c). The significance of student participation is a primary element reiter-
ated in critical theory scholarship (Freire, 1970/1992, 1973; Freire & Faundez,
1989; Shor, 1992; Shor & Freire, 1987). It is also the element that is low in
classrooms employing a transfer-of-knowledge pedagogy. hooks illustrates that
engaging students subverts the norm by empowering and interrogating the
complicity of privileged students:

Unlike the oppressed or colonized, who may begin to feel as they engage
in education for critical consciousness a new found sense of power and
identity that frees them from colonization of the mind, that liberates,
privileged students are often down right unwilling to acknowledge that
their minds have been colonized, that they have been learning how to be

oppressors, how to dominate, or at least how to passively accept the domination of others. (1989a, p. 102)

Overall, student participation in classroom discussion has several benefits: (a) a teacher can better assess the actual cognitive levels of students for purposes of designing individual students' academic progress; (b) students learn to ask questions of themselves, to appropriate information, relating formal subject matter to their experiences both in and beyond the school; (c) teachers and students are both enriched by the interaction; (d) the process builds students' self-confidence; (e) the process nurtures a more democratic learning atmosphere; and (f) curiosity of students challenges teachers to explore new angles in their understanding of subject matter and its transmission (hooks, 1994c). These elements call for a re-conceptualization of both process and content of learning. The role of teachers in a transformative pedagogy is addressed in the next chapter.

hooks' advocacy for learner engagement avoids the marginality of students whose cultural traits and characteristics differ from mainstream values. Expounding on the "exclusion" of voices of marginalized students, she illustrates that most

> students are not comfortable exercising this right [to free speech] especially if it means that they must give voice to thoughts, ideas, feelings that go against the grain, that are unpopular. This censoring process is only one way bourgeois values overdetermine social behavior in the classroom and undermine the democratic exchange of ideas. (1994c, p. 179)

In this context, learner engagement interrogates White supremacy in presenting multiple views of reality. The process deflects attention from "voices" of White, male, and materially privileged students. hooks contends that it is one of the "responsibilities of the teacher to help create an environment where students learn that, in addition to speaking, it is important to listen respectfully to others" (p. 150). Teachers are crucial to establishing a transformative education as the next chapter seeks to illustrate. hooks' use of interviews and dialogues (1994c) in the classroom allows for greater engagement on the part of students and teachers, though some may perceive the process as confusing and chaotic.

The previous discussion has illustrated the rationale hooks advances for learner engagement. hooks notes that most teachers resist engaging students for fear of losing control over the process, and they easily fall back on prescribed content areas and methods of instruction. She points to the inadequacy of most teachers in the area of communication and a degree of comfort with sharing power in the classroom. hooks contrasts her vision of schools to bureaucracies in employing the metaphor of schools as learning communities. Modeled on communities, schools provide avenues for more inclusive discussion in encouraging greater participation and honoring different students' lived realities. In creating "safe" spaces for dialogue, teachers provide avenues for students to question assumptions in classical epistemologies and reconstruct new meanings. Students feel recognized by teachers and subsequently find it easier to integrate subject matter while requesting clarification on matters of ambiguity. As valued participants in a learning process, students feel empowered by the process of engagement and provide feedback. Thus, student participation deconstructs the image of teachers as privileged sources of information. Essentially, students recognize their role as meaning makers. The following discussion explores the significance of incorporating learner experiences in a learning process.

Incorporating Learner Experiences

hooks (1994c) confesses that at the institutions at which she taught, professors preferred an authoritative, hierarchical pedagogical mode, whereby the voice of the professor is the "privileged" transmitter of knowledge. Usually professors devalue personal experience in classroom discussions. Though some professors view the incorporation of students' lived experiences as disrupting the classroom by engaging the professor and students in a struggle for authority, in fact, excitement in classrooms is nurtured by classroom interactions. hooks recounts how the

> telling of personal experience is incorporated into classrooms in ways that deepen discussion. And I am most thrilled when the telling of experience links discussions of facts or more abstract constructs to concrete reality. (1994c, p. 86)

In seeking to incorporate students' lived realities, engaged pedagogy calls for an understanding of teaching that goes beyond "compartmentalized" schooling, beyond the mere sharing of information to a more holistic involvement with students (hooks, 1994c). This proposal is not unique to hooks. Jane Gallop (cited in hooks, 1994c) views the teacher as having an impact that goes beyond the classroom in relating to students as embodied beings with lives beyond the classroom.

hooks challenges herself and her fellow educators to "subvert" the tendency of marginalizing particular students by subordinating "different" voices:

> When those of us in the academy who are working class or from working-class backgrounds share our perspectives, we subvert the tendency to focus only on the thoughts, attitudes, and experiences of those who are materially privileged . . . precisely because it [is] so evident that race, sex, and class privilege empower some students more than others granting "authority" to some voices more than others. (1944c, p. 185)

Similarly, critical and feminist scholarship and multicultural theorists illustrate the significance of incorporating students' lived experience in classroom discussion (Banks, 1988; Freire & Faundez, 1989; Giroux, 1994a, 1994b; Martin, 1992, 1995; Nieto, 1996; Noddings, 1992, 1995a, 1995b; Shor, 1992; Shor & Freire, 1987).

Typically, racial, gender, and class issues are regarded as being too contentious for class discussion even when such issues are central to students' lived realities. This reification of social reality leads to an imposition of a reality alien to most students' day-to-day experience. The process subordinates most students' lived experience, which reinforces these students' senses of marginality. hooks demonstrates:

> To insist on speaking in any manner that did not conform to privileged class ideals and mannerisms placed one always in the position of interloper. It was assumed that any student coming from a working-class background would willingly surrender all values of habits of being associated with this background. (1994c, p. 182)

The "acceptability" or "appropriateness" of certain issues to class discussion results in what Freire (1970/1992), and in agreement hooks (1994c), terms *cultural silence*. To counteract the subordination of "dissenting" voices, hooks (1990, 1994b, 1994c) advocates incorporation of differing voices as a way of giving equal treatment to all students. hooks maintains that critical pedagogies emerge from the struggle of oppressed and exploited groups:

> Critical pedagogies of liberation respond to these concerns and necessarily embrace experience, confessions and testimony as relevant ways of knowing, as important, vital dimensions of any learning process. (1994c, p. 89)

Supporting hooks' contention, Nieto provides clarity on the notion of educational equality. Educational equality goes beyond providing the same resources and opportunities for all students: "Equal education also means that skills, talents, and experiences that all students bring to their education need be considered as valid starting points for further schooling" (Nieto, 1996, p. 10).

hooks sees a ready link between the incorporation of students' lived realities in formal curriculum and the meaningfulness of what is learned in schools:

> Students want knowledge that is meaningful. They rightly expect that my colleagues and I will not offer them information without addressing the connection between what they are learning and their overall life experiences. (1994c, p. 19)

Expounding further on hooks' proposal of linking "outside" classroom experiences to subject matter, Landon Beyer (1995) maintains that combating students' alienation in schools calls for incorporating popular culture—television programs, movies, music, video productions, and comic books into the curriculum. Indeed, all

> students, not just those from marginalized groups, seem more eager to enter energetically into classroom discussions when they perceive it as pertaining directly to them. . . . Students may be well versed in a particular subject and yet be more inclined to speak confidently if that subject matter directly relates to their experience. (hooks, 1994c, p. 87)

Further, "[F]ocusing on experience allows students to claim a knowledge base from which they can speak" (p. 94). Incorporating students' experiences disrupts the impact of cultural hegemony, and resulting "cultural silencing" of members whose traits and characteristics are not reflected in mainstream values and traditions:

> If experience is already invoked in the classroom as a way of knowing that co-exists in a nonhierarchical way with other ways of knowing, then it lessens the possibility that it can be used to silence. . . . It helps create communal awareness of the diversity of our experiences and provides a limited sense of the experiences that may inform how we think and what we say. . . . In our classroom, students do not usually feel the need to compete because the concept of a privileged voice of authority is deconstructed by our collective critical practice. (p. 84)

Incorporating students' lived experience in classroom discussion leads to a greater "engagement" of students in a learning process. A dialogic approach to teaching is an effective way of empowering students. hooks appreciates the feedback her pedagogy elicits:

> When I teach, I encourage [students] to critique, evaluate, make suggestions and interventions as we go along. . . . When students see themselves as mutually responsible for the development of a learning community, they offer constructive input. (p. 206)

Despite the benefits of acknowledging students' presence and their perspectives to make learning more meaningful and enjoyable, not all students readily embrace engaged pedagogy as the following discussion illustrates. Students respond differently to a liberatory education: (a) with enthusiasm; (b) with anger and anxiety, viewing it as a threat to their established values of traditional knowledge and classroom hierarchy; and (c) some with curiosity more than interest.

The notion of knowledge as a process, one in which students and teachers engage and which is achieved through dialogue, through breaking with the past, is not readily acceptable to most students. hooks argues that to

> acknowledge student responsibility for the learning process is to place it where it's least legitimate in their own eyes. When we try to change the classroom so that there is a sense of mutual responsibility for learning, students get scared that you are now not the captain working with them, but you are after all just another crew member—and not a reliable one at that. (1994c, p. 144)

Indeed, most people have been socialized into certain modes of thinking and behaving in which by force of habit they find security. Most students are trained to view themselves as passive recipients of knowledge. This applies especially to students "from working-class, who come to college assuming that professors see them as having nothing of value to say, no valuable contribution to make to a dialectical exchange of ideas" (p. 149).

hooks (1994c) confesses that in her classes some students resist sitting in a circle that would allow for greater interaction. She admits that students often feel they can just get up, walk out, and come back because of her (less rigid) teaching style. In this respect, one has also to take into account the element of cultural binds. The often deeply ingrained hierarchically structured social arrangements in more traditional societies could pose special challenges to a more participative/egalitarian mode of interaction. On the other hand, though unacknowledged, there seems to be an association of Women's Studies to and for women, and thus of little relevance to men. By the same token, it is only in the recent past that classes on Black Studies and/or Third World Literature have attracted students other than those from marginalized groups (hooks, 1994c).

Besides students' resistance to engaged pedagogy, hooks notes the association of the pedagogy to "encounter groups" or "therapy sessions." She contends that despite the reputation of frivolity and unstructured class discussions, the process of interaction between students and learners, and incorporation of lived reality to subject matter, enhances the learning process:

> Within professional circles, individuals often complain bitterly that students want classes to be "encounter groups." While it is utterly reasonable for students to expect classrooms to be therapy sessions, it is appropriate for them to hope that knowledge received in these settings will enrich and enhance them. (1994c, p. 19)

Incidentally, even the shared experiences of students in the classroom are perceived by the others as "good" only by virtue of a teacher's validation. Such judgments make the pedagogy look frivolous and without seriousness. There is an element of truth in the fact that most teachers shy away from confronting the issues of race, sex, and class differences:

> The unwillingness to approach teaching from a standpoint that includes awareness of race, sex, and class is often rooted in the fear that classrooms will be uncontrollable, that emotions and passions will not be contained. (p. 39)

Some people view incorporating new perspectives on gender and race as "diluting" the curriculum and/or questioning old "truths," what hooks calls the deep-seated fear that any "decentering of Western civilizations, of the white male canon, is really an act of cultural genocide" (1994c, p. 32). However, incorporating formerly marginalized groups and/or voices provides avenues for acknowledging "differing" perspectives enhance an intellectual discourse, interrogating the exclusivity in a White supremacist, patriarchal, and capitalist bias (hooks, 1990, 1994b, 1994c). Banks (1988) maintains that to create an egalitarian society would call for a redistribution of power among different ethnic and cultural groupings as a means of broadening the criteria for entry to various social, economic, and/or political institutions or modify the ethnocentrism in prevailing policy makers. Since the first measure is unrealistic and impractical in the short run, a viable option is multicultural education that exposes students to other cultures to nurture respect for multiple views and alternate ways of being. The following discussion presents hooks' rationale (1994c) for cultural pluralism to counteract the monocentrism in school curriculum and pedagogical orientations.

Multicultural Aspect

Though hooks' discussion (1994c) on multiculturalism focuses primarily on ethnic and/or racial cultural differences, Banks' conception of a multicultural approach to education encompasses an "analysis of class, racism, power, capitalism, and other systems that keep excluded ethnic groups powerless" (1988, pp. 165–166). hooks testifies that her awareness of the manner in which class shapes classroom interactions has helped her

> employ pedagogical strategies that create ruptures in the established order, that promote modes of learning which challenge bourgeois hegemony. . . . One such strategy has been the emphasis on creating in classrooms learning communities where everyone's voice can be heard, their presence recognized and valued. (1994c, p. 185)

Students whose cultural traits and characteristics are not adequately represented and/or reflected in the school culture feel alienated or as Banks (1988) terms it, "powerless."

A multiculturalist curriculum reflects the American cultural pluralism and its democratic ideal. hooks calls for the

> sharing of stories that [teach] history, family genealogy, and facts about African-American past . . . [because at present] young black people often have no knowledge of black history and are unable to identify important black leaders like Malcolm X. The arts remain one of the powerful realms of cultural resistance, a space for reawakening folks critical consciousness and a new vision. (1990, p. 39)

Besides empowering marginalized students, sensitivity to cultural pluralism helps develop collaboration and solidarity among students in school (hooks, 1994c). Awareness of one's marginality is central to hooks' (1994b) notion of freedom. It is hooks' contention (1992, 1995b) that a critical analysis of

"Whiteness" is crucial to a process of unlearning [*sic*] White supremacist values and attitudes. hooks argues:

> Whenever those of us who are members of exploited and oppressed groups dare to critically interrogate our locations, the identities and allegiances that inform how we live our lives, we begin the process of decolonization. . . . Acknowledging the truth of our reality, both individual and collective, is a necessary stage for personal and political growth. (1995b, p. 248)

She advocates critical interrogation of the manner in which White supremacy impacts conventional views of social reality and racial/cultural stereotypes:

> All too often we found a will to include those considered "marginal" without a willingness to accord their work the same respect and consideration given other work. In Women's Studies, for example, individuals will often focus on women of color at the very end of the semester or lump everything together about race and difference together in one section. This kind of tokenism is not multicultural education, but it is familiar to us as the change individuals are most likely to make. (hooks, 1994c, p. 38)

A critical interrogation of discriminatory norms and practices ought to help individuals understand the impact of racism and subsequently explore and validate different ways of being, feeling, and knowing (hooks, 1990, 1994b 1994c, 1995b).

In all her writings, hooks notes a prevailing state of cultural domination that makes the articulation and re-definition of social reality both possible and necessary. She argues:

> Accepting the decentering of the West globally, embracing multiculturalism, compels educators to focus attention on the issue of voice. Who speaks? Who listens? And why? (1994c, p. 40)

Subsequently, venturing into new ways of being and definition provides counter-hegemonic discourse as well as visibility for marginalized people whose history for the larger part remains unknown and/or social realities inadequately represented. The process of critical consciousness begins with one envisioning an alternative social reality through use of varied languages, different forms of

English, and employing traditional imagery and metaphors (hooks, 1994b, 1994c):

> In the classroom setting I encourage students to use their first language and translate it so they do not feel that seeking higher education will necessarily estrange them from that language and culture they know most intimately. (hooks, 1994c, p. 172)

Indeed, hooks (1984, 1989a, 1994b; hooks & West, 1991) urges ownership of one's circumstances and process of growth, discouraging a dependency on White and privileged individuals' authorship of texts on marginality. Arguing against essentialism in Cultural Studies programs and subordination of Black experience, hooks maintains:

> Seeking to make a context for critical intervention that is linked with strategies for liberation, cannot ignore the issue of representation, as it determines who gets to speak to, with and for us about culture and be heard [with legitimacy] as cultural studies is more solidly institutionalized and commodified. (1990, p. 9)

Incorporating previously excluded "voices" in traditional discourses affirms a classroom and/or nation's cultural plurality by honoring the rights of marginalized groups as well as ensuring representation of multiple perspectives in a discourse. Supporting hooks' contention regarding an inclusive curriculum and pedagogical orientations, Walter Feinberg contends that the process promotes

> clarity and truth-seeking by assuring that as many different perspectives can be considered in a deliberation. . . . And while removing silences— whether for reasons of rights or for reasons of truth—is likely to improve the lives of children, education is advanced when the former also serves the latter. (1995, pp. 32–33)

Affirming ethnic, racial, linguistic, religious, economic, gender pluralism, multicultural education addresses the alienation experienced by minority students in a school environment that often negates these students' lived experiences, and whereby policies and practices typically reinforce the students' sense of marginality (hooks, 1994b, 1994c). Incorporating students' lived experience affirms the identity of minority students, nurturing an acknowledgment and appreciation of cultures other than each student's own culture (hooks, 1994c). hooks maintains:

Within academic and intellectual climates that are striving to respond to the reality of cultural pluralism, there should be room for discussion of racism that promote and encourage critical interrogation. (1990, p. 124)

She therefore calls for a

recognition of cultural diversity, a rethinking of ways of knowing, a deconstruction of old epistemologies, and the concomitant demand that there be a transformation in our classrooms, in how we teach and what we teach. (1994c, p. 30)

It is also hooks' hope that solidarity is "affirmed by a shared belief in a spirit of intellectual openness that celebrates diversity, welcomes dissent, and rejoices in a collective dedication to the truth" (1994c, p. 33). Similarly, Lawrence Grossberg (1994) notes that Cultural Studies provide a necessary critique to the dominant culture, what hooks (1990, 1994b, 1995b) and Giroux (1994a) discuss under the umbrella of White supremacy. This author contends that the call for connectedness and inclusivity offers a necessary corrective at this particular time in history as many nations (Bosnia, Rwanda, Middle East, Zaire) grapple with issues of cultural, tribal, and religious plurality.

In addressing issues of race, gender, and class discrimination, the multicultural component of hooks' engaged pedagogy (1994c) counteracts the cultural hegemony that develops from a focus on a White supremacy, patriarchal, and capitalist value system. Indeed, looking back to her past experience as a student, hooks notes that Black students

were always having to conquer white supremacist assumptions that [they] were genetically inferior, never as capable as white peers, even unable to learn . . . they were always and only responding and reacting to white folks. (1994c, p. 4)

She highlights the need to incorporate other voices and acknowledge each student's presence, to integrate subordinated cultural histories as a way of awakening critical consciousness, and to create an alternative vision to the prevailing status quo (hooks, 1995a). To illustrate the subordination of Black women's experience and contribution, hooks cites Andrew Ross's "Hip, and the Long Front of Color," in his *No Respect: Intellectuals and Popular Culture*, which

constructs Black experience as though black women have had no role in black cultural production. [Similarly] the end of Meghan Morris' discussion of postmodernism in her collection of *Essays The Pirate's Fiancee: Feminism and Postmodernism*—has no reference to works by black women. (1990, p. 24)

To counteract racial and gender biases in historical accounts, hooks (1984, 1989a) advocates acknowledgment of contribution of female leaders such as Septima Clark, Sojourner Truth, Ann Cooper, Mary Church Terrell, Harriet Tubman, and Daisy Bates. hooks contends that a monocentric curriculum reinscribes colonialism and domination, and recounts her joy at the acknowledgment of cultural diversity in educational settings:

At last, there was the possibility of a learning community, a place where difference could be acknowledged, where we could finally all understand, accept, and affirm that our ways of knowing are forged in history and relations of power. (1994c, p. 30)

hooks recognizes that engaged pedagogy demands more from teachers than a traditional lecture (more impersonal) pedagogy. She also admits that neither she nor most teachers are adequately equipped to accommodate differences of class backgrounds, language, levels of understanding, communication skills, and concerns in a student body. Noting that most teacher-education programs tend toward a functionalist approach and a linear modular thought process that emphasizes hegemony in content, process, and results, hooks maintains that if the

effort to respect and honor the social reality and experiences of groups in this society who are nonwhite is to be reflected in a pedagogical process, then as teachers—on all levels, from elementary to university settings . . . [we] must acknowledge that our styles of teaching may need to change . . . most of us were taught in classrooms where styles of teaching reflected the notion of a single norm of thought and experience, which we were encouraged to believe was universal. . . . Most of us learned to teach using this model. (1994c, p. 35)

Besides inadequacy in teacher-training programs, a teacher's choice in "knowledge" transmission has significance. Some teachers present "knowledge" in a manner that falsely avoids addressing contentious issues in society, which gives some a sense of security. Other teachers adopt an engaging pedagogy that incorporates and honors the contribution of each individual in the class, and critically interrogates issues of power and knowledge as these impinge on students' lives (hooks, 1994c). hooks notes the hesitation of particular Black professors at Yale University who felt it necessary to behave in ways that de-emphasized race, and points to pedagogical orientations that perpetuate hierarchical status:

> Some black professors believe a clear separation reinforced by behavior must be maintained between teacher and student (as in "students must know their place"); the origins of this metaphor are in our history. Such assumptions are based on the very notions of inferior and superior that inform white supremacy. To embrace them is to ally oneself with forces that reinforce and perpetuate domination. (1989a, p. 69)

Over and above the incorporation of differing cultural experiences to mainstream norms, hooks advocates incorporation of works by artists who offer alternative visions. She calls for acknowledgment of

> black artists who successfully attract diverse audiences without pandering to a white supremacist consumer market while simultaneously creating a value system where acquisition of wealth and fame are not the only measures of success. (1990, p. 39)

Changes in any one of the variables necessitate interrogation of habits, values, assumptions that underlie these very patterns. As hooks (1984, 1990, 1992, 1994c) contends, there is need to interrogate "Whiteness" or White supremacy and its impact on marginalized groups. She however insists that racism, sexism, and classism are interlocking dominations. The redress of any one form of necessity calls for a critique of other forms of dominations. Dominations and/or discriminatory norms and practices are based on the hierarchy principle whereby the superiority of an element and/or entity has its inferior coefficient.

The previous discussion demonstrated the role of a multicultural approach to education in honoring the cultural histories of marginalized communities by incorporating these histories and experiences into official curriculum. The process involves a recognition of marginalized cultural histories (beyond Black History months and/or Puertorican Day Parades), establishment of cultural study programs, accommodation of cultural experiences in classroom discussions, and analysis of race, gender, and class biases in educational settings, to counteract White supremacy, patriarchy, and capitalism. Overall, the pedagogy's challenge to critical consciousness is a necessary critique to the pervasive false consciousness evident in people's uncritical allegiance to mainstream values and practices. The legitimacy of materialistic yearning lies in the fact that most cultures define progress in terms of material acquisitions. The following discussion explores hooks' (1994c) proposition for incorporating passion in classrooms to avoid a dualistic thought pattern that privileges rationality over affectivity.

Passion

The author addresses the significance of passion from three main angles: (a) the need to make the classroom experience more exciting, (b) providing an education that honors the affective as well as the rational lives of students, and (c) recognition of interdependence to counteract hierarchical social arrangements. hooks' conceptualization of excitement goes beyond the giddy, "feel good" emotions to encompass a joy in learning and involvement with others, aspects that are normally subordinated in a competitive and individualistic focus on subject matter and acquisition of good grades.

Excitement

Reflecting on her teaching experience, hooks recalls the resistance to incorporating excitement in the classroom in higher education because it was

> viewed as potentially disruptive of the atmosphere of seriousness assumed to be essential to the learning process. [Thus to] enter classroom settings in colleges and universities with the will to share the desire to encourage excitement, was to transgress. (1994c, p. 7)

She contends that the denial of passion is rooted in Western metaphysical dualisms that privilege the public over the private, the rational over the affective, and subsequently, a denial of "bodiliness":

> Trained in the philosophical context of metaphysical dualism, many of us have accepted the notion that there is a split between the body and mind. To call attention to the body is to betray the legacy of the repression and denial that has been handed down to us by our professional elders, who have been usually white and male. (p. 191)

hooks associates both the subordination of affectivity and objectification of teachers and students to the "idea of mind/body split, one that promotes and supports compartmentalization" (p. 16). She however illustrates the fallacy of the dichotomy by arguing that "[R]epression and denial make it possible for us to forget and then desperately seek to recover ourselves, our feelings, our passions in some private place—after class" (p. 192). Supporting hooks' contention regarding the negative effects of denying passion in legitimate venues, Jane Roland Martin (1992) links worker boredom (alienation) to a devaluing of the affective. Martin contends that as

> Workers on assembly lines are benumbed by having to perform a single motion over and over, children are rendered insensible in school by having to memorize facts that have been detached from real-life contexts, fill in answers on worksheets that turn living, throbbing ideas into inert, disconnected facts, and hear the same story again and again. (1992, pp. 134–135)

Holistic Education

hooks contends that the image of students as recipients of compartmentalized bits of knowledge rather than as whole human beings with complex lives and experiences limits student engagement in the learning process. However, this is the very model she saw adhered to in the academy:

> During my twenty years of teaching, I have witnessed grave dis-ease among professors (irrespective of their politics) when students want us to see them as whole human beings with complex lives and experiences rather than simply as seekers after compartmentalized bits of information. (hooks, 1994c, p. 15)

The objectification of students and subject matter is further reinforced by professors who are often

> deeply antagonistic toward, even scornful of, any approach to learning emerging from a philosophical standpoint emphasizing the union of mind, body, and spirit, rather than the separation of these elements. (p. 18)

As far removed from education as the practice of freedom, the abstraction and compartmentalization of knowledge make classrooms "feel more like a prison, a place of punishment and a confinement rather than a place of promise and possibility" (p. 4). It is then no wonder that both teachers and students are typically disinterested in schooling. In this context, passion and dialogical interaction that characterize engaged pedagogy of necessity disrupt the formality assumed to be essential to a traditional approach to the learning process. hooks acknowledges the seriousness of learning but would still maintain that learning ought not be devoid of pleasure and joy. Acknowledging the value of passion in educational settings calls for a paradigmatic shift in attitudes and conceptualization of teaching. hooks illustrates:

> To restore passion to the classroom or to excite it in classrooms where it has never been, professors must find again the place of eros within ourselves and together allow the mind and body to feel and know desire. (p. 199)

Besides subordinating females to whom the affective is typically associated, the false dichotomy between the rational and affective leads to the view that the affective is something to be overcome in one's pursuit of truth. Educational policies reinforce the dichotomy between the rational and affective through school policies:

> Teachers are expected to publish, but no one really expects or demands of us that we really care about teaching in uniquely passionate and different ways. Teachers who love students and are loved by them are still "suspect" in the academy. (hooks, 1994c, p. 198)

Not surprisingly, hooks views the denial of affectivity as a distortion of a learning process:

> Whenever emotional responses erupt, many of us believe our academic purpose has been diminished. To me this is really a distorted notion of intellectual practice, since the underlying assumption is that to be truly intellectual we must be cut off from our emotions. (p. 155)

In schools, the separation of body and mind elevates the rational over the affective in academic circles. This

> meant that whether academics were drug addicts, alcoholics, batterers, or sexual abusers, the only important aspect of our identity was whether our minds functioned, whether we were able to do our jobs in the classroom. (p. 16)

In contrast, hooks (1994c; hooks & West, 1991) enjoins educators to incorporate the affective in classroom activities, to communicate a passion for students and subject matter. Arguing that the acknowledgment of passion is one form of linking theory to practice, hooks contends that incorporating passion for ideas and students makes the classroom a "dynamic place where transformations in social relations are concretely actualized and the false dichotomy between the world outside and the inside world of the academy disappears" (hooks, 1994c, p. 195).

Hierarchical Relations

In hooks' view, a banking system of education that extols the role of the professor is deeply rooted in metaphysical dualism and its hierarchical principle. She maintains that most of her professors "seemed enthralled by the exercise of power and authority within their mini-kingdom, the classroom" (1994c, p. 17). hooks also argues that the "vast majority of students learn through conservative, traditional educational practices and concern themselves with the presence of the professor" (p. 8). In contrast, she advocates incorporating joy in cultural diversity, passion for justice, and love for freedom in educational institutions and society as a way of transforming teaching, working, and living habits.

Passion is one of the elements of hooks' engaged pedagogy (1994c) that educators challenge. Gary Olson (1994) warns against the ready incorporation of passion and intimacy in classrooms because of increasing allegations of child molestations and related abuses by authority figures. However, hooks maintains that to "understand the place of eros and eroticism in the classroom, we must move beyond thinking of those forces solely in terms of the sexual, though that dimension need not be denied" (Olson, 1994, p. 194). Building on Sam Keen's emphasis (cited in hooks, 1994c) on the centrality of passion to an integration of theory to practice, hooks contends that passion infuses a teacher's quest for knowledge and inspires one's teachings.

Supporting hooks' (1994c) advocacy for the incorporation of passion, Martin (1992) and Noddings (1992) contend that focus on the three Cs—care, concern, and connection—provides a necessary vision for society. Organizing education around centers of care avoids the domination of groups in power by seeking to develop relations of mutual intimacy rather than competition and animosity. The focus on collaboration and harmony in a care ethic counteracts school and social hierarchical relations that pit individuals and/or social groupings against each other (hooks, 1994c; Martin, 1992; Noddings, 1992, 1995a, 1995b).

hooks maintains that incorporating passion and desire in the classroom is crucial to learning despite the general weariness with passion and its link to sexual harassment charges leveled against teachers. Joyce Irene Middleton (1994) concedes hooks' analysis (Olson, 1994) of the Western tradition's patriarchal conceptions of hierarchical thinking, privileging, and power relations in schooling and its negative impact on marginalized students. She commends her problem-posing approach to teaching as opposed to a standardized, formulaic pedagogy in its: (a) defining the personal in relation to teaching; (b) shifting the classroom from an either/or, hierarchical paradigm to a both/and learning community paradigm; and (c) confronting negative stereotypes of marginalized groups in texts and classroom practices. Tom Fox (1994) commends hooks for seeking an audience outside the academy and conceiving of her role as educator in broader terms than the usual classroom transmitter of knowledge. He too notes her interactive and inclusive style in teaching, in addition to urging teachers to incorporate passion for purposes of diffusing hierarchical relations in the classroom to create a sense of community.

The previous discussion on the significance of incorporating passion in classrooms builds on hooks' association (1994c) of passion to learner engagement, teachers' love and excitement for students and knowledge, acknowledgment of the affective as well as the rational dimension of learning, and interconnectedness of individuals. Overall, incorporating passion in classrooms avoids a dualistic thought pattern that pits feminine against masculine traits and characteristics, interrogating a patriarchal and capitalistic ideology. The process honors the affective, typically associated with females, and nurtures love and concern between teachers and students and among students. Engaged pedagogy provides an alternative view to the competitive individualism that characterizes capitalistic modes of operation. Indeed, hooks can testify from her past experiences as a student that "excitement [can] co-exist with and even stimulate serious intellectual and/or academic engagement" (1994c, p. 7).

In sum, the components of hooks' engaged pedagogy—inclusive ways of being, feeling, and knowing; link of theory to practice; student empowerment; multiculturalism; and incorporation of passion—in different ways address the issue of student marginality and an alienating curriculum. hooks' engaged pedagogy provides an avenue for addressing issues of race, gender, and class biases in educational settings. Not only do students feel recognized in such venues but they also are able to unite knowledge learned in the classroom with their lived experiences. hooks, similar to critical, feminist, and multicultural scholarship, critiques the view of a static knowledge base. First, an exclusive curriculum privileges students whose cultural history it reflects over students whose experiences are subordinated by the mainstream. Second, hooks (1994b, 1994c) contends that in reflecting White people's values and attitudes, the school culture further alienates students marginalized by an elitist and White supremacist curriculum.

Third, hooks' metaphor of schools as learning communities counteracts the hierarchical, authoritarian model that characterizes most educational settings. The notion of schools as learning communities significantly shapes student-teacher interaction. The implied solidarity in hooks' image of schooling is based on teacher-student common pursuit of knowledge, rather than a hegemonic process based on the suppression of difference. The process serves two functions. The responsibility for creating a conducive learning atmosphere rests on both students and teachers. Further, a greater engagement of students in classroom activities and incorporation of learner experiences enhances students' integration of school subjects to their lived realities while simultaneously empowering students formerly marginalized by virtue of race, gender, and/or class biases in educational settings and the wider society.

A multicultural approach to education addresses student alienation resulting from a monocentric—Eurocentric—curriculum and pedagogical orientations. Multiculturalism honors cultural pluralism through an acknowledgment of different ways of being, feeling, and knowing. Not dissimilar is hooks' proposal for incorporating the affective to counteract a dualistic thought pattern that relegates emotions and other female related traits and characteristics to "non-academic" spheres. hooks calls educators to an expression of passion (beyond sexual feelings) for each other, the subject matter, and the whole teaching/learning process. The rationale for honoring the affective is to build an excitement and joy to counteract the feelings of drudgery, boredom, disinterest that characterize the teaching and learning process. hooks' engaged pedagogy links the pursuit of knowledge to a pursuit for freedom. The awareness of debilitating forces creates in the learner critical consciousness and the stimulus to action. This author supports hooks' faith in the "power" of critical consciousness. Raising the hard questions of biases in one aspect of life typically leads to greater interrogation of other aspects of one's life. Some may be so weary of the demands of a critically conscious mind, that they opt for an "unquestioning" attitude. Thus, the awareness of abuses in power in institutional settings ought to lead to an increasing analysis of one's complicity in maintaining and perpetuating different forms of dominations in different aspects of one's dealing with others. Indeed this is a lifetime venture. The following discussion explores the implications of engaged pedagogy on teachers' role.

CHAPTER 7

Teachers' Role in a Transformative Education

Teacher resistance to a transformative education could be attributed to various reasons besides the potential awkwardness due to a lack of certainty in teaching methods and processes. bell hooks notes that teachers "trying to institutionalize progressive pedagogical practices risk being subjected to discrediting critiques especially from professors resistant to change and unwilling to involve students" (1994c, p. 141). She aptly sums up the essence of engaged pedagogy in stating that it results "in shifts of relations between students and professors and among students" (p. 30). Hierarchical relations in schools and classrooms reinforce society's myths of the inevitability of class divisions: givers and recipients, rulers and the ruled. hooks notes that many

> professors remain unwilling to be involved with any pedagogical practices that emphasize mutual participation between teacher and student because more time and effort are required to do this work. (p. 204)

On the other hand, most students come to class socialized into hierarchical social arrangements. Students know that teachers are the privileged voice and power wielders in matters concerning school policies and practices.

hooks discourages the notion of prescribed pedagogies and calls for a flexibility and appropriateness; to her: "The engaged classroom is always changing . . . when the classroom is engaged, it's dynamic. It's fluid. It's *always* changing" (hooks, 1994c, p. 158; emphasis in original). She urges educators to critically interrogate conventional pedagogies, exploring boundaries of acceptability, creating new visions to make education a practice in freedom by adopting a flexible approach in both their dealings with students and in the presentation of knowledge. She observes:

> We communicate best by choosing [that] way of speaking that is informed by the particularity and uniqueness of whom we are speaking to and with . . . the engaged voice must never be fixed and absolute but always changing, always evolving in dialogue with a world beyond itself. (p. 11)

To further promote flexibility and excitement in classrooms, hooks proposes creating a structure for education where professors can "circulate" in colleges. This avoids the danger of teachers setting up "territories" in any classroom or school that reflect biases or reinforce systems of domination. She also advocates "job-sharing and job-switching in the interest of creating an environment where engaged teaching can be sustained" (p. 165).

Though hooks acknowledges the crucial role of teachers as agents of social change and empowering students in the classroom, she notes:

> Most progressive professors are more comfortable striving to challenge class biases through the material studied than they are with interrogating how class biases shape conduct in the classroom and transforming their pedagogical process. (1994c, p. 187)

The following discussion explores the significance of teachers' attitudes and practices in either reinforcing and/or counteracting discriminatory norms and practices in society. hooks believes that to educate as the practice of freedom

> comes easiest to those [of us] who teach who also believe that there is an aspect of our vocation that is sacred; who believe that our work is not merely to share information but to share in the intellectual and spiritual growth of our students. (p. 13)

She observes that stressing individual "growth" and self-actualization makes the pedagogy both physically and emotionally threatening and demanding. Looking back to her own experience, hooks recalls that many professors sought "security" in more impersonal pedagogical orientations because they lacked basic communication skills, they were not self-actualized, and they often used the classroom to reenact rituals of control that were about domination and unjust exercise of power. (p. 5)

Engaged pedagogy is "transgressive" in advocating greater interaction of teachers with their students as opposed to "standing behind desks or standing at the front, immobilized" (p. 137). On this score, hooks calls teachers to be role models of radical openness and transgression of limiting boundaries, stating that any

> classroom that employs a holistic model of learning will also be a place where teachers grow, and are empowered by the process. That empowerment cannot happen if we refuse to be vulnerable while encouraging students to take risks. (p. 21)

The previous discussion has highlighted the complexity of change involved in acknowledging professors' ambivalence in allowing nondirected thought in the classroom and its interference with the grading process, and in some professors' desire to exercise power and authority within their mini-kingdom, the classroom. This author argues that engaged pedagogy requires a base that hooks (1994c) seems to take for granted or may not consider crucial enough. The pedagogy calls for authentic and self-actualized teachers to broaden the knowledge base in teacher training curriculum (assuming that attitudes/values can be taught!), and making changes in selection and recruitment procedures for teachers. On the other hand, ought one to presume that the recruiters of teachers are any more self-actualized than the teachers? This reasoning partly illustrates the idealism in engaged pedagogy. Finally, it ought to come as no surprise that professors who "are wounded, damaged individuals, people who are not self-actualized . . . will seek asylum in the academy rather than [seek] to make the academy a place of challenge, dialectical interchange, and growth" (hooks, 1994c, p. 165). The following chapter critiques hooks' reliance on schools to direct social transformation.

CHAPTER 8

Limits of Engaged Pedagogy

bell hooks (1994c), similar to Paulo Freire (1970/1992, 1973), maintains that schools are about creating a better society; other scholars espouse contrary views. Similarly, Ira Shor and Freire (1987) contend that in critiquing the myth of social reality as a given, education helps address the issue of prevailing power in schools and society, and shapes students' thinking to influence choices and actions. Nel Noddings too argues that though schools often reflect social values and practices, "schools can help the society to develop individuals who have a clearer, more responsible sense of what it means to live in a democratic community" (1995b, p. 39). However, this is only one side of the story. While hooks (1994c) looks to schools to address social ills, a body of scholarship (Beyer, 1995; Harris, 1995; Noddings, 1992, 1995b) illustrates the flaw in a reliance on education as a lever for social transformation. The following discussion advances arguments against a reliance on schools as levers for social transformation. Landon Beyer maintains that despite the role played by dedicated, hard-working teachers in

> reversing the tendencies toward intellectual apathy and linear thinking . . . the dominant structures and processes of schooling . . . has often served to promote perspectives and values that reproduce these larger cultural and social phenomenon. (Beyer, 1995, p. 259)

Incidentally, even when school boards and parents "allow" for "deviations" in the standard curriculum and teaching methods, the underlying expectations are that these have no adverse effect on students' achievement scores. Commonly, academic achievement is held as the *real* measure of academic success. This raises two issues. First, national concern over decline in America's academic standards and loss of its economic and technological edge necessitates more rigorous academic standards as opposed to stretching scarce resources to develop programs that cater to individual students' needs (Bloom, 1987; D'Souza, 1992; Hirsch, 1987). It is further argued that legitimating cultural and linguistic pluralism undermines a nation's efforts at building national unity (Nieto, 1996).

In *The Imperfect Panacea: American Faith in Education 1865–1990*, Henry Perkinson (1991) illustrates the manner in which the nation previously relied on its education system to address its social, economic, and political issues. The study highlights the fact that education as a socializing agent can only help alleviate, not correct social ills, hence the title—the imperfect panacea. The following discussion first addresses the potential role of education as a tool for social transformation.

Louis Menand illustrates a crucial element regarding a reliance on schools as levers for social transformation. He points out:

> The university has become, at last, too many things to too many people . . . [and yet] unlike the society it simulates, the university is unequipped both administratively and philosophically, to deal with conflicts that cannot be treated simply as conflict of ideas. It has the machinery to arbitrate the sort of disagreements that arise naturally in the pursuit of the university's traditional educational goals; but it is not designed to arbitrate among antagonistic interest groups, or discover ways of correcting inequities that persist in the society as a whole. (1994, p. 97)

It is Menand's contention that as miniature reproductions of society, learning institutions cannot "arbitrate disputes about democracy and social justice, or govern the manner in which people relate socially to one another, or police attitudes" (p. 96). The process of accommodating cultural and linguistic pluralism in school policies and practices may help sensitize students to racial and cultural differences but not eliminate racial and cultural intolerance in schools and society. Similarly, Joel Spring (1978) views the reliance on schools as tools for social transformation as much too indirect an approach to address social ills and, thus, bound to result in failure. Schools are ill equipped to transform social structures of which they are a part. Harris argues:

> No State would consciously and deliberately foster a universal compulsory institution that openly challenged its dominant value, belief, and knowledge systems; or set up and/or sanction an institution likely to produce the kind of future citizens who might overthrow the very State that formed or socialized them. (1995, p. 219)

The above discussion critiques the fallacy behind hooks' (1994c) idealism in expecting to address structural injustices through schools. First, schools are compromised by virtue of their participation in the social structure. The relationship between schools and the wider society makes it difficult for schools to act as agents of social change. In training students for citizenship and future productivity, schools typically reproduce the hierarchical relations of race, gender, and class stratifications in prevailing social structures. Second, knowledge does not necessarily translate into virtue. The Letter to the Romans in the Christian Scriptures best captures this ambivalence between espoused and lived theory: "the desire to do right is there but not the power. What happens is that I do, not the good I will to do but the evil I do not intend" (Romans 7:15.) Further, focusing on schools presumes that racism and discriminatory practices result from individual training rather than discriminatory social structures. Overall, this author supports hooks' contention that schools can provide an avenue for raising awareness to contentious issues in the wider society. It is indeed, a roundabout way of dealing with the issue. But yet, hopefully, critically aware individuals provide a foundation for more sensitive programs, in the sense that these individuals could make policies that are more sensitive to the needs of marginalized students and members of society.

The next chapter provides a short summary of the author's reaction to bell hooks' engaged pedagogy. Indeed, hooks (1981) recognizes the difficulty of changing existing educational structures. The choice to go against the grain, to challenge the status quo often has negative consequences. The discussion addresses the difficulty of changing attitudes and values, the compromised role of schools by virtue of participation in society, and the issues of academic standards. Though hooks' educational critique focuses primarily on higher institutions of learning, the critique is probably more germane to lower institutions of learning whereby schooling is compulsory.

CHAPTER 9

Reflections on hooks' Educational Theory

Difficulty of Changing Attitudes and Values

Though engaged pedagogy addresses what needs to change, why there needs to be a change, and how to effect change, one is still left with a nagging feeling that the process is much more complex than what hooks stipulates. Engaged pedagogy calls for a shift in educational practices that individuals may first and foremost not be ready for and/or necessarily committed to implementing. The theory presumes a willingness in individuals to critique their standpoints with the aim of transforming their consciousness and/or social institutions. This is probably neither true nor practical.

There seems to be in most of us an inherent resistance to change. Notwithstanding the issues of self-actualized professors, bell hooks maintains that individuals who fail to appreciate the underlying contentions in paradigmatic shifts in educational theory and pedagogy often seem to exhibit a gap between espoused and lived principles. The seemingly excessive demands of engaged pedagogy often lead to accommodation and compromise at different levels (hooks, 1994c). It is not uncommon to find teachers who are willing to use different teaching material but who still retain the "politics of domination" in their classrooms or vice versa. As hooks observes, many claim to be committed "to freedom and justice for all even though the way they live, the values and habits of being they institutionalize daily, in public and private rituals, help maintain the culture of domination" (1994c, p. 27). Take the subordination of women and female-related activities. Designing educational programs that avoid trait genderization involves changing existing value hierarchies that attribute inferior work to the traits, tasks, and roles associated with females. What adds to the complexity of making an acknowledgment and/or accommodation of cultural pluralism is that it touches on cultural stereotypes and "acceptable" views. It is hard for people to change behaviors. It is even harder to change attitudes (Fullan, 1976).

Compromising Role of Schools

In her idealism, hooks (1990, 1994b, 1994c) looks to schools to ameliorate the marginality of students and members of the wider society. Employing the Platonian equation of knowledge to virtue, she sees a ready link between acquisition of knowledge and radical choices and/or actions in learners. She maintains that the

> bottom-line assumption has to be that everyone in the classroom is able to act responsibly. That has to be the starting point—that we are able to act responsibly together to create a learning environment. All too often we have been trained as professors to assume that students are not capable of acting responsibly, that if we don't exert control over them, there's just going to be mayhem. (1994c, p. 152)

The presumption of a willingness on people's part to take responsibility raises two issues. On the one hand, not everyone can or does act responsibly. On the other hand, developing critical consciousness in students may not necessarily translate to creating social activists. In schools, students are invited to reflect on the social reality but not mandated to take up arms to correct social ills. Since the roots of inequality, authoritative rule, discipline, alienation, etc., lie beyond the classroom, changing social reality goes beyond classroom discussions and changes in level of consciousness. Schools constitute but one of many social structures and cannot singly transform society.

Humanism over Standards

The lack of a qualitative measure of progress makes multicultural education programs appear to lack concreteness. Most would argue that achievement scores provide a concrete basis of assessing students' goals, progress, and academic achievement, while constructs such as racial harmony and student empowerment have varied interpretations and lack effective measurement scales. The truth of the matter is that there is yet to be a study that provides a causal link between family circumstance, race, gender, or language ability and education achievement. Indeed, constructs such as race, language, and gender are difficult to quantify and/or study. There continue to be charges and counter charges of what does or does not constitute racist or discriminatory practices. There needs to be some measure for assessing students' learning progress. Despite charges of racial and cultural biases on various items, standardized tests are the most concrete measure for "sorting" and "selecting" students.

In sum, engaged pedagogy promises if and when instituted to clearly benefit marginalized groups. hooks (1981, 1984, 1989a, 1990, 1992, 1994b, 1994c, 1995b) creates both a voice and an audience for marginalized groups as she speaks out to and against socially oppressive structures, critiquing the basis of hierarchical teaching practices, the notion of abstract and static knowledge, and the impact of mainstream values and practices on marginalized peoples and cultures. Further, as a teacher of English she calls special attention to the use of language to name and critique prevailing unjust structures. The fact that human beings have the capacity to change is a crucial reminder in a time when most people increasingly feel manipulated by socio-political and economic forces. Herein lies our hope for change. As human beings we owe ourselves at least this much: an acknowledgment of our subjectivity and a critical reflection on our material conditions for the purpose of making necessary transformations. Clearly, to "transgress," to move out of one's place "requires pushing against oppressive boundaries set by race, sex, and class domination" (hooks, 1990, p. 145). Education as the practice of freedom provides the avenue to accomplish this goal.

hooks' whole premise of engaged pedagogy is that, though rarely acknowledged, students "want an education that is healing to the uninformed, unknowing spirit . . . knowledge that is meaningful . . . addressing what they are learning and their overall experiences" (1994c, p. 19). Engaged pedagogy provides the necessary forum to address this very need:

> [T]he academy is not paradise. But learning is a place where paradise can be created. The classroom, with all its limitations, remains a location of possibility. In that field of possibility we have the opportunity to labor for freedom, to demand of ourselves and our comrades, an openness of mind and heart that allows us to face reality, even as we collectively imagine a way to move beyond boundaries, to transgress. This is education as the practice of freedom. (p. 207)

The following part explores the relevance of engaged pedagogy in addressing similar issues of race, sex, and class biases in a Third World context.

PART III

Relevance of bell hooks' Educational Theory to a Third-World Context

Part I analyzed bell hooks' social theory, presenting arguments to support her assessment of the United States' educational system and society, which she contended promoted racism, sexism, and classism in both policy and practice. The part demonstrated the validity of bell hooks' views regarding race, gender, and class discriminatory elements in educational settings and the wider society. Part II analyzed hooks' educational theory based on her book, *Teaching to Transgress: Education as the Practice of Freedom.* The part illustrated that hooks' educational theory, engaged pedagogy, arose from her past experience as a student and present as an educator in a society that sanctions White supremacy, patriarchy, and capitalistic value systems. bell hooks' engaged pedagogy provides strategies for interrogating these biases in educational policies and practices by linking theory to practice, empowering students, honoring cultural experiences of students marginalized in educational settings, and incorporating passion in classrooms. Part III explores the relevance of bell hooks' critique of American society and proposed components of engaged pedagogy to a Third World context, in particular, the author's country of origin, Kenya.

Part III is divided into two major areas of discussion: the relevance of bell hooks' critique of American society to the Kenyan situation, and the relevance of particular components of bell hooks' engaged pedagogy to educational policies and practices in Kenya. Being a theoretical inquiry this part presents supporting arguments drawn from literature on Kenya with regard to race, gender, and class biases in educational settings and the wider society. In addition, the author incorporates personal insights from past experiences in Kenya.

The discussion on the relevance of bell hooks' critique of the American society and its educational system to the Kenyan economy involves a cursory exploration of the impact of colonization in promoting White supremacist values and attitudes, the effect of cultural patriarchal attitudes and practices on women, and the manifestation of a capitalistic mentality in Kenyan people's consciousness. To begin, this author establishes the relevance of hooks' critique of cultural domination in view of Kenya's post-colonial status and current pluralism in educational curriculum and pedagogy. Next, because of Kenya's patriarchal cultural underpinnings, the author analyzes the manner in which certain practices privilege male concerns and interests over female interests and concerns. Then, the author explores the manifestation of a materialistic value system and its increasing role in individual and communal self-definition and social status.

The second area of discussion analyzes the impact of cultural views regarding gender and class, and the focus on testing and grading on schooling. In the Kenyan context, tribal classification often supersedes and/or heightens the impact of racial, gender, and class biases. Membership to the "ruling tribe" ameliorates one's experience of race, gender, and/or class discrimination. Later discussions elaborate on the significance of tribalism in Kenya. In part I, this author illustrated hooks' (1984, 1989a, 1990) contention with regard to the manner in which class determines the degree of one's race and/or gender biases. In Kenya, not only does one's educational status determine one's social status but so does membership in a ruling tribe. Similarly, in a patriarchal society such as Kenya, being male, irrespective of tribal membership, allows one certain privileges, however relative.

Statistics and the Politics of African Leadership

The World Almanac and Book of Facts (Famighetti, 1996) provides the following statistics on Kenya. The country won its independence from Britain in 1963. Situated in the eastern part of the African continent, Kenya has a population of approximately thirty million people. Its neighboring countries are: Uganda to its west, Tanzania to its south, Somali to its east, and Sudan to its north. The country is composed of five major ethnic groups: Kikuyu, 21 percent of the population; Luhya, 14 percent; Luo, 13 percent; Kalenjin, 12 percent; Kamba, 11 percent; and others, including Asians, Arabs, and Europeans. The principal languages include Swahili and English (both official languages), Kikuyu, Luhya, Luo, and Meru. Kenya is a democratic state under the leadership of the twice-elected Daniel Arap Moi. According to the 1993 Census, the literacy rate was estimated at 69 percent.

In *Out of America: A Black Man Confronts Africa*, Keith Richburg, an African American journalist, notes:

> According to the World Bank, Africa is home to the world's poorest nations. . . . Africa's children are the most likely on earth to die before the age of five. Its adults are least likely to live beyond the age of fifty. Africans are, on the average, more malnourished, less educated, and more likely to be infected by fatal diseases than the inhabitants of any other place on earth. (1997, p. 171)

Depressingly, in addition, one is confronted with corrupt practices by the ruling class:

> It has been estimated that Mobutu [Zaire's president] stashed as much as $10 billion in overseas bank accounts, mostly money pilfered from Zaire's copper revenues and from raking off the proceeds of state-run corporations. (p. 173)

The author contends that similar to human rights abuses and other forms of social injustices, little is made public and few people are held accountable for the misappropriation of resources and other abuses of power (Miller, 1984; Richburg, 1997). In this context, soliciting funds from developed countries amounts to little more than a political game. Richburg notes that Daniel Arap Moi, Kenya's current president, continues to cling to power, "still deftly playing the old donors with promises of reform, even while cracking down on his erstwhile critics" (p. 244). "Democracy" has become the West's leverage but also the politician's trump card for soliciting money from the West. Other African leaders also play this game. As Richburg notes, Ibrahim Babangida of Nigeria and Valentine Strasser of Sierra Leone have utilized the same ploy as does Kenyan president Moi, promising political (democratic) reforms in exchange for financial support from the West. In view of the above discussion, hooks and Cornel West's remark concerning the crisis in Black leadership echoes the predicament of leadership in most African countries:

> We have a leadership that is preoccupied with either being elected to office or sustaining the social base of their organizations. . . . There is no one who is willing to be prophetic in a bold and defiant manner with a deep, all-inclusive moral vision and a sophisticated analysis of the distribution of wealth and power and resources in our society. (1991, p. 48)

The following discussion explores the relevance of bell hooks' critique of the United States to Kenya, a Third World country. As is the pattern in Part I on bell hooks' social theory, the discussion explores social myths that legitimize the status quo, the basis and impact of White supremacy, gender, and class/tribal biases in the Kenyan society.

CHAPTER 10

Relevance of hooks' Social Critique

Besides her personal experiences, bell hooks (1994c) attributes the basis of her social theory and critique of American educational policies and practices on insights drawn from Paulo Freire's (1970/1992, 1973) analysis and critique of literacy programs in Brazil. Freire proposed a pedagogy for the oppressed to counteract pedagogies that mirrored and perpetuated the status quo. This author reverses the process yet again in seeking the relevance of hooks' First World critique to a Third World context, Kenya.

Various issues raised by Freire (1970/1992, 1973) with regard to the Brazilian economy resonate with economic and political conditions in most Third World economies: (a) a dependency on raw material export, the demand and pricing of which is determined by external markets; (b) the significantly high illiteracy rates; (c) the defense of a *sui generis* democracy by the elite whereby "health is synonymous with popular silence and inaction . . . [the ruling class purport to] protect the people from what they call 'foreign ideologies' . . . [and] label as 'subversive' all those who enter into the dynamics of the transition and become its representatives" (Freire, 1973, p. 14). Freire viewed society as essentially divided into two primary groupings: the oppressors with access to economic and political power and the "ordinary person . . . crushed, diminished, converted into a spectator, maneuvered by myths which powerful social forces created" (p. 6). Freire's assessment of social inequalities mirrors the Kenyan gap between the "haves" and "have nots" (Miller, 1984). In his books *Decolonizing the Mind: The Politics of Language in African*

Literature (1986) and *Moving the Centre: The Struggle for Cultural Freedoms* (1993), Ngugi Wa Thiong'o raises similar contentions with regard to the West's economic domination, the impact of illiteracy in Third World countries, cultural silencing, and overall disparities in access to resources worldwide.

In analyzing political and economic privilege, this author distinguishes between the White settler group who constituted the dominant elites during the colonial era and the Kenyan dominant elite. Margery Perham (Huxley, 1956), Norman Miller (1984) and Ngugi Wa Thiong'o (1986, 1993) note the bias in economic and political privilege in favor of the White settler group during the colonial era. Miller points out that the "colonial" bias in the allocation of resources prevailed through and after independence:

> Although the end of colonialism was enormously important politically, the economic die that had been cast earlier suggested that Kenya would continue on a capitalistic pathway. So easy was the transition to African capitalism that critics were soon to suggest a black elite had simply replaced the white elite. (1984, pp. 29–30)

The process of exploitation and domination did not end when the country received its independence. In the post-colonial era, the African political leaders, labeled the "Big men," replaced privileged White settlers. Supporting Perham and Miller's assessment, Keith Richburg aptly surmises the politics of African leadership in noting that the practice of economic domination is neither new to Kenya nor does it show any signs of abating:

> The Big men [dominant elites] will still be there, arrogant, extravagant, enjoying the benefits of foreign-aid dollars. They'll still have their marble palaces carved out of the jungle and their bank accounts in Switzerland, their villas in the south of France, and their apartments on the Avenue Foch in Paris. They'll have their fleets of Mercedes limousines and their private jets. They'll build basilicas with their own likeness in the murals with the apostles, and they'll open universities that bear their name but where students can't afford books and will have no jobs if they ever get out. They'll equip their armies with shiny boots and their security forces with the latest weapons, but the hospitals will run short of needles and bandages. (1997, pp. 165–166)

In view of such blatant political and economic exploitation of the masses, many wonder why the Africans do not take to the streets. Two reasons account for the political inactivity of the Kenyan peoples. First, unlike the United States, in Kenya, few people cite the "Constitutional" rights. There are those who neither know nor understand their rights as citizens of the country. High illiteracy rates most probably account for ignorance of political rights. A few know their rights but realize the futility of confronting the system. Those with political contacts know whom to call on when need arises. Second, Mulusa contends: "The poorest of the poor, who should be clamoring for change, have helplessly accepted the status quo as inevitable, or hoped that their chance to escape from poverty is yet to come, but that it is surely on its way" (1992, p. 168). The following discussion explores some social myths that maintain the privilege of the minority—Whites, particular tribes and/or elites—in Kenya.

Social Myths

hooks (1981, 1984, 1989a, 1990, 1994b, 1995b), like Freire (1970/1992, 1973) and Kevin Harris (1995), raises the issue of social myths and the manner in which these myths legitimize an existing order, however oppressive. Their discussions raise two primary issues: (a) the impact of the prevailing culture of domination, manifested in lies and denials of existing injustices; and (b) the impact of stereotypes on social consciousness. As this author illustrated in Part II, hooks links individual and social lies and denial to a culture of domination. hooks contends that the

> contemporary crisis is created by a lack of meaningful access to truth. That is to say, individuals are not just presented untruths, but are told them in a manner that enables most effective communication. When this collective cultural consumption of and attachment to misinformation is coupled with layers of lying individuals do in their personal lives, our capacity to face reality is severely diminished as is our will to intervene and change unjust circumstances. (1994c, p. 29)

Richburg's assessment of "double standards" in African politics (probably not unlike most other countries) resonates with hooks' analysis of a culture of lies and denial:

> Instead of straight talk about Africa, you're more likely to get doublespeak, apologies, excuses—above all hypocrisy. . . . There is a tendency not to want to criticize too openly, too harshly. . . . The reason, of course is that Africans are black. . . . Too much criticism from white countries in the West comes dangerously close to sounding racist. And African

leaders seem willing enough to play that card, constantly raising the specter of "neocolonialism." (1997, pp. 177–178)

He also raises a similar issues in analyzing the degree of corruption in African countries. His experience in Kenya demonstrated to him:

> In many places, it's a national pastime, forced upon people by layers and layers of bureaucracy and archaic, oppressive rules. Even generally honest people learn that you have to find ways to beat the system, or the system grinds you down. (p. 6).

hooks' demonstration of the myth of the inferiority of Black people and women in the United States is readily applicable to a Kenyan context. She maintains:

> Despite so much evidence in daily life that suggests otherwise, masses of white Americans continue to believe that black people are genetically inferior—that it is natural for them to be dominated. And even though women have proved to be equals of men in every way, masses still believe that there can be no sustained social and family order if males do not dominate females whether by means of benevolent or brutal patriarchies. (1994c, p. 200)

What hooks fails to raise in this particular observation is that despite so much evidence, due to internalized racism, a majority of Blacks and women participate in their own subjugation through a sense of inferiority to White people and/or males. She does however note the animosity and wrangling for positions and attention of White folk (hooks, 1990; hooks & West, 1991). First, in Kenya, the myth of White supremacy is reinforced by the West's economic and technological advances and political stability in comparison to African countries. Second, the general association of criticism with ingratitude and/or betrayal of allegiance reinforces cultural "silencing." Other social myths include: (a) the acceptability of nepotism in the public spheres, (b) the belief that the White man's coming destroyed the idyllic communal state, and (c) the idea of elders as the source of wisdom. As a Kenyan citizen and product of the educational system, this author is aware that economic and political circumstances in Kenya breed an allegiance to mainstream norms and practices despite evidence of corruption and abuses of authority as well as human rights abuses. Most Africans are shocked by the atrocities committed by those in power, though this rarely translates into revolutionary action. At least not yet. The seeming inability of Africans to "react" to social injustices caused Richburg great consternation, as he

> traversed the continent, seeing not just famines and massacres but also the everyday human suffering, the abuses of rights, the trampling on individual liberties, the police harassment, the beatings in detention, the closing down and firebombing of newspapers, the arrests of opposition politicians, and the outright murder of those with the courage to speak up against injustice. (Richburg, 1997, p. 164)

The "cultural silence" of the masses extends to educational settings whereby pedagogy is examination oriented, highly authoritative and hierarchical, transmitted in English, a foreign language, and reinforced by a culture that mandates respect and deference to authority (Miller, 1984). Analyzing the inability of the Luos to engage in anti-government uprisings in response to a government-linked assassination of Tom Mboya, a Luo presidential potential, Norman Miller notes:

> One of the reasons for the reaction may have been the age-old Luo respect for authority, a tradition that would have called for [the president] Kenyatta, the Elder, to be treated with respect and to be considered quite justified in administering discipline to unruly youth. (1984, p. 40)

However, the destruction of school property and attacks on "noncooperative" teachers and fellow students during strikes in schools and anti-government riots illustrate the fallacy of a passive acceptance of the status quo. In addition, tribal factions and political instability in Kenya, similar to the situation in most Third World African countries, illustrate contentions over representation and equity in the economic and political spheres. hooks contends that in politically repressive environments "talking back" is a "courageous act . . . it represents a threat. To those who wield oppressive power, that which is threatened must necessarily be wiped out, annihilated, silenced" (1989a, p. 8). hooks' contention regarding the penalty of speaking out echoes Albert Memmi's assessment:

> The colonizer guards against [revolutions] in many ways: by continuous incapacitation of the leaders and periodic destruction of those who, despite everything, manage to come forward; by corruption or police oppression, aborting all popular movements and causing their brutal and rapid destruction. (1965, p. 127)

The Kenyan situation provides ready evidence of hooks' contention both during and after the colonial era.

Ngugi Wa Thiong'o (1986, 1993), Miller (1984) and Perham (Huxley, 1956) note the manner in which the colonial government established repressive mechanisms to discourage dissent among the Africans. Perham points to the police investigations, arrests and trials, and prison sentences of prominent Kikuyu and Kamba leaders. Writing nearly thirty years after Perham, Richburg demonstrates:

> In Africa, the good guys don't win; they usually get tossed in prison, tortured, killed, beaten up, or sometimes just get beaten down. They get beaten so hard they finally give up. And the rest? They just stop trying because they're too busy simply trying to survive. (1997, p. 165)

Elspeth Huxley (1956) argues for patience, lenience, and tolerance toward people who have been subordinated for centuries. There is always the reminder that originally dominated cultural groupings (Blacks in America and/or Africans in the continent) have not fared any better with Black leadership than they did under White people. True, granting the groups the right to vote and/or access, however limited, to political and economic privileges has not necessarily led to greater justice or equality in the world (let alone in many majority Black countries). Huxley's reminder aptly captures the dilemma that faces all of humanity:

> If Africans (or Blacks) are . . . in fundamentals men like ourselves, then like ourselves they are fallible, weak and subject to the power of evil, like ourselves they will, on occasion, seek their own advantage, oppress their fellows, lust after power and riches, lie, cheat, steal, and be stupid; and unlike ourselves, they haven't had a thousand hard and bitter years of trial and error in the arts of government and economy. (1956, p. 224)

However, Richburg raises the issue of success in Asian, in contrast to African, countries. Unlike African countries, Asian countries have somehow managed to pull themselves up by the boot straps of political and economic domination: Malaysia and Singapore, originally occupied by the Japanese during World War II; Vietnam, a former French colony; and Indonesia, formerly occupied by the Dutch. He maintains: "Like Africa, most Asian countries only achieved true independence in the postwar years; unlike the Africans, the Asians knew what to do with it" (1997, p. 172). Indeed, to explain the predicament of the African continent tempts one to fall back on old stereotypes. Richburg voices reservation at laying the blame of Black people's lack of noticeable achievement in different fields after attaining political independence from the "White man." Nicholas Kristof attributes the paradox of Africa's economic underdevelopment and Asia's growth to differences in savings rates, high tariffs on raw materials, differences in levels of foreign investment, access to health and education. He further attributes the poor investment and savings in African countries to political instability and corruption:

> One major reason not to save and invest in Africa has been inflation and instability: when people save money it ends up being confiscated. Victoria Baenongandi, for example, lasted two weeks as an entrepreneur in eastern Congo. She bought a pile of merchandise to resell, but everything was seized by soldiers. So she returned home and gave up on business— and put her savings into beer. (Kristof, 1997, p. 4)

As this author contends, the issue of Black people's continued oppression and abuse of rights between and among themselves raises more questions than promising answers. The good versus bad guys mentality informed by Western metaphysical dualism fails adequately to address the issue of prevailing dominations and injustices in societies. In this context, not all Black men are good, but then too, not all White people are bad either.

The previous discussion briefly presented a rationale for the "cultural silence" in Kenya. This author is in agreement with hooks regarding the association of cultural dominations with lies and denials. Myths of the superiority of the White race, the idyllic traditional communities, the inappropriateness of truth telling, leads to a resignation among the masses to their material conditions, to their marginality. hooks' injunction to truth telling, "talking back," comes at an opportune time. Claiming one's subjectivity requires that one analyze and critique unjust policies and practices however risky the process. In a politically repressive environment the process often involves putting one's life prospects, if not life, on the line.

bell hooks' social theory, as gleaned from writings, demonstrates the often insidious manner in which racist, sexist, and/or classist ideologies are embedded in educational and social policies and practices. The following chapter, patterned after Part I, on bell hooks' social theory, advances arguments to support this author's view of similar ideologies—racist, sexist, and/or classist ideologies in the Kenyan system. The discussion is divided into three topics: the roots of racial biases and the perpetuation of White supremacist attitudes and values in schools and society, the impact of sexist attitudes and values on Kenyan women, and the manner in which capitalism has undermined the traditional community (or rather tribal solidarity) that prevailed before the colonial experience. Overall, the discussions on Kenya explore the historical trend in socio-political and economic forms. This author demonstrates similarities between policies and practices in the pre- and post-colonial eras.

CHAPTER 11

Racism, Sexism, and Classism

Racism

White Supremacy

In Part I, this author demonstrated the basis of White supremacy. White supremacy involves the sanctioning, to the point of idealization, of White people's values and traditions as universal norms. What this translates to are mainstream standards derived from the culturally dominant group's ways of being, feeling, and knowing. Albert Memmi's assessment of the dependence of the colonized on the colonizer provides the rationale for bell hooks' contention regarding the reinforcement of White supremacy:

> All effectiveness and social dynamics . . . seem monopolized by the colonizer's institutions. If the colonized needs help, it is to them that he applies. If he does something wrong, it is by them that he is punished. . . . It is the colonizer's holiday . . . [that] is celebrated brilliantly—Christmas and Joan of Arc, Carnival and Bastille Day. It is the colonizer's armies which parade, the very ones which crushed the colonized and keep him in his place. (Memmi, 1965, p. 103)

The discussion on White supremacy in Part I demonstrated that the negation of Black traits and characteristics is reinforced both by White and

Black members. hooks' corpus of writing raised two issues in interrogating White supremacy. On the one hand, she illustrates the impact of White people's attitudes and values in negating Black people's cultural traits and characteristics through the mass media, and establishment of discriminatory policies and practices. On the other hand, bombarded by culturally negating structures, marginalized groups easily adapt to the prevailing value system, thus valuing dominant cultural traits and characteristics. hooks demonstrates the prize of Black people's attempt to assimilate:

> It was not enough for black people to enter institutions of higher education and acquire the necessary skills to effectively compete for jobs previously occupied safely by whites; the demand was that blacks become "honorary whites," that black people assimilate to succeed. (1995b, p. 189)

The discussion on White supremacy, racial politics, and internalized racism draws primarily from Elspeth Huxley's (1956) *Race and Politics in Kenya: A Correspondence between Elspeth Huxley and Margery Perham*, Memmi's (1965) *The Colonizer and the Colonized*, Norman Miller's (1984) *Kenya: The Quest for Prosperity*, Thomas Mulusa's (1992) "Pluralistic Education in Sub-Sahara Africa: An Overview," Kilemi Mwiria's (1991) "Education for Subordination: African Education in Colonial Kenya," Carolyn Shaw's (1995) *Colonial Inscriptions: Race, Sex, and Class in Kenya*, James Sheffield's (1973) *Education in Kenya: An Historical Study*, Ernest Stabler's (1969) *Education Since Uhuru: The Schools of Kenya*, and Keith Richburg's (1997) *Out of America: A Black Man Confronts Africa*.

The literature of Kenya's pre- and post-colonial circumstances demonstrates the Western impact on both the political and educational systems. Ngugi Wa Thiong'o maintains that the

> real aim of colonialism was to control the people's wealth . . . in other words, the entire realm of the language of real life . . . this involved two aspects of the same process: the destruction or the deliberate undervaluing of a people's culture, their art, dances, religions, history, geography, education, orature and literature, and the conscious elevation of the language of the colonizer. (1986, p. 16)

Subordinating the cultural histories, traits and characteristics of non-White peoples denigrates these elements in the consciousness of both White and Black peoples. Albert Memmi aptly captures the gradual process of marginalizing a cultural heritage:

> Finally, the few material traces of the past are slowly erased, and the future remnants will no longer carry the stamp of the colonized group. The few statues which decorate the city represent . . . the great deeds of colonization. The buildings are patterned after the colonizer's own favorite designs; the same is true of the street names, which recall the faraway provinces from which he came. (1965, p. 104)

Carolyn Shaw demonstrates the implications of Memmi's contention in noting:

> Not only were the Europeans able to imbue their very bodies with authority and potency like brass serpents, but goods associated with them also were festishized. . . . Bottled beer, brewed in British style, easily transportable, always available, for some became a sign of the arbitrary power of the colonialists. (1995, p. 12)

hooks (1994c) and Kathleen Donovan (1994) note the politics of representation in illustrating that "accepting the decentering of the West globally, embracing multiculturalism, compels educators to focus attention on the issue of voice. Who speaks? Who listens? And why?" (hooks, 1994c, p. 40). Literature on pre- and post-colonial events in Kenya support hooks' contention regarding the reinforcement of White supremacist attitudes and values and/or negation of Blackness. George Urch (1968) notes that the early Europeans in Africa held to the superiority of Western culture and viewed their task as a "civilizing mission" on the continent—a successfully accomplished task since the Western-educated African often rejected his primary culture to emulate the European culture for its promise of material and political privilege. Thomas Mulusa contends:

> colonial education was a process of dilution of African traditions and aspirations, and an imposition of European norms and values. Furthermore, colonial education was characterized by discriminatory practices and prejudices based on ethnic, religious and gender differences; disparities in the distribution of educational supply between different regions and communities; and the evolution or enhancement of inequalities between individuals and communities. (1992, p. 159)

Racial representation at the policy-making level shapes and determines official policy and practice (hooks, 1994b). Individual biases easily translate to policies, and subsequently practices, that favor the race and/or cultural groups' values most reflected in social and/or educational norms and practices. Memmi raises a similar issue regarding the Tunisian experience with French colonizers:

> The laws establishing his exorbitant rights and obligations of the colonized are conceived by [the colonizer]. As for orders which barely veil discrimination, or apportionment after competitive examinations and in hiring, he is necessarily in on the secret of their application, for he is in charge of them. (1965, p. 8)

The pre- and post-colonial circumstances in Kenya further demonstrate the validity of this assessment. The correspondence between Huxley and Margery Perham highlights the fact that though racial population was 17,000 White settlers, 40,000 Indians, and 3,000,000 Africans in 1943, the Legislative Council was comprised of eleven elected European members with two representing native interests. The fact that Council discussion followed British guidelines, carried out in English, a language with which most Africans would still have been relatively unfamiliar, exacerbated the marginality of Africans:

> Three million of mostly backward tribal Africans, divided in language and custom (a) cannot understand the issues affecting them [at the Legislative Council], and (b) cannot effectively interpret what they do feel through three or four official or nominated unofficial Europeans. (Huxley, 1956, p. 152)

The matter of racial representation on governing Councils is significant. Supporting hooks' contention regarding the significance of representation, Mwiria (1991) demonstrates that Kenyan economic and political policy and practice were primarily designed by White colonialists to serve the interests of the minority White community. However, critiquing Mwiria's implications of a deliberate move on the White people's part to subjugate Africans, Clive Whitehead advances arguments for the inevitability of White supremacy on the colonies:

> At the turn of the century social Darwinism gave strong support to the widespread belief in European superiority . . . but at the time the technological superiority of Europeans gave them almost unlimited power over African and Asian people alike. It is hardly surprising, therefore, that

Europeans figured prominently in shaping the nature of colonial societies, but this does not necessarily mean that their sole aim was to promote
European interests. (1993, p. 87)

Plausible though Whitehead's rationale for racial inequalities might be, some
of the prevailing attitudes of White settlers illustrate that the exclusion of
Africans on policy-making boards was not coincidental but deliberate. Huxley,
a White settler, finds it outrageous that a "primitive chief with no knowledge
of English and with his hair dressed in mud and sheep's fat should take his
place on the benches of the Legislative Council" (1956, p. 151).

Ironically, this rationale for indispensability on the part of White people,
employed by Whitehead's (1993) and Perham's observation regarding the
minority rule, is not unlike the current president's contention for disallowing
multiparty elections in Kenya. As Richburg observes, it has long

been the argument of the old African strongmen that authoritarian rule
is needed to prevent just those types of tribal blowups. Multiparty
politics, according to this theory, inevitably leads to tribal violence,
because pluralism encourages people to seek protective refuge in their
tribal units. It's virtually inevitable that political parties will be organized
along ethnic, meaning tribal lines. (1997, pp. 105–106)

The evidence in both instances is that the "African" is incapable of self-governance. hooks raises the issue of the significance of representation at policy-making levels. Essentially, somebody, somewhere defines who is or is not qualified
for a particular task. The attitude of racial superiority is heightened by the fact
that White peoples colonized Africa, continue to be a major source of foreign
investment and related donations besides the general feeling that the African
owes gratitude to the West for having saved it from itself.

Besides the reinforcement of White supremacy through commemoration
and celebration of the colonizer's cultural heroes, sages/saints, and political
leaders, White people in Kenya hardly mixed socially with the Africans. Huxley
notes that White people "would not deny a black man's advancement and equal
treatment, but would rather not mix with him socially" (1956, p. 205). Mulusa
attributes the "separatism" to racism. He contends:

To justify political domination by alien minorities and school segregation
in pre-independence sub-Sahara Africa, colonialists invoked the theories
of Caucasian superiority over black races as propounded by various
nineteenth-century scientists in Germany and the United Kingdom and

United States. A black man could not be educated, he could only be trained to work with his hands and eyes. (1992, p. 161)

Some scholars (Memmi, 1965; Mulusa, 1992; Mwiria, 1991; Sheffield, 1973; Stabler, 1969) note two primary ways in which White supremacy was reinforced in Kenya: (a) through access to education, and (b) through a Western-oriented curriculum and pedagogy. Lord Francis Scott, an ex-leader of the White settler community, argued for "compulsory education for all European children on the grounds that [Kenya] was a country of mixed races 'where European children are eventually going to be in a position of authority over other races'" (Huxley, 1956, p. 159). Africans' access to education, however, offered little reprieve. Contending that access to education was limited for the Tunisian, Memmi notes the dilemma of colonized students:

And he who has the wonderful good luck to be accepted in a school will not be saved nationally. The memory which is assigned him is certainly not that of his people. The history which is taught is not his own. . . . Everything seems to have taken place out of his country. . . . The books talk to him about a world which in no way reminds him of his own. . . . His teachers do not follow the same pattern as his father; they are not his wonderful and redeeming successors like every teacher in the world. (1965, p. 105)

Similar to hooks, Memmi notes that in Tunisia, White people acquired the aura of superiority from having their cultural histories, traits and characteristics both idealized in people's social consciousness and through patronage of policy-making positions both in Western and African countries. White supremacy is about access to the power mechanism, political and economic resources with a country. Memmi maintains:

When approaching a colonialist society, one cannot help expecting to find an elite, or at least a selection of the best, most efficient or most reliable technicians. Almost everywhere, those persons occupy, by right or *de facto*, top posts; they know it and claim esteem and honor because of it. The society of the colonizer intends to be a managing society and works hard to give that appearance. (p. 49)

Over thirty years later, Richburg's experience in Kenya and other African countries demonstrates the validity of Memmi's contention. Richburg alludes to the privilege and bigotry in most of the Kenyan White settlers:

Of all the slights one suffers as a black American in Africa, however, none are quite so annoying as the put-downs by whites—the white Africans, or European residents of Africa. Whites in Africa constitute a tiny minority on a black continent, but many act as if colonialism never really ended, that they still really own the place. . . . Once I was waiting in line with an armload of groceries at a shopping center supermarket. Just as it was my turn in front of the cashier, an older white woman stepped directly in front and put her basket of groceries down on the counter in front of me. . . . [Richburg spoke up] She apparently heard my American twang and became flustered. . . . She said in her thick British accent, "I thought you were an African!" (1997, p. 158)

The previous discussion illustrated the basis for the institution of White supremacy on social consciousness. The West colonized most of the African continent. Besides the aura associated with a conquering race and/or nation by the conquered, White people's values and traditions were portrayed as the ideal. "Successful" Africans (the mentality shows little sign of abating) felt the need to emulate White people's values at the expense of their primary tribal values and connections. Relegated to secondary status, the African people's cultural histories and values were viewed as inferior and, therefore, subordinated by "progressive" Africans for purposes of assimilating White people's cultural mores. Further, the minority White rule established laws that suited their interests. Schooling was based on a Western framework; textbooks reflected White people's cultural heroes and histories. Mwiria (1991) contended that in schools the European experiences and superiority legitimated in the geography, history and civics curriculum further reinforced the marginality and/or insignificance of African related studies. The teaching styles reflected missionary models of the "all-knowing" teachers interacting with "ignorant natives." These have abated little after 30 years of independence.

Stereotypes. The following discussion illustrates that in the Kenyan context, colonization did and continues to shape national consciousness with regard to measures of individual worth and social progress. The discussion explores the manner in which White people's values and attitudes are ingrained in national consciousness and the educational system. The discussion explores the internalization of White people's values and attitudes in the Kenyan elites and/or privileged groups.

In *Black Looks: Race and Representation*, hooks analyzes the impact of racial and gender representation on social consciousness. She illustrates that degrading stereotypes and images of Black people presented by the mass media have had significant impact on Black people's self-understanding and the manner in which Black people are perceived and related to by non-Black others:

> Most folks in this society do not want to openly admit that "blackness" as a sign primarily evokes in the public imagination of whites (and all the other groups who learn that one of the quickest ways to demonstrate one's kingship within a white supremacist order is by sharing racist assumptions) hatred and fear. (1992, p. 10)

Similarly, pre-colonial stereotypes in Kenya with regard to the superiority of White people, the savagery of indigenous Black people, and the industriousness of Asians are perpetuated by Blacks who have internalized these negating messages. Memmi argues:

> Willfully created and spread by the colonizer, [this] mythical and degrading portrait ends up being accepted and lived with to a certain extent by the colonized. It thus acquires a certain amount of reality and contributes to the true portrait of the colonized. (1965, pp. 87–88)

The negation of Blackness is also evident in movies such as *Tarzan, The Gods Must Be Crazy, The African Queen, The Jewel in the Nile*, and *Out of Africa*. In most of these movies, Black people are used as a backdrop to main White characters. The movies reinforce the superiority of White people and White culture. Addressing the implications of movie projections on marginalized groups, hooks contends:

> Both African and Native Americans have been deeply affected by the degrading representations of red and black people that continue to be the dominant images projected by movies and television. Portrayed as cowardly, cannibalistic, uncivilized, the images of "Indians" mirror screen images of Africans. (1992, p. 186)

Mass media coverage of the Mau Mau, a Kikuyu-based revolutionary group that initiated the fight for independence, similarly evoked images of cannibalism, primitivity, and decadence (Moore, 1986). Perham criticizes the White settlers' view of Africans as "backward and incomprehensible servants . . . savages [to be] protected and educated" (Huxley, 1956, p. 26). Even Perham, who champions the Africans' cause in the correspondence with Huxley, argues that education ought to help Africans "out of their retarded state and [turn] from savages or serfs into citizens" (p. 220).

George Urch notes a similar negation of the African in his portrayal of the patronizing attitude of the early missionaries: "Not only did the African appear to lack moral principles and character traits deemed necessary to the development of Christianity, but his way of life was considered primitive by Western standards" (1968, p. 103). In effect, the colonizing mission of the West saved the Africans from themselves! Supporting Urch's contention, Shaw argues:

> The social knowledge of these early–twentieth-century colonizers inarticulately constructed a colonized Africa from contradictory images of the African as noble savage and cheap labor, as self-sufficient tribes and incompetent subjects, and as democratic communities composed of immoral and childlike natives. (1995, p. 145)

In a patriarchal society these negating images used to describe Africans/Blacks are also applied wholesale to women. The negation of "Africanness" lies in sharp contrast to the image of White Europeans as "heirs to an inheritance of ingenuity, ambition, restless energy and technical skill [which is] desperately . . . needed in the raw, undeveloped, poverty-ridden territories of Africa" (Huxley, 1956, p. 233). Little has changed in the stereotypes of Blacks and Whites, in both America and Africa, from what Memmi (1965) and more recently, hooks' body of works as demonstrated in the discussion of bell hooks' social theory.

Part I presented hooks' (1989a, 1990, 1992, 1994b, 1995b) evidence of White supremacist attitudes and values, and the reinforcement of these attitudes and values by marginalized persons who internalize dominant cultural values. As a result of the cultural domination of White people's values and attitudes in society, Black and other non-White people internalize a White supremacist's devaluation of Blackness in its association of Blackness with inferiority, victimhood, and inadequacy, valuing, instead, that which is "White" and of White people as later discussions on internalized racism demonstrate. In this context, hooks critiques the movie *Paris Is Burning* in its portrayal of the

> way in which colonized black people . . . worship at the throne of whiteness, even when such worship demands that we live in perpetual self-hate, steal, lie, go hungry, and even die in pursuit. . . . [Which applies to all] black people and people of color, who are daily bombarded by a powerful colonizing whiteness that seduces us away from ourselves, that negates that there is beauty of blackness that is not imitation whiteness. (1992, p. 149)

Reflecting upon her experiences, hooks recognizes how "disempowering it is for people from underprivileged backgrounds to consciously censor our speech so as to 'fit better' in settings where we are perceived as not belonging" (1990, p. 90). Concurring with hooks' assessment regarding the impact of White supremacist cultural hegemony, Carolyn Shaw demonstrates the effect on both the subordinated groups, in this particular case, Africans, and the primary groups associated with the sanctioned values. She notes:

> The paternalistic demand that Africans follow European rules and standards, simply because the orders came from Europeans, inculcated authoritarian discipline in subordinate Africans. By maintaining social distance, political hegemony, control of the distribution of resources, and disciplinary codes of behavior, colonialists gave themselves the aura of gods and brass serpents. (1995, p. 10)

The insidious denigration of Black people throughout most of the continents is reflected in the attention given to issues that directly affect these groups of people. This resonates with West's somber remark regarding the "place" of Black people in society:

> The notion that Black people are human beings is a new notion in Western civilization and is still not widely accepted . . . one of the consequences of this pernicious idea is that it is very difficult for Black men and women to remain attuned to each other's humanity. (hooks & West, 1991, p. 12)

Richburg's (1997) observation regarding the meager attention paid by the world economy to issues affecting most Third World economies demonstrates the validity of West's assessment. Despite the ravages, both from the war and natural causes, Richburg notes the blatant bias in news coverage, which he attributes to a

> "Eurocentric bias" in the American media. . . . Boutros-Ghali himself touched on the disparity, perhaps a bit undiplomatically, when he challenged a Security Council decision to step up costly peace-keeping operations in the former Yugoslavia while relief operations in Africa were left underfunded. Yugoslavia, Boutros-Ghali said, was "a rich man's war." (1997, p. 52)

The previous discussion explored the manner in which Blackness is negated through popular culture and cultural stereotypes and attitudes. The following discussion demonstrates the racial tier that existed during the colonial times in Kenya, which continues in post-colonial times.

Racial Tier. hooks notes the manner in which Third World scholars and African American scholars are pitted against each other:

> We not only compete for jobs, we compete for recognition. . . . In such situations all the necessary elements exist for the re-enactment of a paradigm of colonial domination where non-western brown/black skinned folks are placed in positions where they act as intermediaries between white power structure and indigenous people of color, usually black folks. (1990, pp. 131–132)

Similarly, hooks and West contend that the jostling for positions and recognition from White people is true

> not only between male and female relations but also Black and Brown relations, and Black and Red, and Black and Asian relations. We are struggling over crumbs because we know that the bigger part has been received by elites in corporate America. . . . So, you end up with this kind of crabs-in-the-barrel mentality. When you see someone moving up, you immediately think they'll get a bigger cut in big-loaf America, and you think that's something real because we're still shaped by the corporate ideology of the larger context. (1991, pp. 13–14)

In Kenya, the issue of "separatism" and/or racial discrimination arises from two main angles. The interests and concerns of Africans were historically pitted against White people's and/or the Indians' concerns and interests. The White colonialists brought along Indian workers, who with time functioned as trained workers before taking on supervisory roles. Mulusa illustrates:

> In East Africa, especially in Kenya, separate schools were developed for Europeans, Indians, Arabs and Africans. . . . The European schools, which could afford essential educational facilities, equipment, materials and highly qualified teachers, had a high retention rate, while African schools, with inadequate resources and teachers, had a high drop out rate, especially at the lower levels. (1992, pp. 160–161)

The racial tier in Kenya ranked White settlers' interests first, second preference went to the Indians, with the majority of Africans subordinated to third place:

> Colonial Kenyan society was organized on the basis of race, with three
> social groups—Africans, Asians and Europeans. . . . The racial ideol-
> ogy . . . emphasized the superiority of Europeans over the other two races
> with Africans being relegated to the bottom of the ladder. (Kinyanjui,
> 1979, cited in Mwiria, 1991, pp. 261–262)

The racial tier was evident in the housing, education, political, and other
economic privileges (Eshiwani, 1990; Mulusa, 1992; Mwiria, 1991). What has
emerged between Africans and the Indians is similar to hooks' assessment of
the relations between and among different minority groups in the United
States. Endowed with a wage income, Asians were the first to "buy" out
European settlers. The group had better and earlier access to education than
did the Africans. The Imperial government allowed Indian representation of
the Legislative and Executive Councils well before African representation and
in larger numbers (Huxley, 1956; Sheffield, 1973). Ngugi Wa Thiong'o asserts
that though independence reduced racial barriers to social mobility the pyra-
mid structure remained intact.

> Some Africans could now climb up the pyramid to the middle and top
> zones. . . . [However,] the white community still occupies the room at
> the top, and the Asian community the middle zone. . . . The very things
> that made the people take up arms against colonialism—external domi-
> nation and internal repression—still exist. (1993, p. 90)

Commonly, the Africans' interests were pitted against the settlers' interests
and/or submerged under non-White interests in the same manner Black
women's concerns in the United States have been submerged under the Black
men's interests and/or White women's concerns, as Perham notes with regard
to representation on a newly established

> East African Production and Supply Council, with its independent
> Chairman and its seven Directors of Native and Non-native Production,
> Price Control, Imports and Road and Rail Transport. Two of those are
> unofficials. There are two Commercial Advisers, one of them an Indian,
> and two representatives of each territory nominated by their govern-
> ments. There is, I understand, no African member. (Huxley, 1956,
> p. 202)

The previous discussion on White supremacy demonstrated that the main
aim of colonization was to promote the political supremacy of the White race

(with significant success!). This was accomplished through greater representation of White peoples at governing councils. The concerns and interests
of Indian people were relegated to second place in Kenya's racial tier, while
Africans occupied the bottom rung. The racial tier was evident in housing,
employment, political representation, and educational policies and practices.
Further, the stereotypes of Africans as primitive savages and serfs, child-like
and uneducatable, legitimized their marginality and despite recent economic
and political progress in the pre and post-colonial era, these stereotypes
continue to shape and determine the African's self-conception and the treatment received from non-African others. A similar situation with regard to Black
people's marginality is evident in other Black occupied countries (hooks, 1981,
1984, 1989a, 1990, 1994b, 1995b; Memmi, 1965; Richburg, 1997).

Internalized Racism. hooks' writings associate the negation of "Blackness,"
color-caste hierarchy, and in-group factions to internalized racism in Black
people. She contends:

> Colonization made of us the colonized—participants in daily rituals of
> power where we, in strict sadomasochistic fashion, find pleasure in ways
> of being and thinking, ways of looking at the world that reinforce and
> maintain our positions as the dominated . . . black people in the U.S.
> and black people globally often look at ourselves through images, through
> eyes that are unable to truly recognize us, so that we are not represented
> as ourselves but seen through the lens of the oppressors, or of the
> radicalized rebel who has broken ideologically from the oppressor but
> still envisions the colonized through biases and stereotypes not yet
> understood or relinquished. (1990, p. 155)

A similar argument could be advanced for the internalization of White people's
values and attitudes in Africans (Urch, 1968). Despite the years of White
people's oppression and exploitation of Black people, Africa still looks to the
West to alleviate her social ills. Perham argues: "It is not enough now for nations
to be independent: If they are poor and weak they blame the wealthier and
stronger states, at once asking their help and at the same time trying jealously
to undermine their power" (Huxley, 1956, p. 269). Though the remark was
made during the colonial era, Richburg raises a similar critique of the African
people's failure to take responsibility for their lack of progress and the often
voiced or unvoiced expectation that some fictitious White man is bound to
come along and make things right, again! He argues that the reality of Africa
is that,

in most places, blacks are still waiting to be empowered three decades after the last Europeans packed and went home. Of course, the countries became independent, the flags changed, the names were Africanized, new national anthems were sung, new holidays observed. . . . For the Africans, the ordinary decent, long-suffering Africans, precious little has changed. (1997, p. 169)

Another aspect of the negation of Blackness is the manner in which Africans readily adopt Western ways as a veneer of sophistication. Shaw contends that colonialism turned the Kikuyu into dependent subjects, who imitated the "Europeans in dress, and drink, in progress and prostitution. . . . Africans in the cities are the grotesque imitation of whites, their lives carnivalesque" (1995, p. 164).

Richburg's experience of racial discrimination in a country that is majority Black shocks him. As he recounts:

Simply put, my colleagues in the foreign press corps—my white colleagues—rarely complained of the same hassles as I routinely faced. . . . White people in East Africa are rarely stopped, rarely questioned, rarely instructed to open their bags. They jump to the front lines, they scream and shout for seats on overbooked flights, they walk around with a kind of built-in immunity, the immunity of their skin color. If you are black or Indian, you get stopped. You get the once-over. Your bags get searched. And if you're black, trying to barge your way past an airport customs officer might very well get you a truncheon to the back of your head. (1997, p. 7)

Based on the above discussion regarding the negation of "Africanness" or "Blackness" by Black people, this author supports Richburg's evaluation: "If the [Black] race is ever going to progress, we might start by admitting that the enemy is within" (1997, p. 179). Not only has the impact of colonization marginalized most traditional Kenyan cultural traits and characteristics, but in giving preferential treatment to Whites and/or foreigners, Africans reinforce their own marginality and sanction an oppressive value system. Ngugi Wa Thiong'o bemoans the cultural alienation in Kenya:

The African bourgeois that inherited the flag from the departing colonial powers was created within the cultural womb of imperialism. . . . So even after they inherited the flag, their mental outlook, their attitudes toward their own societies, toward their own history, toward their own languages, toward everything national, tended to be foreign; they saw things through the eyeglasses given them by their European bourgeois mentors. (1993, p. 85).

hooks (1994c) and Abdul Janmohamed (1994) concur in their critique of a Eurocentric bias and its impact on non-White cultural groupings. Even the children born after independence still yearn for the "White man's" ways and use this very framework to define social prestige (Miller, 1984).

hooks (1981, 1984) notes White people's reservation about mixed marriages. She cites Washington to demonstrate White people's resistance to interracial marriages. She contends:

White people [wanted] to prevent inter-racial marriages. They used lynchings, castration and other brutal punishments to prevent black men from initiating relations with white women. . . . [On the other hand, by] perpetuating the myth that all black women were incapable of fidelity and sexually loose, whites hoped to so devalue them that no white man would marry a black woman. (1981, p. 6)

It is increasingly come to public notice that Black women too feel a sense of betrayal and negation of Blackness by Black men having affairs and/or marrying White women. Perham's observation of White settlers' resistance to interracial marriages between Africans and White women is similar to hooks' (1981, 1984, 1989a) contention of race relations within the United States. Perham notes that underlying race relations in East, and even South Africa as in the Southern States of America is the "pathological, sometimes subconscious fear of the white man for his women as it tends to colour his whole attitude towards Africans and to combine a personal fear with one for the future of the race" (Huxley, 1956, p. 209). Ironically, when a law was passed in Kenya, "decreeing death for criminal assaults of Africans upon white women, was announced to the Masai in their council, they got up in disgust and walked out" (p. 210). In effect, what Masai in his right mind would want a White woman!

Color-Caste Hierarchy. In her discussions on the color-caste hierarchy in United States Black communities, hooks (1981, 1984, 1989a, 1990, 1992, 1994b, 1995b) links the preference for lighter-skinned Blacks to the pervasive reverence for "Whiteness" and White people's related traits and characteristics. hooks commends the Micheaux film *Ten Minutes to Live* for "challenging assumptions that whiteness/light skin should be interpreted as signifying innocence. . . . Calling into question the Western metaphysical dualism which associates whiteness with purity and blackness with taint" (1990, p. 135). She further demonstrates that in most Black communities: "Light skin and long hair continue to be traits that define a female as beautiful and desirable in the racist imagination and in the colonized mindset" (1995b, p. 127). Memmi raises a similar contention regarding the colonized adopting the colonizer's tastes and standards. He argues that, in adopting dominant cultural traits and characteristics, the dominated embrace their own condemnation:

> Negro women try desperately to uncurl their hair, which keeps curling back, and torture their skin to make it a little lighter. . . . The women of the bourgeoisie prefer a mediocre jewel from Europe to the purest jewel of their own tradition. . . . Just as many people avoid showing off their poor relations, the colonized in the throes of assimilation hides his past, his traditions, in fact all his origins which have become ignominious. (1965, p. 122)

hooks' contention regarding Black people's reverence for whiteness is readily applicable to the Kenyan context. Richburg recounts the annoyance expressed by Linda Thomas-Greenfield, an embassy official, in her contact with Africans:

> In Kenya, she said, she had never been invited into a Kenyan home. And even going about daily chores, she was met constantly with the Kenyans' own perverse form of racism, a kind of lingering inferiority complex that makes black Kenyans bestow preferential treatment to whites at the expense of their supposed "brothers." (1997, pp. 154–155)

So long associated with power and privilege, "Whiteness" continues to function as the standard for personal and national aspirations. hooks attributes the color-caste hierarchy to internalized racism. Indeed, hooks argues that what

> South Africa is struggling with—that myth of white supremacy—is also being played out by black Americans when we overvalue those who are light-skinned and have straight hair, while ignoring other black people. It also shows how deeply that myth has inserted itself in our imaginations. (1994b, p. 45)

The historical association of "Whiteness" to power and privilege expressed existing circumstances regarding White folk and simultaneously shaped the social order. Both White and non-White cultural groupings bought in to the myth and reinforced it. Existing social structures in the late nineteenth and early twentieth centuries legitimated the myth of White supremacy. In Africa, colonial powers—French, English, German, Portuguese—were White groups. They were foreigners who nonetheless subverted existing tribal structures to emerge as world economic and political powers. Most countries have since attained political independence and increasing numbers of people have gained political awareness. However the myth of White supremacy proves hard to dispel.

The colonized, so long desirous of the colonial power's aura of power and privilege, continue the process of subjugation in subordinating their primary cultural traits and characteristics. Practice lags behind theory. In theory, Africa threw off the shackles of political oppression. In holding onto the myth of White supremacy, however, she views Western ways as superior to her ancestral traditions and values. Economic, political, and cultural freedom are, for most, abstract concepts far removed from day-to-day personal and political choices. On a macro level, political leaders ignore the inconsistency of buying armory from foreign countries to squelch local dissent. The promotion of a Western-oriented educational system falls into a similar category. On a micro level, individual yearnings for Western-labeled goods over local products and services is rationalized as a quest for quality and value for money. Many consider traditional ways primitive relative to Western, civilized ways.

The obsession of Kenyan women with skin color and hair texture is evident in spending patterns on skin bleaching creams (Ambi, Cleartone, etc.) and permanent hair treatments to soften and maintain their hair unnaturally straight. Often little attention is paid to the side-effects of these "beauty" enhancing treatments. Skin lightening creams may contain dangerous amounts of ammoniated mercury. In 1975, a Kenyan woman lost her life after prolonged use of the creams (Waruingi, 1980). Indeed Arthur Kallet and F. J. Schlink contend that "Lead and arsenic, both fatal poisons, the corrosive chemical ammoniated mercury, and a dozen irritants such as salicylic acid and carbonic acid figures prominently in the formulae of [skin bleaching] lotions and creams" (1976, p. 80). They further note that "of all preparations for the care of the skin, freckle-remover and bleachers are probably the most consistently hazard" (pp. 94–95). John G. Fuller too notes that:

The FTC [Federal Trade Commission] reports trouble with bleaching creams, which have habitually contained mercury as a preservative. Nitrates and borates are used in some skin creams for the same purpose, and both are injurious to the liver and kidneys and may be cancer-pro-ducing (1972, p. 251).

bell hooks and Ngugi Wa Thion'go contend that the process of decolonizing one's mind involves personal and political self-recovery and starts with a critical interrogation of one's location as well as the identifications, and allegiances that inform one's life.

Shaw (1995) and Richburg (1997) note a similar preference for White-related traits and characteristics in Kenya. In their analysis of the color-caste hierarchy, both authors demonstrated the negation of "Blackness" in African people. Shaw (1995) notes that the racial nobility given to lighter skin, sharper features, and a taller and leaner body, based on Western aesthetics in colonial Kenya, further subjugated African traits and characteristics. There has been speculation of the Masai being one of the lost tribes of Israel due to their "Caucasian" features—high-bridged, narrow nose, the thin lips, and the elongated bodies" (Shaw, 1995, p. 201). Not surprisingly, the choice of the Miss Kenya beauty contest buys into a similar value system. Richburg notes that the winner of the contest reflected little of the concept of "African" beauty;

> she had light skin, high cheek-bones, a narrow straight nose, soft hair, and something approaching a perfect 36-24-36 figure. . . . Some pageant judges said they thought Miss Kenya had to conform to internationally accepted standards of beauty if she was to have any chance at all in global competitions. But others argued that finding a Miss Kenya who conformed to international standards meant essentially finding a representative who "looked white" and was essentially not a true Kenyan at all. (1997, p. 106)

The previous discussions illustrated the applicability of hooks' contention regarding the persuasiveness and perpetuation of White supremacist attitudes and values in a Third World country. Understandably, the fact of colonization significantly defines and shapes the degree to which "Africans" adapt and adopt to White supremacist attitudes and values. The degree of internalization of racist attitudes and values is demonstrated by African people's allegiance to "colonial" definitions of social reality, the negation of Blackness, the color-caste hierarchy, and in-group factions between and among marginalized groupings. In the African context, hooks' notion of interminority factions translates to tribal factions.

hooks' body of works reiterates the inextricable link among race, gender, and class biases. Her discussions attribute dominations in general to White supremacy and specifically the Western metaphysical dualistic thought pattern. She notes: "Acting in complicity with the status quo, many black people have passively absorbed narrow representations of black masculinity, perpetuated stereotypes, myths" (hooks, 1992, p. 89). This author, however, argues that sexism and sexist attitudes arise from traditional African patriarchal norms that have persisted over the years within African communities. Indeed, hooks acknowledges:

> In the old days, a man who had no money could still assert tyrannical rule over family and kin, by virtue of his patriarchal status, usually affirmed by Christian belief systems. Within a burgeoning capitalistic economy, it was wage-earning power that determined the extent to which a man could rule over a household. (1990, p. 94)

Education of women has probably made a greater impact in terms of interrogating the myth of women's inferiority than have any laws or publicized documents on women's rights. Changes in women's material conditions, consciousness and attitudes, as well as exposure to more egalitarian cultures, impact the status of women in more hierarchically structured communities such as Kenya. As more women reevaluate their status, place, task, and contribution to family, community, and society, many come to realize a destiny beyond bearing and nurturance of children as well as servitude to husbands. The following discussion explores the impact of sexist attitudes in Kenyan cultural norms and practices.

Sexism

The discussion on sexism and sexist attitudes, as expounded in hooks' body of works, demonstrates the impact of socialization patterns (privileging male over female concerns and interests); sexist attitudes and practices heighten the oppression and exploitation of women in most communities. She also raises the fact that the negation of female traits and characteristics is reinforced by women who internalize sexist values and attitudes. The following discussion explores patriarchal biases in Kenya and the impact on women.

In the analysis of the impact of the Columbus myth in America, hooks notes:

> While the African and Native American men . . . did not embody the characteristics of an imperialist misogynist masculine ideal, they shared with white colonizers a belief in gender systems that privilege males. This means that even though there were communities to be found in Africa and the Americas where women did have great privilege, they were always seen as fundamentally different from and in some ways always less than men. (1994b, p. 202)

Scholarship on Kenya demonstrates the validity of hooks' claim. A complexity of socio-cultural and political factors contribute to the low status of women in most traditional communities like Kenya. While men assert their socially sanctioned rights, women as politically inferior beings have obligations and are expected to "negotiate and make claims" (Moore, 1986, p. 172). Given the patriarchal context, many women scheme and cajole to have their needs met, essentially because the system fails to readily honor their rights.

J. R. Eddowes' research findings resonate with hooks' analysis of women's lack of political power. His study of Samburu women in Kenya illustrated that "women have no influence politically and economically" (1988, p. 31). Shaw illustrates that Kikuyu women's roles were limited to the domestic realm while the elder male roles pertained largely to socio-political realms. She contends that the power of Kikuyu women depended on their "spiritual powers, strength of character, ability to use kin lines of influence to their advantage, and knowledge of the indispensability of their household services" (1995, p. 46). Henrietta Moore narrows women's power base even further by illustrating that in effect, the power of women among the Marakwet is "restricted to their ability to influence individual men" (1986, p. 164). Mutindi Ndunda and Hugh Munby, in an analysis of the association between cultural and historical factors and gender biases in education, assert:

> The inherent view that women were less capable than men manifested itself in "son preference": sons have been and still are more valued than daughters. Indeed, even present day monogamous marriages may become polygamous ones if the first wife fails to bear a son. The birth of a son brings pride to the father and respect to the mother, while a woman who does not bear a son is treated with contempt. (1991, p. 686)

Women face dilemmas of identity, social acceptance, and negation of primary traits and characteristics in patrilineal and patrifocal societies. First, the patrilineal system privileges sons over daughters because sons guarantee continuity to a family lineage (Moore, 1986, Shaw, 1995). In accordance with patrilineal systems, sons preserve the family name and possessions while daughters are expected to marry outside the clan, and take on their husband's name, transferring loyalty from their natal to their marital communities. (This has adversely affected the status of women and their access to education, health services, and property.)

Second, families are a primary site for creating and reproducing sexism through sex role learning such as modeling and differential treatment. What starts off as girl's work to help one's mother easily turns to child labor—long hours and servitude. Some families "encourage" daughters to marry at a younger age in order to provide for the brother's bride price.

The litany is endless. Men are expected to be authoritative, assertive, and controlling while women's power comes through service to others. Third, infidelity is tolerated in men, though rarely in women. Mothers allow sons to "entertain" girlfriends. Daughters are expected to maintain their virginity. Promiscuity is a female issue. Infidelity in women is a cardinal offense. Manliness is a privilege. A man may be unemployed but he retains the symbol of breadwinner, decision maker, and protector. Polygamy is permissible, its impact on women and children grossly underrated. Wife-beating is condoned in most Kenyan tribes. Husbands pay dowry to acquire wives; as possessions, wives can be used, abused and discarded. Carol Riphenburg's study (1997) on the status of women and cultural expression in Zimbabwe raises similar issues regarding women's lack of access to property and related legal rights. She argues that women receive little beyond their clothes after a customary divorce. Most of the family property is customarily assumed to be under the husband's jurisdiction. Ironically, women whose managerial capacity is frequently derided shoulder the primary responsibility for raising children.

Shaw surmises from her research findings that though Kikuyu men and women jointly participated in some activities, and positions allocated across gender line, Kikuyu women were excluded from political decision making. Indeed, even in more "flexible" fields such as the gift of prophecy or clairvoyance, the number of men exceeded that of women (Shaw, 1995). Clearly, a woman's identity and worth is dependent on the status of her natal family in her youth and the spouse thereafter.

> Traditionally, only men can inherit property and goods among the Kikuyu, Luo, Luyia, while Kamba women may inherit from their husbands. However, when a Kamba widow dies, her property is inherited by the son of a co-wife, or she may "Marry" another woman whose sons will inherit her land. (Obbo, 1976, cited in Cubbins, 1991, p. 1067)

Supporting hooks' contention regarding the marginality of women, hooks and West argue:

> One of the major means by which Black men are empowered is to have power over Black women. For a people who feel already relatively powerless, it becomes a form of competition to not occupy the bottom rung of the ladder. . . . It is not only the Black male that has subordinated Black women. The Black woman has been subordinated by White and non-White elites in almost every society where Black women live. (1991, p. 107)

West's observation resonates with hooks' reiteration in her corpus of writing that dominations are interrelated. Essentially, the redress of any form of discrimination necessitates redress of other forms of discrimination. A critique of racial oppression requires the redress of other forms of discrimination, such as the critique of sexism in Black communities.

In most African communities, polygamy is a norm rather than the exception. Making a distinction between civil and customary laws in Zimbabwe, Carol Riphenburg argues that Black men conveniently appeal to customary laws to justify personal choices. "Men married under civil law, for example, occasionally marry second wives under customary law, although technically such marriages are bigamous" (1997, p. 36). On the other hand, despite the exposure to alternative views and awareness of the obligations of married couples toward each other, most African women tolerate polygamy as one more case of male frivolity. Mbye Cham's interview (1994) of Anne Mungai, a movie and video artist, illustrates Kenyan women's ambiguity over the issue. Anne Mungai's dismissive and apologetic stance toward polygamy and sexism in general is instructive. She dismisses it as a male issue. Men take wives and married men keep girlfriends. There is little acknowledgment of how men/husband's choices impact women.

Keith Richburg contends:

> African men come from a recent past where polygamy was the norm, and siring dozens of children was the only way of insuring that at least a few would survive past infancy. So today, monogamy still seems an alien concept. (1997, p. 124)

Arguing in its defense, Louis Leakey, the "White Kikuyu," contends that "polygamy and other Kikuyu customs were similar to those of the Old Testament, and therefore worthy of respect" (Shaw, 1995, p. 140). Richburg notes: "Taking new wives and siring children accorded respect, even in a squatter slum. Whether one could afford the additional burdens of a new family was never part of the equation" (1997, p. 34). This author contends that whether polygamy is biblically or culturally based, the practice reinforces the marginality of women. The practice serves male interests more than female interests. It is ironic that though women are viewed as totally dependent on men, children survive on the mother's "strength and resourcefulness" (p. 29). Moore demonstrates:

> Men not only depend on their wives for labour to produce the crops which feed their children and provide the grain for beer, but in addition

are crucially dependent on women as reproducers, reproducing both clan and labour force. (1986, p. 113)

Various factors make the subordination of women appear natural and inevitable. The invisibility of women in public life can be attributed to the "invisible" nature of their contributions which in turn reinforces the social perception that women are "dependents" rather than "producers" (Jacobson, 1992). First, sexist attitudes and practices reinforce the marginality of women who are already clustered in less prestigious occupations. Derogatory comments about women, overemphasis on beauty and youth, and intimations of their lack of focus undermine their potential and overall productivity. Second, because women's economic contribution typically involves non-monetary exchange, it receives little recognition and often goes unaccounted, if not undervalued and unrecorded, in economic statistical data. Third, legal and customary barriers limit women's access to land, natural resources, credit, technology and other means of production. Jodi Jacobson argues:

As a result of privatization favoring male land-holders, the amount and quality of land available to women food producers in the Third World is declining. Legal and cultural obstacles prevent women from obtaining land, and therefore, from participating in cash crop schemes. Land titles invariably are given to men because governments and international agencies routinely identify men as heads of their households, regardless of whether or not they actually support their families. Women's rights to land are now subject to the wishes of their husbands or the whims of male-dominated courts and community councils. (1992, p. 26)

Disputing the fact that colonialism had a detrimental effect on African communities, with men being taken away from the farms to work in urban centers and/or for White settlers, Huxley argues that:

Practically all the work of cultivating the soil and harvesting the crops fell on the women. Their job was to hoe the land, plant the seed, keep down the weeds, cut the crop, thresh and winnow the grain, carry and store it, and, of course, do all the work of preparation for food. They also chopped and carried firewood, fetched the water, made baskets and pots. . . . The function of the older men was to hear and settle disputes, and arrange marriages, circumcisions and other business and ceremonial affairs, while the small boys looked after the goats. (1956, p. 92)

Analyzing the unequal gender relations in Zimbabwean traditional family structures, Carol Riphenburg points out that although male-headed families are the ideal family model, with males having the ultimate decision making power, the man "simply makes the major decisions and owns whatever property has been in the family that is managed by his wife or wives. The women, with the help from their children, develop and maintain property that is officially in their husband's names" (1997, p. 34).

No wonder Huxley cited the Kikuyu proverb: "A young man is a piece of God" (1956, p. 92). Moore came to a similar conclusion with regard to patriarchal bias among the Marakwet of Kenya. Indeed, Moore illustrated that "maleness [is] associated with a series of things like 'big,' 'up,' 'sky,' 'right': while femaleness is associated with their opposite, 'small,' 'down,' 'earth,' 'left'" (1986, p. 168).

Television both reflects and offers legitimization for stereotypical roles in society. First, children's stereotypical perceptions and role expectations can be attributed to gender bias in television imagery. Mary Mwangi's (1966) analysis of 105 television advertisements aired on Kenya's television networks (KBC and KTN) during an 8-week period revealed stereotypical portrayal patterns similar to those observed in First World countries (McGhee and Freuh, 1980; Craig, 1992). Women's roles are confined to the less prestigious occupations: low-paying, lower status, staff and administrative positions. While women are depicted in subservient roles to men, dependent, less authoritative, and passive, the fictional hero is always a man—protector, avenger, achiever, and so on. The gender bias in mass media sanctions the mythical superiority of men and, by extension, the inferiority of women. These distinctions and genderized social status are made to appear inevitable and natural:

> Culturally dominating representations acquire their status precisely be-
> cause they are widely and consistently believed in, and because, in spite
> of contradictions, they retain the ability to remain highly effective in
> providing people with explanations and definitions of themselves and
> others. Women . . . are socialized just as forcibly as men, into accepting
> social norms and values. (Moore, 1986, p. 184)

Women's acceptance and/or adoption of male norms does not of necessity imply that women's interests are identical to those of men or that these women desire to be men. Internalizing sexism, similar to the process of internalizing racist attitudes and values, expresses a yearning on the part of the marginalized to possess the advantage of the "master." This rationale undergirds hooks' discussions on internalized racism. hooks maintains that women are socialized into linking their self-esteem to their capacity to serve others, a process that reinforces their sense of subordination and marginality:

> And those of us who have been socialized from childhood on to feel that women's "personal power" only comes through serving others may have the most difficult time learning to see that personal power really begins with care of self. (1993, p. 89)

She terms this, "the black woman's martyr syndrome" (p. 89).

Critiquing the ideology of patriarchy, hooks contends:

> Black male phallocentrism constructs a portrait of woman as immoral, simultaneously suggesting that she is irrational and incapable of reason. Therefore, there is no need for black men to listen to women or to assume that women have knowledge to share. (1990, p. 103)

hooks' observation resonates with the conception of African women by African men as the following discussion illustrates. In most Kenyan communities the higher status of older people is attributed to the acquisition of traditional knowledge and skills, property and power (Simons, cited in Eddowes, 1988). However, Moore's ethnographic findings demonstrate that among the Marakwet of Kenya:

> Knowledge, like language, is thought to be a male attribute, and although some older women are highly rewarded and recognized as knowledgeable they still do not possess the peculiarly social knowledge which is the inheritance of men. Access to knowledge, like the control of language, is a prerequisite for full adult, male status. The process of becoming adult, of assuming social responsibility is closely tied to the acquisition of certain esoteric knowledge. (1986, pp. 164–165)

Patriarchy endows authority and power to male elders who are revered and respected and being a patrilineal society, sons are a source of honor to the clan (Miller, 1984; Riphenburg, 1997, Shaw, 1995). Similar to most cultures, once married, women relinquish their primary culture, clan, customs, and name. Further, the practice of paying bridal wealth in exchange for a wife reinforces women's secondary status—property, source of income, and labor ("Making Education Meaningful," 1994). It is argued that lineage and inheritance are limited to the male line as a means of safeguarding a family and/or community's wealth. Were women to inherit, the argument goes, the wealth of the clan would be depleted with the marriage of daughters; each taking a part of it to the spouse's clan. A similar reasoning has limited most Kenyan communities' investment in women's education. Even after independence, Ndunda and Munby note:

> The advantage given males by colonial education and the traditional son preference still influence rural parents, who remain unwilling to invest in their daughters' education because the investment is considered wasteful or frivolous. The disparities resulting from the interaction of traditional culture and colonial exploitation are in employment statistics. (World Bank Country Study, cited in Ndunda & Munby, 1991, p. 687)

Besides the impact of patriarchy in society and within schools, three issues hinder the development of women's education: (a) difficulty of access to education, (b) early drop-out, (c) and poor participation in "hard" subjects such as mathematics and science (Miller, 1984; Ndunda & Munby, 1991; Obanya, 1992). In a keynote address to a seminar on "Girls Education in Anglophone Africa," Hilary Ng'weno argues that the male chauvinism in most traditional societies accounts for the lack of women's access to education:

> We usually say that girls drop out of school at a higher rate than boys. But the fact is not that they drop out. They are forced out of school. Forced out by ignorant tradition-bound parents. Forced out by an indifferent, insensitive male dominated society determined to assign girls, and women in general, a permanently inferior status. ("Making Education Meaningful," 1994, p. 24)

The article further illustrates the sexism in educational settings, the syllabi, teacher expectations, and pedagogy. In *Changing Images: Portrayal of Girls and Women in Kenyan Textbooks*, Anna Obura demonstrates the validity of Hilary Ng'weno's claim regarding structural obstacles to girls' education. Poor academic achievement in females arises from a complexity of socio-cultural factors. In most traditional communities which rely on oral history, the written word is not just novel in approach and content but acquires an aura of political invincibility as well. School textbooks have an immense impact on the socialization of children. "Children are arguably more exposed to textbooks at the early primary stages than to any other print or electronic material. Textbooks are Africa's mass medium for children" (Obura, 1991, p. 10). Indeed, *The World Almanac and Book of Facts 1998* gives the following facts on Kenya's communication network: One television set per 91 persons, one radio per 11 persons, and one phone per 111 persons.

The school curricula and pedagogy reflect and reinforce the marginality of women. Most women's rights continue to be curbed, their mobility restricted by spouses. Women cannot initiate a divorce or own property and they have limited access to the legal system. Anna Obura's analysis of gender portrayal in mathematics, science, technical, language, and social science textbooks illustrates the prominence of male figures, the use of male pronouns, and elevation of male-associated characteristics. The numerical infrequency of adult role models for girls in textbooks reinforces their insignificance. History books focus on the activities and achievements of men. Only one female freedom fighter, Mme Katilili, is mentioned on the last page of the Standard 4 textbook. The first eight pages of *Standard 3 Mathematics* employs seventeen characters in the math problems, all of whom are male. The Standard 4 *Longman Agriculture for Primary Schools* textbook mentions girls 7.6 percent of the times while boys are mentioned 76.9 percent of the time. Even though women predominate as mothers who bear and raise children and perform the housework chores in *Home Science: A Complete Textbook for KCPE* (Kenya Certificate for Primary Education), "only 21 out of 114 pronouns are female. . . . The masculine gender pronoun is used when referring to people in general" (Obura, 1991, p. 58). Science books portray women as restricted to the domestic sphere, subordinate to men in general, powerless, passive and absent from adult activities, indigent and in need of male protection, dull and lacking in initiative (Obura, 1991). Not surprisingly, the secondary school dropout rate of girls is over 30 percent.

Anna Obura argues that, given such a patriarchal context, girls feel like intruders and misfits in the school system. Reinforcing the marginality of women in society, school textbooks at primary levels present an exclusive world of men, made by men and for men. Property ownership is patrilineal, men are gatekeepers to the world, exposing children to a world beyond the home. Unlike women, men's decision-making impact pertains both to the domestic and public sphere. Men are recognized as breadwinners. Even though 80 percent of agricultural labor is performed by women, men are portrayed as farmers with women and children as an appendage. The options of girls in such a male-dominated society are either as wage earners or spouses to wealthy men. The latter receives cultural endorsement and thus is viewed by many women as less threatening. The factors for female subjugation are in place as early as primary (American: grade) school.

While male figures are portrayed in expansive roles in public"—members of Parliament, managers, physicians, dentists, surgeons, teachers, headmasters,

chemists, agricultural officers, potters, merchants, paid cooks, wood carvers—
female figures, if mentioned at all, forever remain in the margins. In these
textbooks men, not women, buy land, houses, farms, cattle, vehicles, food,
clothing and so on. Men generate power, use modern equipment, travel to
places beyond the confining home of women and children, and are custodians
of the national heritage. Women's contributions to the domestic and public
sphere are ignored. "There is no large-scale farmer among the women, no trader
or coffee or cattle, no businesswomen, no headmistress, no woman leader"
(Obura, 1991, p. 32). However, contrary to this documentary invisibility of
women, "there are large-scale women farmers; there are women agricultural
officers, financiers, agricultural researchers, institution managers; and above all
there are women subsistence farmers" (Obura, 1991, p. 54).

Cheru (1987) makes a similar observation regarding the gender bias in
educational policy and practice in Kenya. Economic, cultural, and political
inequalities in society related to class and gender differences impact schooling:

> Traditionally, Kenyan education prepared youth for gender-specific roles
> as adults in their society; girls were prepared to be wives and mothers and
> were taught specific feminine roles, and the boys were taught specific
> masculine roles. The formal educational opportunities made available to
> Africans by the Europeans were developed along similar gender lines.
> (Ndunda & Munby, 1991, p. 692)

Ndunda and Munby surmise that in schools: "Science education appears to
perpetuate and reinforce the traditional Kenyan ideology of male supremacy
and dominance" (p. 698). Similar to Ndunda and Munby's contention regarding the genderization of educational opportunities and advancement, Mulusa
notes: "Women are still discouraged from learning intellectually rigorous
subjects such as mathematics and physical sciences in favour of '
feminine courses' associated with domestic work like sewing, knitting and
cookery" (1992, p. 166).

Studies show that factors in both homes and schools work against girls'
education so that boys perform better than girls academically. There are
inherent limitations to the education of women. Over and above the unequal
access to educational opportunities, teachers' interaction with girls in schools
and low expectations of girls to excel academically pose a formidable handicap
to women's educational and economic progress. Ciarunji Chesaina notes that
despite the "Women's Decade" (Kenya hosted the 1985 Women's Decade
Conference in Nairobi):

There were no efforts made to improve the facilities of girls' secondary schools, which have always been less well equipped than boys' schools. There were also no significant steps taken to encourage girls to enter areas traditionally regarded as male dominated domains, such as science and technically based disciplines. (1994, p. 186)

Traditionally, girls were primarily prepared to be wives and mothers. In contemporary society educational opportunities continue along gender specific lines. Female children have limited access to education and spend fewer years in school than their male counterparts. Not only do boys/men have greater access to formal education but men spend more years in school and are therefore better equipped for one only prestigious professional occupations. Because women face high rates of illiteracy, low levels of education, and limited access to prestigious occupations, most cluster in lower-paying, lower-status, staff and administrative occupations such as teaching, nursing, secretarial and clerical jobs.

Mwiria attributes the dominance of females in literacy programs to the patriarchal system that privileges male over females concerns:

Kenyan women have historically had less access to formal educational opportunities than men. . . . Poor families have been known to prefer educating their sons to daughters because of the perceived long-term economic security sons are seen as likely to guarantee. And in some communities, especially the Muslim-dominated ones, many parents worry that education will make their daughters discontented or immoral and eventually come in the way of marriage . . . a good proportion of schoolgirls are forced to leave school for marriage because of the relatively high incidence of female student pregnancies. (1993, p. 186)

Ndunda and Munby further illustrate the manner in which sexism is reflected in pedagogy. A male student observed that besides directing most of the questions to male students

[T]he physics teacher did not engage the girls in class, the girls were blamed for being silent in classes. The teacher appeared to endorse cultural teachings—to be gentle in manner, not to raise the eyes or voice when talking to men in public—thus projecting cultural male dominance into the girls' science experiences. (1991, pp. 690–691)

hooks (1981, 1984, 1989a, 1990) and feminist literature (Lorde, 1984; Martin, 1984, 1992; Minnich, 1990; Noddings, 1984, 1992, 1995a, 1995b; Pagano, 1995) note the subordination of female traits and characteristics in educational settings and the wider society. Moore too raises the issue of a general negation of female-related traits and characteristics. She contends that the hierarchy between what is "male" and what is "female"

> implies a set of valuations such that male qualities are positively valued, in contrast to those associated with the female, which are not. Women themselves may be positively or negatively valued, but that which is "female," or partakes of a female quality, always retains a negative connotation. (1986, p. 163)

The previous discussion provides various illustrations of sexism and sexist attitudes and values in Kenya. Patriarchy privileges male concerns and interest while simultaneously relegating female traits and characteristics to secondary status. The negation of womanhood, similar to the negation of Blackness, is reinforced by sexist stereotypes of women as irrational, childlike, emotional, and lacking in political agency. The fact that social knowledge is culturally understood to be a male construct reinforces the marginality of women. The justification for polygamy (and from a White settler at that) illustrates society's attempts to accommodate male interest and concerns, with carrying on the family—male—lineage commonly cited as justification. There is little discussion of its impact on women. Not for long, from the given cultural/political trend. The fact that Charity Kaluki Ngilu and Wangari Mathaai vie for presidency in Kenya's "deeply patriarchal and sexist society" (McKinley, 1997b, p. 3) illustrates the inroads political awareness can make in cultural norms. Indeed, the mere thought of recognizing the leadership ability of women is dramatic in itself.

It is within the past ten years that gender issues as matters of national concern are frequently raised in national papers. This is not surprising. Mrs. Tabitha Seii contests against an incumbent cabinet minister, Nicholas Biwott. Ms. Martha Karua is numbered among the formidable opposition women leaders. Mrs. Grace Mueni Mwewa and Maryam Mohammed Matano have infiltrated the political world of men. Most of the female parliamentary candidates promise to liberate women from their social and economic stigma by improving women's representation at top echelons. Cultural and social influences, however, prove hard to dispel. Mrs. Zipporah Kitony, a nominated member of parliament and head of the women's development movement Maendeleo Ya Wanawake, chastises presidential women candidates Charity Ngilu and Wangari Mathaai for overstepping cultural boundaries. It is "unAfrican" for girls to have designs on elder's (read: men's) seats of authority. The presidency, she argues, is for elders, not girls. The following discussion analyzes class biases in Kenya.

Classism

Part II demonstrated the manner in which White people's (bourgeois) values and attitudes are sanctioned and presented as mainstream values in the wider society and, as well, reflected and perpetuated in educational policies and practices. hooks' corpus of writing critiques the manner in which one's social standing is defined by material possession and/or educational status as opposed to his/her contribution to individual communities. She notes:

> For so long, Black folks have felt that our longing for goods is a justifiable longing because the desire for material well-being is the crux of the American dream. . . . We deal with white supremacist assault by buying something to compensate for feelings of wounded pride and self-esteem. When we don't receive racial respect, we try to regain feelings of worth through class competition and material possession. Goods function as an equalizer, allowing a person to falsely believe that there is opportunity through consumer choice. (hooks & West, 1991, p. 98)

Her writings highlight the manner in which social divisions are determined by one's access to resources. hooks notes the promotion of bourgeois norms in educational settings and the wider society:

> I still find that most academics, irrespective of their politics, whether they identify as conservative, liberals or radical, religiously uphold privileged class values in their manner and style in which they teach, when it comes to habits of being, to mundane matters like dress, language, decorum, etc. (1995b, p. 174)

Most people in Kenya seek to emulate values and attitudes of the West and the materially privileged class. Arriving at an assessment similar to hooks' regarding Black people's emulation of White people's ways of being, feeling, and knowing, George Urch contends that what initially intrigued the African was the White man's possessions rather than his god:

> He was willing to listen to the teaching of the missionary if it brought him the power of the European with his elaborate clothing and equip-

ment, for the African already had a religion, but he did not have the riches of the Westerner. (1968, pp. 114–115)

hooks' writings raise the issue of the significance of education to the political plight of African Americans. hooks notes:

> Education represented a means of radical resistance but it also led to caste/class divisions between the educated and the uneducated, as it meant the learned person could more easily adopt the values and attitudes of the oppressor. Education could help one assimilate. (1989a, p. 98)

The association of "Whiteness" to privilege and power mirrors post-colonial racial divisions while reinforcing more recent practices that marginalize the underprivileged in most communities in Kenya:

> Schools were developed which divorced the pupil from African culture and the common yardstick of prestige became success in the Western oriented system of education. School examinations were designed which reflected a European rather than an African background. . . . Secondary education schools were organized as boarding schools which increased the cultural gap between home and school. (Urch, 1968, pp. 5–6)

On the political level, Shaw (1995) illustrates that colonial Kenya further subverted indigenous social arrangements by pitting the new wealthy elites against traditional elders, the poor against the landowners, and the local Africans against the colonialists. The pre-colonial social divisions pre-shadowed later divisions, making way for development of an African bureaucratic elite. Stabler notes:

> As young Africans saw their missionary teachers living in comfortable bungalows furnished in European fashion, or Government officials even more comfortably housed and driving motor cars, their appetite grew for an education that might lead them to a similar way of life. (1969, p. 11)

In contemporary times, Keith Richburg makes the contrast between the materially privileged African sector and majority underprivileged Africans:

> The picture of the Big Man replaced the portrait of the Queen. But in country after country, power simply passed from a white colonial dicta-

torship to an indigenous black one—and the result has been more repression, more brutality. (1997, p. 169)

Materially privileged Kenyans disassociate themselves from underprivileged members of the community. Albert Memmi's analysis aptly captures the process of assimilation in the colonized:

The recently assimilated place themselves in a considerably superior position to the average colonizer. They push a colonial mentality to excess, display proud disdain for the colonized and continually show off their borrowed rank, which often belies a vulgar brutality and avidity. Still too impressed by their privileges, they savor them and defend them with fear and harshness. (1965, p. 16)

Urch (1968) notes that besides an alienating education, the emergence of a capitalism value system disrupted the traditional corporate society bringing in its wake a dysfunctional tribal system, competition, and classism. In educational settings, the English language is reinforced as the language of the elite class. Further, White people's values and attitudes are reinforced in practices such as manner of eating (fork, knife, and spoon for proper etiquette), dress codes (in spite of extremely high temperatures during the dry season, the African businessman still wears tie and suit for elegance), and manner of speech (an English accent makes all the difference in business interactions). Shaw contends: "European class prejudices were overlaid on racist notions overdetermining the style and rhetoric of subordination of Africans by European colonialists" (1995, p. 186). During the colonial period, in arguing for racial separation on the basis of "comfort level" with one's own kind, Perham raises the issue of racial mixtures stating that the

colonist regards the African as backward: he sees how poor he is: he does not like what he has seen or heard of his customs, especially, perhaps, in the all-important question of sex. In England, most people of the middle and upper classes would not ask into their houses as a guest some rough working-man, a man who, in their view, might be dirty and have no manners. . . . It is not surprising that, when to this class-feeling are added the extra barriers made by race, colour, language and custom, the average colonist rules out even the possibility of social equality with Africans. (Huxley, 1956, p. 208)

Mulusa illustrates: "The wealthy and powerful have used the existing socioeconomic institutions to propel themselves into their present positions and cannot introduce laws and regulations that might destroy such institutions" (1992, p. 168). Supporting Mulusa's contention, Richburg (1997) illustrates the disparities in living conditions in Nairobi, Kenya's capital. Richburg argues:

> Corruption is the cancer eating at the heart of the African state. It is what sustains Africa's strongmen in power, and the money they pilfer, when spread generously throughout the system, is what allows them to continue to command allegiance long after their last shreds of legitimacy are gone. (1997, p. 173)

He contrasts the privileged members in their new Mercedes and BMWs, the symbol of Kenya's corrupt class, to the filthy beggar children of indeterminate sex begging for money in Nairobi's streets.

In her critique of mainstream feminism, hooks notes that women "chose to define liberation using terms of white capitalist patriarchy, equating liberation with gaining economic status and money power" (1981, p. 145). Similar to the argument raised by hooks (1984, 1989a, 1990, 1992, 1993) regarding the equation of "freedom" to material privilege, Perham (Huxley, 1956) notes that what the Africans sought at independence was not freedom in which to work out their own salvation but rather access to material privilege. Citing the *Area Handbook for Kenya*, Miller notes:

> The elite began to regard themselves as a cohesive group that deserved prestige and economic well-being. . . . They adopted British standards in clothing, housing, furniture, and entertainment. They lived in red tiled bungalows with well-tended gardens in Nairobi's residential sections. They played tennis, drank whiskey, and owned high-priced cars. (1984, p. 72)

While the access of higher education is typically associated with middle- and upper-level social stratas of society, in Kenya the accessibility to resources is significantly determined by one's tribal membership. Richburg makes an insightful remark in stating that in "Africa, you belong to a tribe; without a tribe, you don't belong" (1997, p. 110). To expound on the insight, the following discussion on tribalism, nepotism, and corruption demonstrates the impact of tribal divisions on social policy and practices in Kenya.

Tribalism, Nepotism, and Corruption

Given the cultural domination and alienation in American context, hooks advocates a degree of physical and emotional "separatism," what this author terms, "voluntary apartheid." hooks argues that the idea of "homeplace" creates "separate places, the times apart from whiteness . . . for sanctuary, for reimagining, for re-membering" (1995b, p. 6). Richburg advances arguments to illustrate:

> It's virtually inevitable that political parties will be organized along ethnic, meaning tribal lines. And that's not too different from tribal voting patterns in American big cities, where you can count on the black vote, the Irish vote, the Polish vote, the Jewish vote. (1997, p. 106)

Indeed, tribal separatism can serve the positive function raised by hooks. However, in Kenya, the process has lead to discriminatory policies and practices, manifested in abuses by the tribal grouping with access to economic and political power, as the following discussion demonstrates. Mulusa equates tribalism to racism:

> Like racism, tribalism is based on unfounded beliefs about the superiority of one's ethnic group over other groups and the fear of losing privileges enjoyed or being exploited by more powerful tribal groupings. Tribal groupings are often intensified when members of the same ethnic group live in the same geographical region or belong to the same religious organization, political party or other social movement. (1992, p. 161)

Though tribal divisions may have originated in the pre-colonial era, the colonial government exploited the divisions, setting up hierarchies among tribes of different nations. In the pre-colonial era, tribal differences arose from the scramble for scarce resources. Tribal groups were reinforced religiously through taboos, fetishes, and protective medicines:

> The tribal god or gods not only brought kinsmen together, but helped unite and mark the member as separate from other groups, for the brotherhood of man only extended to members of the tribal structure. (Urch, 1968, p. 115)

The impact of cultural alienation in hooks' corpus of writing could be applied to an analysis of tribal factions in most African countries. In this case, the term *dominant group* applies to racial as well as tribal dominations. During the colonial era, Kenya's distribution of wealth and political resources were in inverse ratio to the population's composition of Africans, Indians, and Whites. The post-colonial era favored the interest of White settlers; Perham (Huxley, 1956) and Mwiria (1991) illustrate that the racial division of labor mirrored a similar hierarchy in the education system and other social amenities in colonial Kenya. Besides grooming the Indians for supervisor roles, in trying to create effective tribes to rule, the colonial government reinforced

> internal political and economic differences, by recognizing big men or wealthy landowners over elders' councils and men over women, by establishing feudal relations to whole groups of people through the vassalage of their appointed leader. (Shaw, 1995, p. 5)

There is a close connection between the policy-makers' composition and the president's tribe in Kenya. Citing the Scandinavian Institute Studies, Miller (1984) notes that the domination of Kikuyus in government was a major concern. In 1972 the Kikuyu who constituted 20 percent of the population held 40 percent of senior government offices while the Luo, the second-largest ethnic group with 18 percent of the population, held only 8.5 percent of the senior government offices. Expounding on the informal political and economic process in Kenya, Miller notes:

> In Kenyatta's regime all major decisions flowed from the top and were taken either by Kenyatta or his close lieutenants. The inner circle that held real power was the family. . . . Any real or imagined tie to Kenyatta was tantamount to political power, and a great deal of business moved on the basis of "the wishes of the president." Kenyatta's word was law, and no one was prepared to challenge him directly. (1984, p. 61)

For the greater part, most schools were located around the Missions. The Mission stations were not evenly distributed in the country. Mulusa (1992) and Urch (1968) illustrate the significance of the distribution of educational institutions in Kenya:

> Tribal groups which had access to many schools built up the literacy level of their members rapidly, produced teachers and other social workers for the local area and tended to dominate both the public service and the national business sector. The educational gap between the tribes thus

developed during the colonial period became an economic gap in the post-independence period. (Mulusa, 1992, p. 162)

The Kikuyu tribe had greater access to political, educational, and economic advances during the term of the late Jomo Kenyatta, Kenya's first president. However, the situation changed drastically during Moi's presidency. Miller (1984) demonstrates that in promoting the interests of his Kalenjin tribe, Moi's presidency has been criticized for similar excesses of corruption and nepotism typical of Kenyatta's regime. Supporting Miller's contention, Barkan and Chege assert:

In 1978, when Moi assumed the presidency, he initially maintained Kenyatta's broad[er] ethnic-regional base of political support and patronage. But by the early 1980s, Moi had purged many Kikuyus and non-Kikuyu allies of Kenyatta from both central cabinet and senior posts located within administrative districts. Evidence also is clear that government funds, previously allocated to a variety of regions for roads, commercial and social-sector development, became more concentrated in Moi's home Kalenjin district (in Western Kenya) and benefitted a narrow set of ethnic allies. (Bradshaw & Fuller, 1996, p. 89)

Mulusa argues by illustration that the tribal biases translated to educational biases:

Since education is seen as a tool for development and domination of the less developed, parents, teachers and community leaders in the grip of tribalism have tended to encourage children from their tribe to perform well educationally, using both conventional and unconventional methods and preventing children from other tribal groupings from taking advantage of educational opportunities in their districts or states. (1992, p. 168)

Exploiting the divisiveness resulting from tribal contentions and subsequent separatism, most African leaders conveniently play on the ethnic fear to remain in power (Richburg, 1997). The current Kenyan president presents his regime as a protection from a Kikuyu takeover. At the base of the tribal contentions is a perceived injustice in the allocation and access to the country's resources. Ironically, each grouping feels justified in their demands and/or protection of their rights. Richburg relates the tribal conflicts in Kenya to the tensions between the Tutsi and Hutus in Rwanda. He therefore surmises that:

the Hutu who participated in the killings were slashing at centuries of stereotypes and discrimination. . . . They were slashing at their own perceived ugliness, as if destroying this thing of beauty, this thing they could never really attain, removing it from the face of the earth. (1997, p. 108)

This discussion on social divisions based on class differences highlights the fact that in Kenya, class, or specifically access to education, economic, and/or political resources, is closely aligned to one's tribal standing. As the history of Kenya's post-independence years illustrates, tribal membership significantly impacts one's social mobility in a country rife with tribal divisions and resource allocation disparities. hooks advocates the notion of a "homeplace" as a place of psychological recovery for people bombarded by culturally negating messages. However, in Kenya this separatism has caused tribal rivalry, resulting in bloodshed and loss of lives. Tribal "separatism" provides an avenue for "recovery" in a culturally alienating milieu. Tribal separatism on the African continent has created tensions rather than nurturing tribal harmony through equal representation (Miller, 1984; Richburg, 1997; Urch, 1968). What adds to the complexity in the Kenyan tribal context is the link to economic and political power distribution. A ruling tribe exploits its position by amassing national resources and reinforcing its institutions by electing members to policy-making levels. Memmi attributes the "grab while you can" mentality in most African leadership, to the transience in power. This author links tribal abuses of power and privilege to what Memmi surmises of the French colonialists in Tunisia: "The colonialist does not plan his future in terms of the colony, for he is there only temporarily and invests only what will bear fruit in his time" (1965, p. 69). However, discounting the attribution of national tensions to tribal conflicts, Ngugi Wa Thiong'o asserts:

The misleading stock interpretation of the African realities has been popularized by the western media which likes to deflect people from seeing that imperialism is still root cause of many problems in Africa. (1986, p. 1).

Although Ngugi Wa Thiong'o attributed Kenya's political, economic, and social divisiveness to colonialism and its arm, White supremacy, tribalism plays a significant role in the ongoing separatism. The 1997 Kenyan general campaigns and elections demonstrated the impact of tribal divisiveness. The electoral majority denounced the appropriation and mismanagement of funds, political oppression, and nepotism characteristic of the current presidency of

Daniel Arap Moi, but this failed to translate in a combined majority vote among the opposition parties. The presidential vote was divided among fifteen presidential candidates mostly along tribal lines. The Kikuyu vote was divided among Mwai Kibaki, Koigi Wa Wamwere, and Wangari Mathaai. The Luhya vote was divided between Martin Shikuku and Wamalwa Kijana. The Luo and Kamba vote went respectively to Raila Odinga and Charity Ngilu.

In sum, this author argues that bell hooks' critique of the United States is pertinent to a Third World country such as Kenya. The contention is primarily based on three factors: (a) Western civilization has significantly altered the histories of both the United States and Kenya; (b) both exhibit sexist attitudes and values; and (c) both employ a capitalistic model to define social prestige. The following discussion provides a brief synopsis of the historical and cultural impact on Kenya's educational system in trying to assess the manner in which prevailing educational policies and practices either maintain or critique the social order through the curriculum and/or pedagogical orientations.

CHAPTER 12

Relevance of hooks' Engaged Pedagogy

Part I analyzed bell hooks' social theory and demonstrated the validity of her critique of the racism, sexism, and classism in educational settings and the wider society. hooks (1994c) contends that race, sex, and class privilege empower and grant authority to particular students and deny authority to marginalized students. hooks' (1994c) contention regarding biases in school norms and practices resonates with critical, feminist, and multicultural scholarship with regard to the marginality of students whose cultural traits and characteristics are not adequately reflected in mainstream norms and practices (Freire & Faundez, 1989; Giroux & McLaren, 1994; Martin, 1984, 1992; Nieto, 1996; Noddings, 1992, 1995a, 1995b; Shor, 1992; Shor & Freire, 1987). To interrogate and transform the privileges of Whites, males, and materially privileged individuals, hooks proposes curriculum policies and pedagogical orientations that decenter the focus on White people's cultural histories, traits, and characteristics, male-based norms and practices, and an individualistic, competitive, and materialistic value system.

In the Kenyan context, James Sheffield (1973) and Ernest Stabler (1969) note the alienating factor in the Kenyan curriculum and school culture. Both scholars argue that Kenya's educational system has been a mirror image of European systems. Their criticism

focused on two main problems: the alienation of the educated minority from its traditional culture and values, and the irrelevance of an academic curriculum to the economic needs of a largely agricultural society. (Sheffield, 1973, p. 98)

Marginality is exacerbated in students from materially underprivileged backgrounds. The students come to school "not accustomed to using knives and forks or sleeping between sheets, while others [have] grown up in Nairobi in a thoroughly urban style of life" (p. 99). Sheffield's and Stabler's contention regarding an elitist curriculum and school culture demonstrates the relevance of the components of hooks' educational theory (1994c), engaged pedagogy: (a) conceptualization of the knowledge base, (b) linking of theory to practice, (c) student empowerment, (d) multiculturalism, and (e) incorporation of passion. To different degrees and in different ways, the strategies address the marginality of most students whose ways of being, feeling, and knowing are subordinated and/or excluded in educational settings. The whole basis of an alienating curriculum and school culture arises from the origins of formal education in Kenya.

The British missionaries introduced Western education around the mid-nineteenth century. The Western-oriented framework of education purposes and goals has persisted over the years (Ngugi Wa Thiong'o, 1986, 1993; Sheffield, 1973; Stabler, 1969). The missionaries monopolized the control of formal schooling institutions between 1846–1911 (Mwiria, 1991). Besides its proselytizing aim, Missionary education initially emphasized the teaching of Catechesis, eventually expanding its curriculum to include technical and vocational training. On the other hand, government and non-religious–sponsored schools promoted the idea of vocational training for the Africans (Richburg, 1997; Sheffield, 1973). Overall, education has been a shared responsibility between the local and colonial government, religious and non-religious organizations (NIER, 1995). Each group had different educational goals and purposes. Missionary education helped maintain law and order in Africans, and provided the colonial government with clerks, policemen, and interpreters. The government looked to education to train its workforce. George Urch contends:

Through the years education in Kenya vascillated between the desires of the African, who felt the road to success hinged on emulation of the European, those of the missionary teacher, who viewed education as a by-product of Christianity, and those of the government anxious to develop a system . . . to help the African become part of the modern world. (1968, p. 9)

Notwithstanding the difference in educational purposes, Sheffield notes:

The three-tiered pattern which emerged in Kenya, with community development for the majority, technical training for a minority, and academic secondary education for a tiny fraction of the African population, was reinforced by subsequent policy statements of the British Colonial Office. (1973, p. 24)

After attaining its independence from Britain in 1963, Kenya replaced the racially segregated education system with a more open system whose "aim was to produce properly socialized individuals [with] the necessary knowledge, skills, attitudes and values to facilitate their full participation in nation building" (p. 83). To address previous racial and social inequalities in access to economic and political power, the new education system was founded on the universal principles of political, economic, and social equality (Merryfield, 1989). An "Africanized" education was primarily viewed by the new government as a means of rejecting subservience to foreign masters and an assertion of the rights and interests of the African (Urch, 1968). However, in spite of post-colonial African nationalistic ambitions to make Kenya's education more reflective of traditional norms and values, the original principles of a liberal education in its focus on the academic over the practical continues to dominate and inform educational policy and practices (Mulusa, 1992; Mwiria, 1991; Sheffield, 1973). Kilemi Mwiria notes that after independence

Africans rejected [technical and agricultural] education and called for academic education because the colonial economy assigned a low value to manual work and offered more compensation to those who had literary as opposed to technical education. (1991, p. 269)

Kenya has a central body that oversees its education system. As such, any changes in national policy and/or practice significantly impact educational policies and practices. The management of formal education in Kenya is the responsibility of the Minister of Education operating through the Ministry of Education and its legal organizations: the Kenya Institute for Education (KIE), responsible for the curriculum development; the Kenya National Examination Council (KNEC), responsible for the development and administration of national examinations including certification; the Teachers Service Commission (TSC), responsible for the recruitment and employment of teachers; the Jomo Kenyatta Foundation (JKF) and the Kenya Literature Bureau (KLB), publishers of textbooks and other educational materials to facilitate curriculum implementation; the Kenya Educational Staff Institute (KESI), which organizes in-service courses, seminars and workshops for educational leaders including heads of schools, inspectors, and other field personnel; and the Kenya Institute of Special Education (KISE), which trains teachers and other personnel to handle education for the disabled (NIER, 1995, p. 83). The following discussion explores the relevance of hooks' social and educational critique to Kenya's educational system.

The analysis of the relevance of hooks' engaged pedagogy to a Third World context establishes the applicability of the following components of her pedagogy: (a) conceptualization of knowledge, (b) linking theory to practice, (c) student empowerment, (d) multicultural approach to education, and (e) the incorporation of passion. The discussion explores past and current educational policies and practices while simultaneously raising means by which hooks' engaged pedagogy critiques and offers transformational strategies for addressing prevailing inadequacies in the educational system.

Conceptualization of Knowledge

The previous part explored hooks' contention (1994c) regarding the basis of power in classrooms. An elitist conceptualization of knowledge gives "power" to the designator of "official knowledge," and privileges official over experiential knowledge, from which most students claim a foundation for understanding academic concepts. The focus on academic knowledge subordinates other forms of acquiring knowledge. In Kenya, intellectual knowledge (typically offered in major universities) has acquired greater status compared to practical knowledge offered in "perceived" second-rate vocational colleges (Mwiria, 1991; Richburg, 1997; Sheffield, 1973; Stabler, 1969).

hooks notes: "Education was considered to have the potential to alienate one from one's primary community and awareness of our collective circumstances as black people" (1989a, p. 99). Sheffield's remark (1973) regarding Kenya's universities as ivory towers for the elite echoes hooks' contention regarding the potential dangers of formal education. He maintains that Kenyan universities have over the years acquired an "ivory tower complex" that proves hard to dispel. What with most students' limits in resources and the accessibility of a university education, successful candidates feel a "cut" above the ordinary *mwananchi*, or local citizen. Albert Memmi raises a secondary issue to the fallacy of education in the colonies: "One of my former schoolmates told me that literature, art and philosophy had remained foreign to him, as though pertaining to a theoretical world divorced from reality. It was only after a long visit to Paris that he could really begin to absorb them" (1965, p. 105). Ngugi

Wa Thiong'o raises a similar contention with regard to Kenya's colonial education: "The alienation became reinforced in the teaching of history, geography, music, where bourgeois Europe was always the centre of the universe" (1986, p. 17). Education prepares children for a country to which they do not belong and/or white-collar jobs to which few of them have access.

In the previous part, the author illustrated hooks' contention regarding the manner in which an abstracted knowledge base reinforces social inequality by privileging students, usually from dominant groups. The discussion demonstrated that an elitist (abstracted) knowledge is based primarily on values and traditions of dominant cultural groups. In a racist, sexist, and classist society the social knowledge would be primarily Western, masculine oriented, and reflective of bourgeois values. Critiquing the Eurocentric bias in Kenya's educational curriculum after independence, Mwiria notes:

> In literature classes students were forced to memorize William Shakespeare, George Bernard Shaw or T. S. Eliot. In music they sang "London Bridge is burning down" and "God save the King" as they honoured the Union Jack. (1991, p. 270)

Henrietta Moore's analysis of the politics in a conceptualization official knowledge resonates with hooks' contention regarding the "politics" of social knowledge. Among the Marakwet, a sexist conceptualization of knowledge reinforces the marginality of women. Moore illustrates that "since women are thought to have an incomplete command of language, and since they do not, by definition, possess social [that is, male] knowledge, they are excluded from the exercise of power, whether it be political or ritual" (1986, pp. 165–166). To address the marginality of cultural groups whose "knowledge" is subordinated in mainstream forms of knowledge, hooks (1994c) advocates linking theory to practice and accommodating "differing" ways of being, feeling, and knowing in official curriculum and pedagogical orientations. Similar to feminist scholars, hooks (1994b, 1994c) argues that the focus on academics over practical and experiential knowledge, and objectivity and rationality over connectedness and affectivity leads to the transmission of partial knowledge and, therefore, exclusive ways of being, feeling, and knowing.

An analysis of curriculum in Kenya must of need incorporate the religious factor. Education curriculum offered by the Christian missionaries was primarily of a religious nature, its aim being proselytization of the African (Eshiwani, 1990; Mwiria, 1991; Urch, 1968). Indeed, the criteria of selection for European teachers bound for the colony was religious affiliation rather than their teaching ability (Urch, 1968). The fight for independence was closely linked to a fight for a less religious-oriented curriculum (Urch, 1968). Since the initial contact between the indigenous peoples and the White culture was via the missionaries, many African nationalists viewed the Church as an agent of European imperialism (Mulusa, 1992; Mwiria, 1991; Urch, 1968). The church made little attempt to affirm the African culture—portraying the African as inferior, primitive, and pagan. The converts' choice for Christianity amounted to a choice against their traditional beliefs and communities:

> In many instances they were ostracized from their traditional surroundings and it became necessary for missionaries to gather them around the mission center. (Urch, 1968, p. 117)

Supporting hooks' contention (1994c) of official curriculum and conventional pedagogical orientations, Part I of the Ominde Report, whose aim was to reduce the Eurocentric bias in education, critiqued prevailing teaching methods and the focus on academics and examinations. The report viewed the Cambridge School Certificate (taken after seven years of primary and four years of secondary schooling) as the "real enemy [to education], for it is entirely possible to pass in subjects merely by amassing knowledge, cramming book learning that has little educational significance in itself, except perhaps as a training of the memory" (Ominde Report, cited in Sheffield, 1973, p. 96). Ironically, Sheffield, similar to hooks (1994b, 1994c), notes the African students' resistance and hostility toward "departures from traditional methods" (Sheffield, 1973, p. 96).

hooks critiques the traditional notion of a teacher in the classroom "behind a desk or standing at the front immobilized. . . . [Noting that as] long as the mind is still working elegantly and eloquently, that's what is supposed to be appreciated" (1994c, p. 137). hooks' critique applies to the Kenyan context whereby most primary teachers and parents would be content if pupils "acquire mechanical skills in reading, writing, and arithmetic and memorize a few facts in history and geography" outlined in a syllabus by the Ministry of Education (Stabler, 1969, p. 35). On the one hand, the image of teachers as the privileged voice in schools is drawn from the colonial framework (Urch, 1968). The authoritarian teaching style was further reinforced by a prescriptive approach to tribal instruction, with the youth seated at the feet of the elders who it was assumed had absolute authority, power, and wisdom. Indeed, teachers engaging in radical teaching, opposing school policy, or organizing students risk loss of employment, transfer and/or demotion, etc. The case of university professor Edward Oyugi best illustrates the prize of critical thought in a politically oppressive environment:

[He] ran afoul of President Daniel arap Moi, who saw the universities as a major source of subversion. . . . So, like others among Kenya's best and brightest, Oyugi left the country, for Germany. He returned a year later, when he was allowed to resume his old post at Kenyatta [University], but in 1990, with multiparty fever sweeping the country, he was arrested again, no evidence, just plain harassment. This time charged with trying to overthrow the government. (Richburg, 1997, p. 186)

In spite of politically repressive forces in both the academy and the wider society, hooks contends that "talking back" is a necessary element of claiming one's subjective identity. She maintains that one cannot enter the struggle as an "object" with the intention of emerging as a "subject":

Moving from silence into speech is for the oppressed, the colonized, the exploited, and those who stand and struggle side by side a gesture of defiance that heals, that makes new life and new growth possible. It is that act of speech, of "talking back," that is no mere gesture of empty words, that is the expression of our movement from object to subject— the liberated voice. (1989a, p. 9)

The previous discussion has demonstrated the politics of social definitions of knowledge and the impact on marginalized groups. hooks advocates re-con-ceptualization of knowledge from two primary angles: broadening prevailing curriculum and recognizing alternative ways of being, feeling, and knowing. Notwithstanding the elitism in Kenya's official curriculum, the competitive-ness resulting from a focus on national examinations undermines team spirit among students and exalts the rational over the affective. hooks' critique of a Western and male-oriented curriculum and pedagogical orientations avoids dualisms by honoring the affective as well as the rational in learning environ-ments. What hooks proposes is a broadened canon to include both White and non-White people's cultural histories and traditions. In addition, the issue of the impact of a reification of knowledge from students' lived realities was raised. Moore (1986) demonstrates the impact of the privileging of male forms of knowledge and ways of knowing in her ethnographic study of the Marakwet of Kenya. First, an elitist education grants greater status to rationality (i.e., academic orientations), while simultaneously subordinating experiential knowledge from which students can at least claim a base. Second, given the promotion of racist, sexist, and classist ideologies in educational settings and the wider society, policies and practices tend to reflect values of dominant groups. The legacy of an elitist education inherited from the colonial period plagues Kenya, hindering the development of an agriculturally oriented curriculum. Moore's study (1986) illustrates the validity of hooks' contention based on the Marakwet of Kenya. The patriarchal system privileges masculine ways of being, feeling, and knowing. Sexist attitudes and norms relegate female ways of being, feeling, and knowing to the margins, undermines women's efforts at self-actualization, and exalts masculine traits and characteristics. The following discussion explores the relevance of hooks' advocacy for linking theory to practice.

Linking Theory to Practice

bell hooks' primary premise (1990, 1994b, 1994c) of linking theory to practice is to avoid the reification of official knowledge from contentious issues of race, gender, and sexual biases in educational settings and the wider society. She critiques the fallacy of divorcing theory from practice. In her view, the separation of theory from practice is employed by the academy to

> set up unnecessary and competing hierarchies of thought which reinscribe the politics of domination by designating work as either inferior, superior, or more or less worthy of attention. . . . [Further, it] is evident that one of the many uses of theory in academic locations is in the production of an intellectual class hierarchy where the only work deemed theoretical is work that is highly abstract, jargonistic, difficult to read, and containing obscure references. (1994c, p. 64)

Sheffield's (1973) view of the elitism in Kenyan universities resonates with hooks' contention regarding the intellectual class hierarchy in academic settings.

hooks' (1990, 1994b, 1994c) critique of an elitist education and her proposed strategy for linking theory to practice addresses the issue of an elitist education and alienating school culture both in the United States and in Kenya. In Kenya, the (United Nations Economic and Social Council) UNESCO-sponsored Tananarive Conference (1962, cited in Sheffield, 1973) discouraged an elitist education detached from the society in which it was situated. The recommendations appear to have gone unheeded:

> To the African it appeared as though the West had achieved its power and wealth particularly as a result of its classical education. He did not want a type of education which he felt made him intellectually inferior

and economically subservient, but instead sought an educational parity. (Urch, 1968, p. 252)

Indeed, to the African, Western education promised both financial reward and social prestige. However noble hooks' advocacy for linking theory to practice, the suggestion faces various barriers in a Kenyan context. During the colonial era, academic knowledge was seen as a prerogative of the White people and on rare occasions, the Indians. Sheffield (1973) notes that the three-tier education granted an academic-oriented education greater status in limiting its access to the White settler populations. Sheffield's observation explains the continued gap between theory and practice as manifested in the devaluation of technically based and/or experiential knowledge. Both Lisa Cubbins (1991) and Mwiria (1991) support Sheffield's contention regarding the devaluation of technical and agricultural fields of knowledge. Mwiria argues:

> In keeping with the ideology which stressed the role of the African as that of service of the white man, technical and agricultural (as opposed to academic) education was recommended for Africans by missionaries, colonial authorities and external educational commissions. (Anderson; Sifuna; both cited in Mwiria, 1991, p. 268)

The association of academics with higher intelligence and vocational training with the uneducatable Africans persists in the minds of most Kenyans to this day, which explains why

> [T]he vocational bias of African education, regardless of its motivation, was understandably seen by the Africans as a second-rate, inferior education designed to keep him in his place. . . . Widespread opposition developed among the Africans to the missionary educators' introduction of school gardens, with an emphasis on "traditional" agriculture. (Richburg, 1997, p. 20)

Similarly, Part I of the Ominde Report attributes the resistance of educated youth of Kenya to engaging in agricultural education and, subsequently, agriculturally oriented occupation to a "dissatisfaction with a way of life, bound by traditional social and economic habits, and offering little financial incentive, with which farming was generally associated" (cited in Sheffield, 1973, p. 99). Until agricultural education translates to a higher economic status by way of improved financial remuneration, a Eurocentric, academic-oriented educational system will prevail and enjoy a high social status in African countries (Sheffield, 1973; Stabler, 1969; Urch, 1968):

> When education is adapted, African style, to rural development . . . and when evidence mounts that it is possible to make a decent living on the land, and when young people withdraw from the gamble of finding a job in town as they see there are prizes to be won at home—then, perhaps only then, the political and social pressures for expanding secondary education will decrease. (Stabler, 1969, p. 172)

Only the valuation of an agricultural education could dissuade the African from yearning for a white-collar job and a vision of a good life modeled after a Western European value education system. Meanwhile, though schools seek to inculcate in students the following qualities: (a) mutual respect between parents and children, (b) sensitivity to other's needs and problems, (c) sense of responsibility, (d) sensibility about environmental protection, (e) respect for human dignity and human rights, and (f) devotion to the cause of peace, most students consider math and science more prestigious in contrast to social and cultural studies (Obanya, 1992). Supporting Obanya's observation, Stabler maintains that what belies individual efforts at change is the commonly held belief: "Behind the emphasis on academic standards lies a high regard for scholarship and a belief in the intrinsic value of the liberal arts and sciences" (1969, p. 100). Overall, as hooks argues: "Reinforcing the split between theory and practice . . . [denies] both groups the power of liberatory education for critical consciousness, thereby perpetuating conditions that reinforce our collective exploitation and repression" (1994c, p. 69).

Based on the previous discussions, this author maintains that various factors limit the process of linking theory to practice in a Kenyan educational context. Since its independence, Kenya has endeavored to develop a curriculum reflecting socio-political change: from an initial dependency on Western ideologies and practices to a national identity that reflects indigenous values and experiences. Before independence, White settlers like Huxley advocated: "Children [should] be taught more African history, and more about their African surroundings" (1956, p. 216). What Huxley failed to mention was that her proposed curriculum changes applied only to African schools. In leading European schools, African history, speech, or customs made no appearance in the syllabus (Huxley, 1956). However, Huxley's ideas constitute a noble ideal. Apart from history and social studies curricula (most African schools provide enough avenues to vent one's anger against the bad, "White people," probably less risky than critiquing existing oppressive regimes) and technical subjects, official knowledge is often presented as neutral, objective, devoid of contentious issues of race, class, and/or gender injustices in educational settings and society at large.

The previous discussion provides the complexity of linking theory to practice in a Kenyan context. The historical racial-tiered education relegated the development of practical skills—agriculture and vocational training—to secondary status. The practical-based education was offered to Africans who were perceived as less intellectually inclined. The impact of the colonial subordination of an agriculturally based education is evident in the continued preference for an elitist, academic-oriented education, and white-collar– as opposed to blue-collar–oriented occupations. In the previous part, this author explored three primary ways proposed by hooks (1994c) to empower students in a classroom environment: (a) the image of schools as a learning community, (b) a greater engagement of students in classroom activities, and (c) incorporating students' lived realities in class discussion to make a teaching/learning process more interactive and meaningful. The following discussion explores the relevance of hooks' proposed efforts for student empowerment given Kenya's educational system in its focus on national exams.

Student Empowerment

hooks' concept of a community of learners suggests more than equality in student/teacher relations. She illustrates that students and teachers are equal to the "extent that [they] are equally committed to creating a learning context" (1994c, p. 153). hooks notes the significance of education in Black communities after manumission:

> Within [these] segregated schools, black children who were deemed exceptional, gifted, were given special care. Teachers worked with and for us to ensure that we would fulfill our intellectual destiny and by so doing uplift the race. My teachers were on a mission. (p. 2)

Her proposed strategy of student engagement faces student, parent, and community resistance given the national focus on adequate preparation of students for national examinations. For Kenyan students, doing well on nationally administered exams and, therefore, progressing to the next academic rung is a primary means of escaping a life of poverty and a means for economic advancement. In the majority of cases, education is for social mobility (Miller, 1984).

Reflecting upon her past experience as a student, hooks admits:

Learning early on that good grades were rewarded while independent thinking was regarded with suspicion, I knew that it was important to be "smart" but not too "smart." . . . For a smart child to ask too many questions, to talk about ideas that differed from the prevailing world view, to say things grown Black folks relegated to the realm of the unspeakable was to invite punishment and even abuse. (hooks & West, 1991, p. 149)

Further, hooks argues that most teachers feel wedded to a "conservative banking system of education which encourages professors to believe deep down in the core of their being that they have nothing to learn from their students" (1994c, p. 152). In contrast, hooks' metaphor of schools as learning communities promises greater student engagement in classroom activities, provides an avenue for incorporating students' lived realities to make learning more interactive and meaningful. hooks' engaged pedagogy underscores an understanding of a dynamic teaching/learning process:

Teaching is a performative act. And it is that aspect of our work that offers the space for change, invention, spontaneous shifts, that can serve as a catalyst drawing out the unique elements in each classroom. To embrace the performative aspect of teaching we are compelled to engage "audiences," to consider issues of reciprocity . . . [calling] everyone to become more engaged, to become active participants in learning. (p. 11)

She contrasts an engaged pedagogy to a transfer-of-knowledge pedagogy. hooks (1994c), similar to Freire (1973), argues that the latter best serves the interests of the ruling elite in maintaining the status quo. In Kenya, most school leavers often realize that much "'learning' has been by rote with little competence developed in creative thinking, initiative, problem solving, or technical intuition" (Miller, 1984, p. 79). The fact that most schools in Kenya are characterized by the authoritative rather than an interactive/engaged pedagogy could be attributed to reasons beyond the maintenance of the status quo. Barbara B. Brown (1994) surmises from an international National Council for the Social Studies (NCSS) that the largeness of class sizes and lack of basic materials limit the degree to which schools move from teacher-centered to child-centered pedagogy.

Passive students embody the ideal classroom environment and are the norm in most Kenyan schools. hooks' recount of hierarchical and authoritative social arrangements in the U.S. Southern Black community mirrors most of traditional cultural communities in Kenya, whereby "back talk" and the "talking back" meant speaking as an equal to an authority figure. . . . To make yourself heard of if you were a child was to invite punishment, the back-hand lick, the slap across the face that would catch you unaware, or the feel of switches stinging your arms and legs. (1989a, p. 5)

In Kenya, one may "outgrow" the switches, but never the covert forms of punishment, such as the ostracism that results from a failure to defer to "authority," be it within families or the public/political sphere (Miller, 1984). There are indeed positive and negative repercussions to the process. Besides the maintenance of order and discipline, enforced respect belies individual attempts at critical thought, and subsequently the redress of social injustices. Stabler's illustration highlights the oft-cited benefits of a well-"disciplined" student body:

Classes of forty or more are not uncommon but African children are well behaved, eager to answer, and usually stand up and deliver their answers in complete sentences. They are both less restless and less critical than the precocious sceptics of Britain and America. They give the impression of being glad to be at school, grateful that their parents can pay the 60/yearly fee, and anxious to learn whatever their elders tell them to learn because education and examinations are keys that will unlock the way to a better life. (1969, p. 33)

hooks critiques the veneer of order and contentment in educational settings and the wider society. She associates the fallacy of this deference to "colonization of the mind." Teachers who feel comfortable with a "peaceful" student body are similar in attitude to

White people [who] are much more comfortable with a black person who doesn't ask any direct questions, who acts like they don't know anything—who appears *dumb*—in the same way that men are comfortable with a woman who doesn't appear to have knowledge, strength, [and] power. . . . And when that person becomes empowered, it can totally freak out the people they're with, and around, and work for. (1994b, p. 222; emphasis in original)

hooks' idea (1994c) of education as the practice of freedom takes on a totally different meaning in a Kenyan context. Freedom to most students promises relief from hunger, disease, and ignorance and not necessarily a critical interrogation of injustices embedded in prevailing social structures (Eshiwani, 1990). On the other hand, hooks notes teachers' preference for "order" in classrooms. This often translates to a "safe" environment in which the "professor lectures to a group of quiet students who respond only when they are called on" (1994c, p. 39). This author contends that in politically repressive environments, critical thought is definitely not a primary educational objective. Oginga Odinga noted the uncritical nature of pedagogy in Kenya:

> The teaching in the classrooms stressed memory rather than reasoning, repetition by rote instead of thinking and originality. . . . The purpose of education was not to train for independence but for subservience. (Mwiria, 1991, p. 270)

In Kenya, a critique of the economic exploitation and abuses of power may lead to a criticism of some of the national leaders with dire consequences (Huxley, 1956; Richburg, 1997; Stabler, 1969).

hooks (1994c) advocates the image of schools as learning communities, maintaining that such environments nurture greater interaction between teachers and students. One of the primary aims of hooks' engaged pedagogy is to subvert hierarchical social relations, the privileging of teachers' voices, and the classroom "authority" of students from dominant cultural groups. She argues that the devaluation or rather failure to incorporate students' contributions in classroom discourse maintains and perpetuates domination and colonization by reinforcing the superior image of teachers. The responsibility for enhancing learning by creating a conducive environment rests on both teachers as well as students. hooks maintains that the

> exciting aspect of creating a classroom community where there is respect for individual voices is that there is infinitely more feedback because students feel free to talk—and talk back. And, yes, often this feedback is critical. (1994c, p. 42)

hooks' call for greater learner engagement through increased student participation in classroom discourse is a necessary critique to prevailing pedagogical orientation in most Kenyan schools. Stabler's observation (1969) of a Kenyan "disciplined" and "orderly" classroom may be most teachers' dream class. However, the process of enforced discipline undermines learner engagement and promotes passivity in learners. Further, the focus on students' performances on national exams significantly affects teachers' choices of content and pedagogy:

The learning process is modified to fit the cut-throat competition for high grades in public examinations. The teachers use all the tricks they can to enable their children to perform well in public examinations, including drilling them on how to answer examination questions and giving frequent trial tests, known in Kenya as mock examinations. (Mulusa, 1992, p. 162)

hooks' metaphor of schools as a community of learners that empowers both students and educators could be misconstrued in a Kenyan context. While hooks defines freedom in terms of one's ability to interrogate biases in social policy and practice in materially underprivileged circumstances, freedom could rightly be understood as the absence of hunger, disease, and/or ignorance. hooks needs to clarify the distinction between desirable and undesirable goals in education. Teacher/student focus on preparation for national exams is a collective effort in itself, though this author doubts that this is what hooks had in mind in her conceptualization of collective effort for social transformation. Further, in a politically repressive environment, it may be "safer" not to be too critical of social injustices without guaranteed "protection."

The Kenyan educational system's focus on performance on national examinations determines and shapes official curriculum, pedagogical orientations, and social mobility (Sheffield, 1973). Mwiria contends that the examination ideology was initially established to promote racial inequality:

Examinations were very much part and parcel of the restrictive machinery used by the colonial authorities in Kenya to deny Africans formal education. At the very early stage of their education Africans, unlike other races, had to sit for one of the most competitive selection examinations ever administered in the history of Kenyan education. . . . Out of classes of thirty and more it was not unusual to see only one or two students pass and qualify to proceed to the next level. (1991, p. 265)

Teachers give greater attention and time to memorizing the "subject matter" for examination purposes: "entry to white-collar employment and further technical and professional training was determined by competitive exams which were based on a literary curriculum" (Stabler, 1969, p. 11). Stabler demonstrates the degree of competition involved in progressing from one academic rung to the next:

At the end of primary school all children write the same Kenya Preliminary Examination, preliminary, that is, to secondary education for those who can secure places. At the moment some 10 to 15 percent of primary leavers find places in aided secondary schools, and thus in its importance in deciding a child's future the KPE is little short of the Final Reckoning. (p. 31)

hooks' engaged pedagogy (1994c), based on a community model of learning, advocates student empowerment through greater student engagement, and acknowledgment of the significance of learner experiences in enhancing an integration of subject matter. Underlying hooks' advocacy of student empowerment is the whole notion of dialogue and learner/teacher interaction in an environment of mutual inquiry. This is one of hooks' components of engaged pedagogy that would face considerable obstacles in the Kenyan educational system. Empowering students takes the form of preparing them for exceptional performance on national exams as opposed to involving them in meaning making and/or effecting a greater integration of subject matter to students' lives. Sheffield contends that the "formal system [of education] is highly competitive and has retained its strong academic orientation" (1973, p. 94).

The previous discussion illustrated that hooks' notion (1994c) of education as the practice of freedom and her metaphor of schools as communities of learners could be viewed in a variety of ways. Most Kenyan communities manifest a collective effort in social undertakings because of the cultural emphasis on obligations to associates, family, or kin members. There is indeed a collective effort. The difference, however, is that Kenyan teachers and students would just as readily interpret hooks' injunction regarding a "freeing" education to mean freedom from hunger, disease, and ignorance as opposed to hooks' idea of a development of critical consciousness. It could be argued that Third World nationals are faced with more basic and immediate concerns (Maslow's hierarchy of needs) as opposed to First World nationals. The Kenyan view of progress, which hooks would critique, defines progress in terms of a White supremacist, capitalistic model. Both notions express some form of freedom. The following discussion explores hooks' proposal for policies and practices that accommodate cultural pluralism in educational settings and the wider society.

Multiculturalism

The previous part's discussion on the significance of accommodating cultural pluralism in educational settings and the larger society presented hooks' contention (1990, 1994b, 1994c) regarding sensitivity to cultural pluralism in developing collaboration and solidarity among students. hooks claims that Cultural Study programs provided avenues for transgressing boundaries, in terms of enabling students to "enter passionately a pedagogical process firmly rooted in education for critical consciousness, a place where they felt recognized and included, where they could unite knowledge learned in the classroom with life outside" (1994b, p. 3). Acknowledging a nation's cultural pluralism validates different ways of being, feeling, and knowing not necessarily reflected in mainstream values. The discussion on multiculturalism goes beyond tribal distinctions to encompass race, gender, and class differences.

In Kenya, the colonial government groomed particular tribal groupings, reinforced patriarchy in allocating administrative posts to men rather than women, and finally, created a class structure by granting audience to educated Christians over cultural leaders who may not have been as disposed to White people's cultural values and attitudes (Huxley, 1956; Miller, 1984; Shaw, 1995). The colonial era set a precedent that Africans have brought to full fruition. In contemporary times, one's tribe, and/or specifically the tribe to which the ruling class (most especially the president) belongs, significantly determines the access to economic and political resources beyond what one's educational status prescribes. From his three-year experience as a journalist in Kenya, Richburg contends:

Tribalism remains the single most corrosive, debilitating influence plaguing modern Africa in its quest for democracy and development. To blame Africa's ills on tribalism is a cliché, to be sure. But like many clichés, this one has a basis in truth. (1997, p. 240)

Richburg attributed most of the political instability and economic disparities to tribal contentions. He notes:

Even in a modern state like Kenya, tribal animosities bubble just an inch beneath the surface. The Kikuyu are the largest tribe and until Moi took over, had been at the forefront of the country's independence struggles and its early postcolonial politics. Jomo Kenyatta was a Kikuyu, and he was by all accounts a particularly harsh autocrat, a tribal chieftain of the first order who believed it was the Kikuyus' natural right to rule. Many Kenyans, non-Kikuyu, are deathly fearful of another Kikuyu presidency, and Moi has managed to tap into that fear and present himself as the only alternative. (1997, p. 26)

The observation echoes the history of most continents as the mass media illustrate. In America, it is the old story of Black against White; in the Middle East, it is Arabs against Jews; in Bosnia, it is Christians against Moslems; in Nigeria, it is the Moslems against the Christians, the North against the South; in Kenya, it is the Kikuyu against the Luo or the Kalenjin to which the current president belongs; and in Rwanda, it is the Hutus against the Tutsi.

In Kenya, an acknowledgment of cultural pluralism honors different tribal cultural histories and decenters attention from White people's values and traditions. Affirming formerly subordinated cultural experiences, multiculturalism empowers students from these groupings. Stabler notes:

> if on the first day in school [the student] is asked to put aside his mother tongue and adopt another language for learning, [the student] may be driven to feel that there is something inferior about his language and, perhaps, himself. (1969, p. 39)

To counteract the Eurocentric bias in school culture, hooks (1990) advocates a multicentric curriculum. Huxley urged White settlers in Kenya

> to build up in [the Africans'] mind an idea of the African as a fellow citizen, with his own problems, his own hopes and fears, his own history and traditions, and his own contribution to make to the future of the country whose fortunes they both share. (1956, p. 216)

However, despite such eloquent and noble sentiments and the country's desire to forge a new identity, its social structures continue to reflect the post-colonial academic-oriented education system. Kenya struggles to establish a body of cultural knowledge that reflects and accommodates its cultural diversity (Merryfield, 1989). This is not unlike the United States' contention over a cultural literacy canon. Over and above the propaganda on the significance of Social and Cultural Studies, marketability of math and science skills dictates a hierarchy in academic disciplines (Obanya, 1992).

hooks' advocacy (1994b, 1994c) for accommodating linguistic pluralism in the school's official curriculum despite its questionable feasibility is a relevant issue to Kenya's educational system, whereby English has and continues to function as a business language alongside the national language, Swahili. hooks views the emphasis on Standard English as a form of cultural imperialism. Supporting hooks' thesis, Ngugi Wa Thiong'o maintains that the colonial regime exalted the English language to the level of sacrality; all other languages deferred before it:

In my view language was the most important vehicle through which that power [of the colonizer] fascinated and held the soul prisoner. The bullet was the means of subjugation. Language was the means of spiritual subjugation. (1986, p. 9)

Similarly, Albert Memmi (1965) supports hooks' contention regarding the significance of acknowledging languages other than the colonizer's. The superiority of the colonizer is reinforced through cultural hegemony. The "Master's" language appears to take precedence over tribal languages.

The Binns Report, which tried to ameliorate relations between state and church in education, discouraged the teaching of Swahili, arguing that "its use as a lingua franca impeded the learning of both the vernacular and English" (cited in Sheffield, 1973, p. 46). Following not too far on The Beecher Report, which dealt with the scope, content, and method of African education, and The Binns Report, which sought to promote an Africans-oriented education, the Cambridge Conference (cited in Sheffield, 1973) advocated tribal-language and English-language usage in teaching as early as primary grades. Part I of the Ominde Report (cited in Sheffield, 1973) recommended English as the medium of instruction but made learning Swahili compulsory for the primary school levels. Notwithstanding the contention over the degree of incorporation of Swahili in school curriculum is the whole issue of tribal languages. Kenya is a country with over forty tribal languages (Miller, 1984). The educational system is centrally controlled by the Board of Education and Examination Council. How does one go about developing teaching materials to accommodate tribal pluralism while simultaneously maintaining set educational standards and/or literacy levels? Thomas Mulusa's observation raises a similar issue: "Since most African countries already have difficulties in providing sufficient reading materials in the present official languages, they would have even greater difficulties in trying to develop several languages to be used in the school system" (1992, p. 165).

Presently, most academic textbooks are written in English as are all national exams. Stabler notes:

No one, of course needs to remind a parent that his son or daughter will take the preliminary examination in English at the end of Standard VII, and that his success in that examination will determine whether or not he gets a secondary school place. (1969, p. 44)

The degree to which local languages are incorporated in the national curriculum dates back to the post-colonial era. Similar to hooks' contention regarding the impact of a Western-oriented education on Black and other marginalized cultural groups, Memmi argued for some recognition of the mother tongue: "The entire bureaucracy, the entire court system, all industry hears and uses the colonizer's language. Likewise, highway markings, railroad stations signs, street signs and receipts make the colonized feel like a foreigner in his own country" (1965, p. 107). Further, Urch (1968) predicts that the current Western bias in school subjects will no doubt persist until African writers and researchers emerge to offer an alternative view of reality.

What has limited the promotion of Swahili in schools is the unavailability of textbooks, lack of trained personnel, and the local perception of Swahili as a working- and low-class language (Huxley, 1956; Sheffield, 1973). English retains its aura of privilege as an international medium of communication and the language of instruction in most Kenyan schools. On the other hand, Tanzania, Kenya's neighboring country, has broken this trend in legitimating Swahili as the medium of instruction and subverting tribal divisions and contentions. Richburg points to Tanzania to illustrate the significance of a national language in reducing the degree of tribal factions:

> Under Julius Nyerere and his ruling socialists, the government was able to imbue a true sense of nationalism that transcended the country's natural ethnic divisions, among other things by vigorous campaigns to upgrade education and to make Swahili a truly national language. . . . Tanzania is one place that has succeeded in removing the linguistic barrier that separates so many of Africa's warring factions. (1997, p. 241)

In the previous part this author noted hooks' call for

> recognition of cultural diversity, a rethinking of ways of knowing, a deconstruction of old epistemologies, and the concomitant demand that there be a transformation in our classroom, in how we teach and what we teach. (1994c, p. 30)

Kenya has managed to accomplish, in terms of multiculturalism, an incorporation of African/Black scholarship in Literature and History syllabi (Sheffield, 1973). Jamieson McKenzie (1990) concludes from his educational tour of Kenya that the primary aim of its educational system was to build a just and decent society as opposed to a focus on tests of basic skills. But that is one side of the story. Theoretical ideals do not as readily translate to practical applications. In fact, the late Tom Mboya (cited in Sheffield, 1973) called for changes in the educational system to counteract the colonial psychology and atmosphere characteristic of a system of education that would eliminate the colonial biases by instilling in boys and girls an independent psychology that nurtured students' pride in their cultural uniqueness, their cultural history, and African personality. Mboya's contention is similar to Molefi Asante's (Marriott, 1991) advocacy for an Afrocentric curriculum that affirms Black people's experience in America. What belies efforts aimed at changing the curriculum and/or pedagogical orientations and developing an agriculturally based education (more consistent which an agrarian society, which Kenya is) is that such efforts are seen by students and parents alike to be promoting a "second-rate education, as [the British] had done during the colonial era" (Sheffield, 1973, p. 66).

The previous discussion demonstrated the relevance of hooks' advocacy of a curriculum and pedagogical orientation that reflects a nation's cultural pluralism. She bases her critique on racial differences in America and the manner in which educational policies and practices reinforce White supremacist, patriarchal, and capitalist values. hooks' critique is readily applicable to a Kenyan context, given the prevailing tribal contentions. Tribes have functioned as individual and social definers. Tribal membership significantly determines one's social mobility (Richburg, 1997; Sheffield, 1973; Stabler, 1969). Kenya's system of education faces the challenge of developing a curriculum that is reflective of its tribal pluralism. A multicultural approach to education honors tribal cultural histories and traditions, while simultaneously counteracting racist, sexist, and classist tendencies in educational settings and the wider society. However, Urch (1968) and Mulusa (1992) illustrate the impracticality of honoring tribal pluralism in educational settings because of the limits in resources and existing social policies and practices. The desire for an incorporation of tribal knowledge in the official curriculum hinges on its marketability to corporations. Currently, tribal cultural practices are mostly valued in tourism and tourist-related industries. The following discussion offers an alternative model to the traditional focus on rationality and academic disciplines.

Incorporating Passion

The previous part's discussion on the need to incorporate passion in classrooms raised three main issues: (a) the need to make the classroom experience more exciting, (b) the provision of an education that honors both the affective and the rational aspects of students' lives, and (c) a recognition of interdependence to counteract hierarchical social arrangements. hooks associates the denial of the significance of passion in the academy with Western metaphysical dualism in its subordination of the affective and distinctions of elements in nature. Contrasting Paulo Freire and the Buddhist Thich Nhat

Hanh, hooks asserts: "While Freire was primarily concerned with the mind, Thich Nhat Hanh offered a way of thinking about pedagogy which emphasized wholeness, a union of mind and body, and spirit" (1994c, p. 14). Indeed, hooks admits that the Buddhist's view helped her overcome her socialization to a dualistic thought pattern that pits the rational and the affective in academic settings. She argues that learning is not "just for knowledge in books, but knowledge about how to live in the world" (p. 15).

hooks (1994c) illustrates that the denial of passion in classrooms results in students seeking to recover themselves, their feeling, and passions in "private" places after class. In a country that offers little by way of part-time occupations such as Kenya, academic performance has a tremendous impact on economic and social mobility. hooks' proposal for making education more student centered faces limitations given Kenya's educational system. The competitive nature of the educational system and the scarcity of resources and personnel make individualistic pursuits and an examination-oriented pedagogy inevitable (Miller, 1984). National exams are administered at the end of each calendar year and results are released at the beginning of the preceding year in time for student placement. Schools are ranked and results published in the press on the basis of student performance on National Exams. At the end of an eight-year cycle of primary school, students sit for a national examination on the basis of which 40–45 percent move on to secondary education. Students who fail to qualify for the next academic rung either enter vocational training centers or engage in different forms of employment in the agricultural, typically domestic sector (NIER, 1995; Sheffield, 1973; Stabler, 1969). Miller illustrates the consequences of an exam-oriented educational system in analyzing the "ivory tower" image of universities: "Kenya's university students are an elite. They have survived a grueling series of examinations that have eliminated their former schoolmates" (1984, p. 102). Overall, pedagogy is often driven by national examinations, the availability of resources, and community needs (Merryfield, 1989). Acknowledging the impact of an examination-oriented pedagogy, Stabler notes:

> The anxieties of teachers and students over examination results [have a] profound effect on secondary education. A grim adherence to the syllabus, the working over of old examination papers, and the memorization of dictated notes all become familiar routines. The choice of subjects in most schools was narrow, and practical or vocational subjects had not found a place in the curriculum. (1969, p. 78)

Not surprisingly, most schools focus on academic excellence. Though most schools discourage cramming, school officials recognize the importance of examinations in the lives of students (Stabler, 1969). The underside of the emphasis on grades is that students' exceptional discipline, cooperation, and eagerness in school provide little indication of their desire to acquire knowledge per se. Overall, hooks raises significant issues in encouraging the incorporation of passion in the classroom to avoid the false and unnecessary dichotomy between classroom activities and students' lived realities where interactions are more affective and community oriented.

The previous discussions on the relevance of the components of hooks' engaged pedagogy to a Third World context demonstrated that the problems hooks seeks to address in a United States context are not dissimilar to the problems faced in Third World countries. First, a Western-oriented, elitist knowledge base and school culture have alienated most students whose primary traits and characteristics are at variance with most school norms and practices. Second, the idea of linking theory to practice faces great resistance given Kenya's colonial policies that promoted technical and vocational training for Africans while providing a liberal arts education to the White populations and on occasion the Indians. It was also illustrated that the focus on national tests drives curriculum and pedagogy in most of Kenya's educational systems. This author notes that hooks' idea of "collective effort" and "Education for Freedom" needs to be qualified and/or clarified. There is indeed a collective effort when students and teachers work toward improved performance on national examinations. Further, the notion of education for freedom could in a materially underprivileged environment readily translate to education for freedom from poverty, disease, and ignorance, the Kenyan mantra (Sheffield, 1973). Finally, this author raised the issues of the implications of developing critical consciousness in students in a politically oppressive environment. The following discussion presents the author's reaction to some of hooks' propositions.

CHAPTER 13

Reflections on hooks' Relevance to a Third-World Context

The discussions regarding the relevance of bell hooks' social and educational theories to a Third World context demonstrate the similarities between socio-political issues in Kenya and the United States. The whole notion of a sanctioning of White supremacist attitudes and values and the manner in which these attitudes and values determine and shape policies and practices in educational settings applies to both the United States and Kenyan context. Both countries experienced Western influence in terms of colonization. The prominence of Western civilization, as exhibited by the priority of academic disciplines and a dualistic thought pattern in elements and nature (body/mind, rational/affective, private/public), prevails in both economies.

hooks links the process of coming into a new identity to critical consciousness. She contrasts her notion of "talking back" with marginalized people's speech aimed at explaining, placating, and appeasing: "words that express the fear those in a lower position within a hierarchy have for addressing those in higher positions of authority" (1989a, p. 15). This is a crucial reminder to the African populace, most of whom, for security purposes, look to the West to correct social, economic, and political abuses by political leaders. It is needless to add that this is not an unfounded expectation, the West has on occasion "intervened" to help correct political abuses on the local scene. Keith Richburg's contention resonates with hooks' challenge regarding individual subjectivity and responsibility for correcting social ills:

Africans might start the process, the reexamination, by taking a cold, hard look at themselves. They might begin by looking at their own maddening propensity to accept all kinds of suffering while waiting for some outside deliverance. . . . As a reporter, I saw people take to the streets against authoritarianism and oppression in Haiti, and later in Burma. I got a glimpse of the tail end of the popular protests that changed the system in Korea. . . . But in Africa, it's a rarity to see people take to the streets for their rights. In Africa, there is no People Power. (1997, p. 181)

Kenyans are taking to the streets too. Long schooled in a deference for authority, Kenyans realize the fallacy of depending on self-fulfilling leaders. The casualties and bloodshed from ethnic cleansing rituals incited by more politically powerful ethnic groups testify to the dismissal of democratic charades harboring political maneuvers, oppression, and economic exploitation of the masses by the status quo. Under the guise of ethnic cleansing, houses and property of tribes opposing the mainstream are looted and burned to squelch dissent in the masses as well as curtail unwanted criticism. However, political upheavals all over the African continent demonstrate citizens' discontent with supposedly well-intentioned and paternalistic, though actually self-serving, regimes. Stories abound of political silencing—disappearances, arrests, torture, and sometimes murder of political activists. The doors to most Kenyan universities are closed more months in a year than they are open. Student demonstrations go beyond mere discontent with university conditions. Pressured by exams, disillusioned by the political apparatus, and with few prospects of securing occupations reflective of their academic achievements and sacrifices, university students' unrest mirrors the overall social unrest of many African citizens. Their plight is not unique.

This author agrees with Ira Shor and Paulo Freire's critique (1987) of hooks' idealism (1994c) in its reservation about relying on schools to transform society:

The liberatory approach can create conditions for some illumination, some systematic study . . . [only] organized opposition can achieve these goals. . . . [However,] the dialogical method contradicts the logic of domination, contradicts the dichotomized curriculum, and challenges the social relations of learning which inhibit democracy and critical thought. (1987, p. 138)

Similar to Shor and Freire, Richburg advocates measures that go beyond altering school practices:

Government control over the media needs to be broken, and that especially applies to radio, which most Africans rely on for their news. Security and police forces, now mostly tools of repression, need to be brought under neutral command and control. Election laws that are impartial must be drafted. Voters must be properly registered. Mechanisms must be put in place to monitor funding, to prevent entrenched Big Men from simply printing money to buy votes. (1997, p. 238)

hooks (1990, 1994b, 1994c, 1995b) reiterates the need for an interrogation of "Whiteness" and its impact of the construction of social consciousness in both White and non-White peoples, the definition and/or understanding of individual and social status, the conceptualization of what constitutes knowledge and/or literacy, and determination of social values. The colonial experience left Kenya with a White supremacist legacy that has proved hard to dispel. The entire socio-political bureaucracy reflects Western frameworks. Except for social studies, most schools rely on Western literature (Eshiwani, 1990; Mulusa, 1992; Urch, 1968). No doubt the reliance on Western scholarship reinforces White supremacy. Inadvertently, in reacting to the discriminatory practices during the colonial period most African people adopt self-defeating policies and practices. The denial of the elitist education to Africans during the colonial era has reinforced its superiority/prestige and its demand among most students. The colonial racial tier in education reinforced the marginality of the indigenous people. Subsequently, Kenyan students clamor for a Western elitist education denied the Africans during the colonial period. This author argues that the transformation of prevailing beliefs regarding the social prestige of an elitist over a technically or agriculturally oriented curriculum poses great challenges to the Kenyan economy. Margery Perham (Huxley, 1956) contends that the process involves an acknowledgment of changes in the conceptualization of humanity (both White and non-White) and redefinition of what makes for "proper" living as opposed to an uncritical allegiance to an individualistic, competitive, and materialistic value system.

In raising the issue of race/culture, gender, and class biases, hooks critiques existing ideologies in calling for critical interrogation of the manner in which White supremacacy, patriarchy, and capitalism determine and shape conventional understanding of official knowledge and pedagogy. Her critique illustrates that in reflecting dominant cultural traits and characteristics, institutionalized ideologies privilege particular students while simultaneously marginalizing students whose cultural traits and characteristics are inadequately represented and/or excluded in mainstream values. hooks' critique, similar to critical, feminist, multicultural scholarship, illustrates the link between knowledge and power.

Knowledge and power are intrinsically linked as Henrietta Moore's study (1986) of the Marakwet of Kenya demonstrates. An exclusive representation on policy-making bodies significantly influences the quality and form of decisions that affect other people's lives and self-understanding. Forms of knowledge that are included in the mainstream acquire status while excluded and/or subordinated ways of being, feeling, and knowing remain marginalized. Keith Richburg (1997), James Sheffield (1973), and Ernest Stabler (1969) demonstrate the need for cultural criticism in Kenya. Thirty years after attaining its independence, most of Kenya's schools adhere to the West's educational framework, a process that promotes overt and subtle White supremacy. Further, given its patriarchal system, female-related traits and characteristics are relegated to secondary status. Mutindi Ndunda and Hugh Munby (1991) illustrate the genderization of educational opportunities and privileges in Kenya. Finally, employing material privilege to assess an individual's "success" reinforces a capitalistic value system while under-mining humanistic values such as individual character and virtue, as well as community-building efforts.

As an educator, hooks looks to educational settings to address issues of social injustice. Schools may not solve social problems, but in providing an avenue for intellectual discourse, schools provide a stimulus for action. In critiquing the cult of professionalism, hooks recognizes other forms of knowledge while simultaneously linking theory to practice, academic activities to the lived reality with its race, gender, and class contentions. Further, her critique of conventional representations of "truth" encourage a hermeneutics of suspicion, continued interrogation of ways of being, feeling, and knowing. The discussion illustrated the often subtle, uncritical allegiance of the African to the West and Western institutional frameworks of operation. hooks' association to the West—the American identity over and above her African identity—and her professional status grant her and her social critique a degree of legitimacy. However, hooks as a Black woman would most likely face obstacles that a White male would not in similar circumstances because of Kenya's patriarchal bias.

The following questions require further research: (a) How does one address the issue of "Whiteness"?; (b) Does hooks lay too heavy a burden on education in expecting it to correct unjust social structures?; and (c) What would enhance the effectiveness of the engaged pedagogy theory? It is this author's contention that Kenya, similar to other formerly colonized African countries, needs to address the issue of the impact of colonialism on the national consciousness before embarking on the process of envisioning effective strategies for developing a truly unique national identity. To borrow Moyosore Okediji's terminology (1995), Kenya ought to aim for an auto-hegemonic as opposed to an counter-hegemonic national image.

Epilogue

In Germany they first came for the Communists and I didn't speak up
because I wasn't a Communist. Then they came for the Jews, and I didn't
speak up because I wasn't a Jew. Then they came for the trade unionists,
but I didn't speak up because I wasn't a trade unionist. Then they came
for the Catholics, and I didn't speak up because I was a Protestant. Then
they came for me—by that time no one was left to speak up.

(Adena Peters, 1988, p. 2)

The quotation from one of Pastor Martin Niemoller's speeches after World
War II aptly defines bell hooks, the objective of her corpus of writing, her
teaching assignments, her lectures, and conference presentations. The composition of policy makers significantly impacts social policy and practice. hooks
reiterates that institutions by virtue of their existence enact rules and regulations that typically mirror policy-makers' interests and backgrounds while
simultaneously marginalizing concerns of particular members in society. In this
context, one's values and aspirations determine personal choices and actions.

On an institutional level, decision makers, who have primarily been White,
materially privileged men, establish policies to address issues of more immediate concern to them. In the United States, political and economic power was
for the major part shared among White folk. The trend is reenacted in majority
Black countries in Africa that have been colonized by the West. Thus, "power,"
the ability to influence other people's lives, was and continues to be executed

by White privileged males. In a country such as Kenya, the ruling tribe acquires the social status that is the prerogative of White males in the Western world. (In patriarchal societies, a degree of power is invested in males irrespective of race and/or class.) Further, when the dominant group's cultural traits and characteristics are sanctioned and exalted as the norm, the group in possession of the traits takes on an "aura" of superiority, the traits and characteristics presented as assimilation ideals. The "reverence" for White people and related traits and characteristics provides clear evidence of this. This raises another issue. Most African countries have by now gained political independence and yet continue in their "reverence" for "Whiteness," even though most nationals would claim that one of the primary aims of political independence was to shake off the White man's shackles.

hooks speaks for individuals and groups marginalized by virtue of race/culture, gender, and/or class. This author finds the following issues of marginality raised by hooks commendable, insightful, and challenging. Undergirding hooks' interrogation of each of the marginalizing elements are mass media representations, the portrayal of different cultural groups, and the manner in which the representations determine and shape social consciousness. The underside of this process is the subordination and/or subjugation of cultural groups—non-White, females, and the materially underprivileged. A sense of cultural superiority, what hooks terms White supremacy, is reinforced in cultural groups—White, male, and/or middle and upper class—whose traits are reflected and promoted in mainstream values. Thus, the maintenance of racist attitudes in mainstream America over and above the fallacy of racial equality and democratic ideals promoted by the American and/or for that matter the Kenyan constitution is borne out by the experiences of marginalized groups and, as bell hooks put it, those who stand side by side with us in the struggle. Ironically, Michele Wallace (1995a, 1995b) is vehemently opposed to hooks as a champion for the marginalized. In her view, hooks is a self-proclaimed spokesperson with little credibility as a scholar. Wallace (1995b) contrasts hooks' path with the high road, intellectual/creative route traveled by scholars who have carved their path with every step earned and copiously contextualized such as Alice Walker, Toni Morrison, and Toni Cade Bambara. The low road,

> the gospel according to bell hooks firmly in hand, the path etched in the vertiginous stone of rhetoric, hyperbole, generalizations, platitudes, bad faith, phony, prophetism, and blanket condemnation. (1995b, p. 23)

hooks' insistence on the need to interrogate "Whiteness" is an issue this author has grappled with in the research process, never having reflected on "Whiteness" beyond White people and colonialism in the African continent. Reading hooks' writings has led the author to develop a "hermeneutics of suspicion." This author is critical of issues and understandings previously taken for granted, more reflective of the significance of personal choices and those which reinforce belief systems of domination and those which support a greater appreciation of "Blackness." hooks' corpus of work makes one question personal and communal decisions, most of which are taken for granted, including conventional norms, the power of metaphor and imagery, and institutionalized ideologies and their impact of social consciousness.

The research process has led this author to conclude that a lot of issues raised by hooks are applicable to a Third World context. hooks' analysis of the United States resonates with cited literature on the Kenyan situation in terms of cultural, gender, and class biases. hooks, similar to Paulo Freire, recognizes the dual role of education, either as legitimating existing institutions and/or providing intellectual avenues for addressing the "hard" questions of life and within society. The research findings demonstrated the fallacy of equity and/or democracy in educational settings and the wider society. Essentially, social institutions, as state apparatus, reflect national policy and practice, even when the social values and practices marginalize non-White, female, and materially underprivileged members of the community. hooks' critique of the focus on White people's cultural histories and traditions in genderized educational practices and the association of social prestige to material acquisitions applies to both Kenya and the United States. What hooks' engaged pedagogy avoids is the whole notion of schizophrenic scholars—students whose lived realities have little if any connection to classroom learning. Torn between two loyalties, these students maintain lives of two existences. These students' primary cultural traits and characteristics are subordinated by the dominant culture. Thus, denying what comes naturally to them, the students yearn, and they attempt to embody an existence that brings little affirmation or accommodation. Cast between a rejected past and longing for an unwelcoming future, students struggle to integrate the two realities while simultaneously grappling with what the official curriculum has to offer.

The whole premise of hooks' engaged pedagogy is the development of critical consciousness. The emphasis on one's ability to interrogate and transform one's social consciousness and ultimately one's material conditions assumes a constitutional backing of a freedom of speech, which the United States can boast of unlike most other countries. hooks' engaged pedagogy presumes the right of people to free speech. This author argues that the assumption of a freedom of speech (often stated in print), as a "basic" human right, is not a lived reality in most countries. Similarly, political oppression, what hooks (1990, 1994b, 1995b) terms *dominations*, not only undermines the rights of certain groups but reinforces social, political, and economic inequalities by providing a justifiable rationale for the state of affairs (Freire, 1970/1992; hooks, 1990, 1994b, 1995b). "Oppression" not only justifies the existence of a particular social order, it enforces the existing order. This author argues that the politically oppressive environment by its very nature undermines the whole premise of hooks' engaged pedagogy. Most countries establish policies and engage in practices that maintain the social order through officially instituted mechanisms and/or undercover practices. In Kenya, "silence" and obedience to authority and/or one's elders is the norm of the day both during the colonial era and contemporary times with African leadership. Notwithstanding the cultural norm of loyalty and allegiance in most Third World traditional communities, critics (labeled political dissenters) of prevailing systems often "find" themselves on the wrong side of the law for what may amount to trumped-up charges (try proving the contrary) but which determine one's future prospects, if one lives long enough to worry about one's future.

This author contends that the idea that "it's anybody else's fault but mine" is not only escapist but self-defeating. The issue ought to be not so much who is the more guilty party, but rather what needs to be done to right the historical injustice. A wider range of literature by Kenyan scholars (except those in exile) provides a litany of the ills of the White man, most especially during the colonial period. As a native of the country, this author would like to think that it is more for security reasons, than that we, as Kenyans, fail to be more critical of our "own." Or is it perhaps that dirty linen is best kept in closets, away from company. It could also be that historical detachment allows one a level of objectivity unequaled at closer, and in more immediate, circumstances.

In sum, the study has been enlightening though disturbing. This author often wonders what it is about human nature that seems to desire some form of privilege over another being. The dualisms and hierarchical conception of elements and entities in Western metaphysical thought have had a profound impact on the understanding of humanity, life, progress, and intellectualism. This raises another issue. Most African countries have by now gained independence and yet the persistence of the reverence for "Whiteness" persists in social consciousness, even though most nationals would claim that a primary aim of political independence was to shake off the White man's shackles. What the author found most overwhelming was the negation of Blackness. hooks' engaged pedagogy provides possible strategies for social injustices through educational policies and practices. Further research is called for to assess the impact of White supremacy on Black people's psyches, and the process of decolonizing the colonized. Not unlike Ngugi Wa Thiong'o (1986, 1993), the Kenyan cultural critic, hooks surmises:

> The system of white-supremacist capitalistic patriarchy is not maintained solely by white folks. It is also maintained by all the rest of us who internalize and enforce the values of this regime. This means that black people must be held accountable when we do not make the needed critical interventions that would create the "revolution in vision." (1995a, p. xii)

Not underrating the disparities in the situation of the colonized Blacks in the United States and Kenyans, the parallels in cultural and political experiences of both groups as subjects of a white politically and economically dominant rule allows some sort of comparison and application of emerging frameworks of cultural pluralism in America. hooks' social and educational critique provide a necessary framework for analyzing existing structures despite the chronicled limitations to a wholesale application of engaged pedagogy to a Third-World context. Decolonization of the mind involves first and foremost an acknowledgment of our complicity as marginalized people in legitimating and promoting oppressive structures and practices. Subsequently, integrating formerly subordinated ways of being, feeling, and knowing to official school curricula creates a forum for critiquing cultural and political biases as well as envisioning a more democratic system, an aim increasingly espoused by most societies. Undoubtedly, this poses the arduous task of continual reflection and action on an individual as well as collective level. The commitment to bell hooks' engaged pedagogy and its primary aim of developing critical consciousness is both a challenge and hope for any marginalized group irrespective of location.

References

Alston, Kal. (1995). The difference we make: Philosophy of Education and the Tower of Babel. In Wendy Kohli, ed., *Critical Conversations in Philosophy of Education* (pp. 278–297). New York: Routledge.

American Council of Education, Education Commission of the United States. (1988). *One third of a nation. A report of the Commission on Minority Participation in Education and American life.* Washington, DC: American Council on Education.

Archdeacon, Thomas J. (1983). *Becoming an American: An ethnic history.* New York: The Free Press.

Arcilla, René V. (1995). For the stranger in my home: Self-knowledge, cultural recognition, and philosophy of education. In Wendy Kohli, ed., *Critical conversations in philosophy of education* (pp. 159–172). New York: Routledge.

Aronowitz, Stanley, & Giroux, Henry A. (1988, May). Schooling, culture, and literacy in the age of broken dreams: A review of Bloom and Hirsch. *Harvard Educational Review* 95(2), 172–194.

———. (1991). *Postmodern education: Politics, culture, and social criticism.* Minneapolis, MN: University of Minnesota Press.

Banks, James A. (1988). *Multiethnic education: Theory and practice* (2nd ed.). Boston: Allyn and Bacon.

Belenky, Mary F., Clinchy, Blythe M., Goldberger, Nancy R., & Tarule, Jill M. (1986). *Women's ways of knowing: The development of self, voice, and mind.* New York: Basic Books.

Berry, Mary F., & Blassingame, John W. (1982). *Long memory: The Black experience in America*. New York: Oxford University Press.

Beyer, Landon E. (1995). Beyond the formal and psychological: The arts and social possibility. In Wendy Kohli, ed., *Critical conversations in philosophy of education* (pp. 258–277). New York: Routledge.

Bloom, Allan. (1987). *The closing of the American mind*. New York: Schuster.

Bowers, C. (1995). Toward an ecological perspective. In W. Kohli, ed., *Critical conversations in philosophy of education* (pp. 310–323). New York: Routledge.

Bradshaw, York W. (1993, December). State limitations, self-help secondary schooling, and development in Kenya. *Social Forces* 72(2), 347–378.

Bradshaw, York W., & Fuller, Bruce. (1996, June). Policy action and school demand in Kenya. *International Journal of Comparative Sociology* 37(1–2), 72–76.

Brown, B. B. (1994, October). Africa: Myth and reality. *Social Education* 58(6), 374–375.

Brown, E. B. (1989, Summer). African-American women's quilting: A framework for conceptualizing and teaching African-American history. *Signs* 14(4), 921–929.

Burbules, N. C. (1995). Reasonable doubt: Toward a postmodern defense of reason as an educational aim. In Wendy Kohli, ed., *Critical conversations in philosophy of education* (pp. 82–102). New York: Routledge.

Cassara, B. B., & Reche, G. N. (1990, June). Traditional adult education in Kenya: Some thoughts for today's world. *Adult Learning* 8(8), 14–15.

Cham, Mbye. (1994, Fall). African women and cinema: A conversation with Anne Mwangi. *Research in African Literatures* 25(3), 93+.

Champagne, John Gerard. (1993). *The ethics of transgression: Criticism and cultural marginality*. Unpublished doctoral dissertation, University of Pittsburgh, Pennsylvania.

Cheru, Fantu. (1987). *Dependence, underdevelopment and unemployment in Kenya: School leavers in peripheral capitalistic economy*. Lanham, MD: University Press of America.

Chesaina, Ciarunji. (1994). The development of women's studies in Kenya. *Women's Studies Quarterly* 3 & 4, 180–196.

Collins, E. (1994). Intellectuals, power and quality television. In Henry A. Giroux & Peter McLaren, eds., *Between borders: Pedagogy and the politics of cultural studies* (pp. 56–73). New York: Routledge.

Cooper, Constance M. (1994). *Race and gender: The question of authorship in African-American women's history*. Unpublished doctoral dissertation, University of Windsor, Ontario, Canada.

Covi, Giovanna. (1996). *The slow process of decolonizing language: The politics of sexual differences in postmodernist fiction*. Unpublished doctoral dissertation, State University of New York at Binghamton.

Coyle, Sandra Mcleod. (1996). *Bringing bell hooks to the classroom: Toward an understanding of "intellectual work" and its relationship to process.* Unpublished doctoral dissertation, University of South Carolina, Columbia, South Carolina.

Craib, Ian. (1984). *Modern social theory: From Parsons to Habermas.* New York: St. Martin's Press.

Craig, Stephen R. (1992). The effects of television day part on gender portrayals in television commercials: A context analysis. *Sex Roles* 26(5/6), 197–211.

Cubbins, Lisa A. (1991, June). Women, men, and the division of power: A study of gender stratification in Kenya. *Social Forces* 69(4), 1063–1083.

Dewey, John. (1902). *The school and society.* Chicago: University of Chicago Press.

———. (1916). *Democracy and education.* New York: Macmillan.

———. (1963). *Experience and education.* New York: Collier. (Original work published 1938).

Donovan, Kathleen M. (1994). *Coming to voice: Native American literature and feminist theory.* Unpublished doctoral dissertation, University of Arizona, Tucson.

D'Souza, Dinesh. (1992). *Illiberal education.* New York: Vintage Books.

Dworkin, Martin S. (1959). *Dewey on education: Selections.* New York: Teachers College Press.

Eddowes, J. R. (1988). *Role and status continuity: A study of the aging women in traditional Samburu society.* Philadelphia: University of Pennsylvania. (ERIC Document Reproduction Service No. ED 314 325).

Education, the key to a better life: Education of girls promotes economic growth and reduces poverty. (1994, May 20). *The Weekly Review*, pp. 24–25.

Elias, John L., & Merriam, Sharon (1980). *Philosophical foundations of adult religious education.* Malabar, FL: Robert E. Kreiger.

Erikson, Kim. (1997, May/June). Make-up call. *The Environmental Magazine* 8(3), 42–43.

Eshiwani, G. S. (1990). *Implementing educational policies in Kenya* (World Bank Discussion Papers, African Technical Department Series). Washington, DC: World Bank.

Faichney, Gavin (1994, October). Educating and challenging the world. *Social Education*, 58(6), 372–374.

Famighetti, R. (1996). *The world almanac and book of facts 1996.* Mahwah, NJ: Funk & Wagnalls.

Feinberg, Walter. (1995). The discourse of philosophy of education. In Wendy Kohli, ed., *Critical conversations in philosophy of education* (pp. 24–33). New York: Routledge.

Feinberg, Walter, & Soltis, Jonas F. (1992). *School and society* (2nd ed.). New York: Teachers College Press.

Fordham, Signithia. (1996). *Blacked out: Dilemmas of race, identity, and success at Capital Hill.* Chicago: University of Chicago Press.

Fox, Tom. (1994). Literacy and activism: A response to bell hooks. In Gary A. Olson, ed., *Philosophy, rhetoric, literary criticism: (Inter)views* (pp. 105–111). Carbondale, IL: Southern Illinois University.

Fraser, Nancy. (1994). Rethinking the public sphere: A contribution to the critique of actually existing democracy. In *Between borders: Pedagogy and the politics of cultural studies* (pp. 74–100). New York: Routledge.

Freire, Paulo. (1973). *Education for critical consciousness.* New York: The Seabury Press.

———. (1992). *Pedagogy of the oppressed* (M. Bergman Ramos, trans.). New York: Continuum. (Work originally published 1970).

Freire, Paulo, & Faundez, Antonio. (1989). *Learning to question: A pedagogy of liberation.* New York: Continuum.

Fullan, Michael. (1976). *The meaning of educational change.* New York: Teachers College Press.

Fuller, John G. (1972). *Two hundred million guinea pigs.* New York: G. P. Putnam's Sons.

Fuss, Diana. (1989). *Essentially speaking: Feminism, nature, and difference.* New York: Routledge.

Giarelli, James M. (1995). Educating for public life. In Wendy Kohli, ed., *Critical conversations in philosophy of education* (pp. 201–216). New York: Routledge.

Giroux, Henry A. (1983). *Theory and resistance in education: A pedagogy for the opposition.* Boston, MA: Bergin & Garvey.

———. (1994a). Living dangerously: Identity, politics and the new cultural racism. In Henry A. Giroux & Peter McLaren, eds., *Between borders: Pedagogy and the politics of cultural studies* (pp. 29–55). New York: Routledge.

———. (1994b). Reading texts, literacy, and textual authority. In D. H. Richter, ed., *Falling into theory: Conflicting views on reading literature* (pp. 63–74). Boston: Bedford Books of St. Martin's Press.

Giroux, Henry A., & McLaren, Peter, eds. (1994). *Between borders: Pedagogy and the politics of cultural studies.* New York: Routledge.

Giroux, Henry A., & Simon, Roger. (1989). *Popular culture, schooling and everyday life.* Granby, MA: Bergin & Garvey.

Goodlad, John I. (1984). *A place called school: Prospects for the future.* New York: McGraw-Hill.

Greene, Maxine (1995). What counts as philosophy of education? In Wendy Kohli, ed., *Critical conversations in philosophy of education* (pp. 3–23). New York: Routledge.

Grossberg, Lawrence. (1994). Introduction: Bringin' it all back home—Pedagogy and cultural studies. In Henry A. Giroux & Peter McLaren, eds., *Between borders: Pedagogy and the politics of cultural studies* (pp. 1–25). New York: Routledge.

Harris, Kevin. (1995). Educating for citizenship. In Wendy Kohli, ed., *Critical conversations in philosophy of education* (pp. 217–228). New York: Routledge.

Havinghurst, Robert J., & Neugarten, Bernice L. (1992). *Society and education* (8th ed.). Boston: Allyn & Bacon.

Haywood, Chanta Mariena. (1995). *Prophesying daughters: Nineteenth-century Black women preachers, religious conviction and resistance.* Unpublished doctoral dissertation, University of California, San Diego.

Hirsch, Eric Donald. (1987). *Cultural literacy: What every American needs to know.* Boston: Houghton Mifflin.

hooks, bell. (1981). *Ain't I a woman: Black women and feminism.* Boston, MA: South End Press.

———. (1984). *Feminist theory: From margin to center.* Boston, MA: South End Press.

———. (1989a). *Talking back: Thinking feminist, thinking Black.* Boston, MA: South End Press.

———. (1989b, Spring-Summer). Writing from the darkness. *Tri-Quarterly* (75), 71–77.

———. (1990). *Yearning: Race, gender and cultural politics.* Boston: South End Press.

———. (1992). *Black looks: Race and representation.* Boston: South End Press.

———. (1993). *Sisters of the yam: Black women and self-recovery.* Boston: South End Press.

———. (1994a). Eros, eroticism and the pedagogical process. In Henry A. Giroux & Peter McLaren, eds., *Between borders: Pedagogy and the politics of cultural studies* (pp. 113–118). New York: Routledge.

———. (1994b). *Outlaw culture: Resisting representations.* New York: Routledge.

———. (1994c). *Teaching to transgress: Education as the practice of freedom.* New York: Routledge.

———. (1994d). Toward a revolutionary feminist pedagogy. In David H. Richter, ed., *Falling into theory: Conflicting views on reading literature* (pp. 74–79). Boston: Bedford Books of St. Martin's Press.

———. (1995a). *Art on my mind: Visual politics.* New York: The New Press.

———. (1995b). *Killing rage: Ending racism.* New York: Henry Holt.

———. (1996a). *Bone Black: Memories of childhood.* New York: Henry Holt.

———. (1996b). *Reel to real: Race, sex, and class at the movies.* New York: Routledge.

hooks, bell, & West, Cornel. (1991). *Breaking bread: Insurgent Black intellectual life.* Boston: South End Press.

Huxley, Elspeth J. G. (1956). *Race and politics in Kenya: A correspondence between Elspeth Huxley and Margery Perham.* London: Faber & Faber.

Jacobson, Jodi L. (1992, September). *Gender bias: Roadblock to sustainable development.* Worldwatch paper 110.

Jaeger, Richard M., ed. (1988). *Complementary methods for research in education.* Washington, DC: American Educational Research Association.

Janmohamed, Abdul. (1994). Some implications for Freire's border pedagogy. In Henry A. Giroux & Peter McLaren, eds. *Between borders: Pedagogy and the politics of cultural studies* (pp. 225–241). New York: Routledge.

Johnson, Elizabeth. (1992). *She who is: The mystery of God in feminist theological discourse.* New York: Crossroads.

Kallet, Arthur & Schlink, F. J. (1976). *One hundred million guinea pigs: Dangers in everyday foods, drugs, and cosmetics.* New York: Ayer.

Kaplan, Abraham. (1964). *The conduct of inquiry: Methodology for behavioral science.* San Francisco: Chandler.

Kohli, Wendy. (1995a). Educating for emancipatory rationality. In W. Kohli, ed., *Critical conversations in philosophy of education* (pp. 103–115). New York: Routledge.

————, ed. (1995b). *Critical conversations in philosophy of education.* New York: Routledge.

Kozol, Jonathan. (1991). *Savage inequalities: Children in America's schools.* New York: Crown.

Kristof, Nicholas D. (1997, May 25). Why Africa can thrive like Asia. *The New York Times,* pp. 1, 4.

Leach, Mary S. (1995). Turning tricks. In Wendy Kohli, ed., *Critical conversations in philosophy of education* (pp. 355–363). New York: Routledge.

Leen, Mary. (1995). *Theories of storytelling: Surviving the gaps and rhythms of migration in the gift of homeplace.* Unpublished doctoral dissertation, Illinois State University, Normal.

Lentricchia, Frank. (1983). *Criticism and social change.* Chicago, IL: University of Chicago Press.

Lorde, Audre. (1984). *Sister outsider.* Trumansburgh, NY: The Crossing Press.

Making Education Meaningful. (1994, May 27). *The Weekly Review,* pp. 24–29.

Marriott, Michel. (1991, November 11). Afrocentrism: Balancing or skewing history? *The New York Times,* pp. 1, 18.

Martin, Jane R. (1984, Fall). Bringing women into educational thought. *Educational Theory* 34(4), 341–353.

————. (1989, March). The 3Cs plus the 3Rs: Reeducating our children in the womanly qualities. *Radclife Quarterly,* pp. 10–11.

————. (1992). *The schoolhome: Rethinking schools for changing families.* Cambridge, MA: Harvard University Press.

————. (1995). Educating for domestic tranquility in critical theory. In Wendy Kohli, ed., *Critical conversations in philosophy of education* (pp. 45–55). New York: Routledge.

McCarthy, Cameron, & Apple, Michael W. (1988). Race, class, and gender in American education research: Toward a nonsynchronous parallelist position. In Lois Weis, ed., *Class, race and gender in American education* (pp. 9–31). Albany, NY: State University of New York Press.

McGhee, Paul E. & Freuh, Terry. (1980). Television viewing and the learning of sex-role stereotypes. *Sex Roles* 6(2), 179–188.

McGinnis, K. (1995, March). Settling down in a new place. *Pace* (24), 21–27.

McKenzie, Jamieson A. (1990, October). An educational safari. *Phi Delta Kappan* 72(2), 156.

McKinley Jr., James C. (1997a, July 8). Crackdown bleeds Kenya's democracy movement. *The New York Times,* p. 3.

———. (1997b, August, 3). A woman to run Kenya? One says, 'Why not?' *The New York Times,* p. 3.

McLaren, P. (1989). *Life in schools.* White Plains, NY: Longman.

———. (1994). Multiculturalism and the postmodern critique: Toward a pedagogy of resistance and transformation. In Henry A. Giroux & Peter McLaren, eds., *Between borders: Pedagogy and the politics of cultural studies* (pp. 192–222). New York: Routledge.

McNaught, Sandra Elaine Cole. (1996). *Alterity/identity: A postcolonial critique of educational policies and practices in the United States.* Unpublished doctoral dissertation, University of Miami, Oxford, Ohio.

Memmi, Albert. (1965). *The colonizer and the colonized.* Boston: Beacon Press.

Menand, Louis. (1994). What are universities for? In David H. Richter, ed., *Falling into theory: Conflicting views on reading literature* (pp. 88–105). Boston: Bedford Books of St. Martin's Press.

Meriwether, James Scaite, III (1993, June). *Unity, duality, and multiplicity: Toward a model for post-modernism.* Unpublished doctoral dissertation, Florida State University, Tallahassee.

Merryfield, Merry M. (1989, November). *Cultural literacy and African education.* Paper presented at the 32nd annual conference of the African Studies Association, Atlanta, GA. (ERIC Document Reproduction Service No. ED 319 663).

———. (1996, November-December). The process of Africanizing the social studies. *Social Studies* 86(6), 260–269.

Middleton, Joyce Irene (1994). bell hooks on literacy and teaching: A response to bell hooks. In Gary A. Olson, ed., *Philosophy, rhetoric, literary criticism: (Inter)views* (pp. 100–104). Carbondale, IL: Southern Illinois University.

Miller, Mark Crispin. (1988) *Boxed in: The culture of TV.* De Kalb, IL: Northern Illinois University Press.

Miller, Norman N. (1984). *Kenya: The quest for prosperity.* Boulder, CO: Westview Press.

Mills, Chester St. H. & Caisson, Rebecca A. (1996). In Mary Cross, ed., *Advertising and culture: Theoretical perspectives* (pp. 113–124). Westport, CT: Praeger.

The Ministry of Education. (1994). *Education in Kenya: Information handbook.* Nairobi, Kenya: The Ministry of Education.

Minnich, Elizabeth K. (1990). *Transforming knowledge.* Philadelphia: Temple University Press.

Mohanty, Chandra T. (1994). On race and voice: Challenges for liberal education in the 1990s. In Henry A. Giroux & Peter McLaren, eds., *Between borders: Pedagogy and the politics of cultural studies* (pp. 145–166). New York: Routledge.

Moore, Henrietta L. (1986). *Space, text and gender: An anthropological study of the Marakwet of Kenya.* New York: Press Syndicate of the University of Cambridge.

Morrow, Raymond Allan, & Torres, Carlos Alberto. (1995). *Social theory and education: A critique of theories of social and cultural reproduction.* Albany, NY: State University of New York Press.

Mulusa, T. (1992). Pluralistic education in Sub-Sahara Africa: An overview. *Prospects* 22(2), 159–170.

Mwangi, Mary W. (1996). Gender roles portrayed in Kenyan television commercials. *Sex Roles* 34 (3/4).

Mwiria, K. (1991, September). Education for subordination: African education in colonial Kenya. *History of Education* 20(3), 261–273.

———. (1993, May). Kenyan women adult literacy learners: Why their motivation is difficult to sustain. *International Review of Education* 39(3), 183–192.

National Institute for Educational Research (NIER), Tokyo, Japan. (1995, September). *Educational reform and educational research: New challenges in linking research information and decision-making.* Document summary of proceedings of a meeting held in Tokyo, Japan. (ERIC Document Reproduction Service No. ED 393 196).

Ndunda, Mutindi, & Munby, Hugh. (1991, November). "Because I am a woman": A study of culture, school, and futures in science. *Science Education* 75(6), 683–699.

Nelson, Jack L., Carlson, Kenneth, & Palousky, Stuart B. (1996). *Critical issues in education: A dialectical approach.* New York: McGraw-Hill.

Ngugi Wa Thiong'o. (1986). *Decolonizing the mind: The politics of language in African literature.* Portsmouth, NH: Heinemann Educational Books.

———. (1993). *Moving the centre: The struggle for cultural freedoms.* Portsmouth, NH: Heinemann Educational Books.

Nieto, Sonia. (1996). *Affirming diversity: The sociopolitical context of multicultural education* (2nd ed.). White Plains, NY: Longman.

Noddings, N. (1984). *Caring: A feminine approach to ethics and moral education.* Berkeley, CA: University of California Press.

———. (1992). *The challenge to care in schools: An alternative approach to education.* New York: Teachers College Press.

———. (1995a). Care and moral education. In Wendy Kohli, ed., *Critical conversations in philosophy of education* (pp. 137–148). New York: Routledge.

———. (1995b). *Philosophy of education.* Boulder, CO: Westview Press.

Obanya, P.A.J. (1992, August). *Education and cultural development: Policies and practices in the African region.* Paper presented at the 43rd International conference on Education, Geneva, Switzerland. (ERIC Document Reproduction Service No. ED 369 704).

Obura, Anna P. (1991). *Changing images: Portrayal of girls and women in Kenyan textbooks.* Nairobi: African Centre for Technology Studies (ACTS) Press.

Ogbu, John U. (1992, November). Understanding cultural diversity and learning. *Educational Researcher,* pp. 5–14, 24.

Ohmann, Richard. (1996). *Selling culture: Magazines, markets, and class at the turn of the century.* New York: Version.

Okediji, Moyosore Benjamin. (1995). *Semiopotics of anamnesia: Yoruba images in the works of Jeff Donaldson, Howardena Pindell and Muneer Bahauddeen.* Unpublished doctoral dissertation, the University of Wisconsin, Madison.

Olson, Gary A., ed. (1994). *Philosophy, rhetoric, literary criticism: (Inter)views.* Carbondale, IL: Southern Illinois University.

Pagano Jo Anne. (1995). Matters of the mind. In Wendy Kohli, ed., *Critical conversations in philosophy of education* (pp. 340–354). New York: Routledge.

Perkinson, Henry J. (1991). *The imperfect panacea: American faith in education (1965–1990)* (3rd ed.). New York: McGraw-Hill.

Peters, Adena. (1988, July-September). Niemoller and the Nazis. In Israel Gutman, ed., *The Encyclopedia of the Holocaust* (Vol. 3, pp. 2–3). New York: Macmillan.

Phillips, D. C. (1995). Counting down through the millenium. In Wendy Kohli, ed., *Critical conversations in philosophy of education* (pp. 34–42). New York: Routledge.

Popkewitz, Thomas S. (1991). *A political sociology of educational reform: Power knowledge in teaching, teacher education, and research.* New York: Teachers College Press.

Pursuing non-sexual images. (1994, May 20). *The Weekly Review,* pp. 23–24.

Richburg, Keith B. (1997). *Out of America: A Black man confronts Africa.* New York: Basic Books.

Richter, David H., ed. (1994). *Falling into theory: Conflicting views on reading literature.* Boston: Bedford Books of St. Martin's Press.

Riphenburg, Carol. (1997). Women's status and cultural expression: Changing gender relations and structural adjustment in Zimbabwe. *Africa Today* 4(1), 33–50.

Robertson, Emily. (1995). Reconceiving reason. In W. Kohli, ed. *Critical conversations in philosophy of education* (pp. 116–126). New York: Routledge.

Ross, Andrew. (1989). Hip, and the long front of color. In Andrew Ross, ed., *No Respect: Intellectuals and Popular Culture.* New York: Routledge.

Ryle, Gilbert. (1949). *The concept of the mind.* London: Hutchinson's University Library.

Scapp, Ronald M. (1990). *A question of voice: The search for legitimacy.* Unpublished doctoral dissertation, State University of New York at Stony Brook.

Schuyler, Sarah Elizabeth (1990). *Running hot and cold: A cultural history of late-modern bodies.* Unpublished doctoral dissertation, University of Washington, Seattle.

Sergiovanni, Thomas L. (1987). *The principalship: A reflective practice perspective.* Boston: Allyn & Bacon.

———. (1990). *Value-added leadership: How to get extraordinary performance in schools.* San Diego, CA: Harcourt Brace Jovanovich.

———. (1992). *Moral leadership: Getting to the heart of school improvement.* San Francisco: Jossey-Bass.

Shaw, Carolyn M. (1995). *Colonial inscriptions: Race, sex, and class in Kenya.* Minneapolis, MN: University of Minnesota Press.

Sheffield, James R. (1973). *Education in Kenya: An historical study.* New York: Teachers College Press.

Shor, Ira. (1992). *Empowering education: Critical teaching for social change.* Chicago: The University of Chicago Press.

Shor, Ira, & Freire, Paulo. (1987). *A pedagogy for liberation: Dialogues on transforming education.* South Hadley, MA: Bergin & Garvey.

Siegel, Harvey. (1995). Knowledge and certainty: Feminism, postmodernism, and multiculturalism. In Wendy Kohli, ed., *Critical conversations in philosophy of education* (pp. 190–200). New York: Routledge.

Simon, Roger I. (1994). Forms of insurgence in the production of popular memories: The Columbus quincentenary and the pedagogy of countermemoration. In Henry A. Giroux & Peter McLaren, eds., *Between borders: Pedagogy and the politics of cultural studies* (pp. 172–142). New York: Routledge.

Soltis, J. F. (1978). *An introduction to the analysis of cultural studies* (2nd ed.). Reading, MA: Addison-Wesley.

Spelman, E. (1988). *Inessential woman.* Boston: Beacon Press.

Spring, Joel. (1978). *American education: An introduction to social and political aspects.* New York: Longman.

———. (1994). *Deculturalization and the struggle for equality.* New York: McGraw-Hill.

Stabler, Ernest. (1969). *Education since Uhuru: The schools of Kenya.* Middletown, CT: Wesleyan University Press.

Starratt, Robert J. (1990). *The drama of schooling: The schooling of drama.* London: The Falmer Press.

———. (1993). *The drama of leadership.* London: The Falmer Press.

———. (1995). *Leaders with vision: The quest for school renewal.* Thousand Oaks, CA: Corwin Press.

Stevens, Leonard B. (1996, June). The place of race in America. *Education Week* 15(39), 41, 52.

Stone, Lynda. (1995). Narrative in philosophy of education: A feminist tale of "uncertain" knowledge. In Wendy Kohli, ed., *Critical conversations in philosophy of education* (pp. 173–189). New York: Routledge.

Stotts, Alexandra Lynn. (1993). *Possibilities of liberation in dialogue: A critical interpretation of hooks and Bakhtin (Mikhail Bakhtin).* Unpublished doctoral dissertation, Michigan State University.

Trend, David. (1994). Nationalities, pedagogies and media. In H. A. Giroux & P. McLaren, eds., *Between borders: Pedagogy and the politics of cultural studies* (pp. 225–241). New York: Routledge.

Urch, George E. F. (1968). *The africanization of the curriculum in Kenya.* Unpublished doctoral disseration, University of Michigan at Ann Arbor.

Urdang, Laurence. (1968). *The Random House dictionary of the English language* (college ed.). New York: Random House.

Wallace, Michele. (1995a, October). Art for whose sake? *The Women's Review of Books* 13(1), 8.

———. (1995b, November). For whom the bell tolls: Why America can't deal with Black feminist intellectuals. *The Village Voice* 40(45), 19–24.

Waruingi, Chege B. (1980). *The consumer and the marketing system in a developing country: Kenya.* Unpublished doctoral dissertation, Indiana University, Bloomington.

Weinstein, M. M. (1997, October). 'The bell curve,' revisited by scholars. *The New York Times,* p. A10.

Whitehead, Clive. (1993). Education for subordination? Some reflections on Kilemi Mwiria's account of African education in colonial Kenya. *History of Education* 22(1), 85–93.

Willis, Lucinda Evelyn. (1996). *Womanist Intellectuals: Developing a tradition.* Unpublished doctoral dissertation, University of North Carolina, Greensboro.

Index

Africa, 26, 145, 149, 152, 153, 157, 158, 159, 161, 163–167, 170, 171, 172, 177, 180, 188, 214, 219

Africans, 5, 10, 16, 18, 34, 64, 89, 145, 146, 148–152, 157–170, 172, 173, 176, 177, 179, 182, 185–187, 189, 191, 192, 196, 197, 200, 202–205, 207, 209, 211–214, 219–222, 224

Ali, Shahrazad, 49

Alston, Kal, 89, 90

American nationalism, impact, 14–18. *See also* Assimilation; Standard English

Archdeacon, Thomas J., 14

Arcilla, Renée, 90

Asante, Molefi Kete, 89–90, 215

Assimilation, 9, 14, 15, 16, 28. *See also* American nationalism; Standard English

Babangida, Ibrahim, 146

Baldwin, James, xvii–xviii, 1, 64, 66

Bambara, Toni Cade, 224

Banks, James, 14, 15, 17, 25, 27, 28, 29, 30, 54, 58, 73, 88–89, 115, 118, 119

Baraka, Amiri, 46

Bates, Daisy, 46, 123

The Beecher Report, 213

Belenky, Mary, et al., *Women's Ways of Knowing*, 39, 50, 68, 90

Berry, Mary F., 14

Beyer, Landon, 59, 99, 102, 116, 135

The Binns Report, 213

Bird, Caroline, 60

Black: in-group factions, 35; men, 22, 42, 43, 44, 45, 47, 48, 49, 50, 51, 60, 71, 166, 169, 175; women, 18, 19, 31, 42, 43, 45, 46, 49, 50, 51, 55, 57, 61, 66, 122, 123, 166, 169, 175

Blackness, negation, 24, 32–33, 63–65, 69, 73, 88, 150, 156, 157, 159–166, 168, 169, 172, 184, 222. *See also* Stereotypes

135–137, 139–141; incorporating learner experiences, 114–119; learner engagement, 110–114; multiculturalism, 86–88, 119–125, 210–215; passion, 125–129, 215–218; reconceptualization of knowledge, 95–100; student empowerment, 105–117, 205–210; and student resistance, 117–118
Eshiwani, G. S., 166, 199, 208, 221

Famighetti, R., 144
Fanon, Franz, 40
Feinberg, Walter, 121; and Jonas Soltis, 1, 58, 73
Fordham, Signithia, 56, 65, 73
Fox, Tom, 105, 129
Fraser, Nancy, 87
Freidan, Betty, 60
Freire, Paulo, xvii, xviii, xxi, xxiv, xxv, 21, 24, 25, 27, 29, 31, 36, 55, 64, 66, 68, 70, 77, 79–86, 99, 102, 111, 112, 115, 135, 147, 149, 195, 206, 215–216, 225, 226; and Antonio Faundez, xxi, 21, 27, 32, 36, 59, 84, 102, 112, 115, 195
Fullan, Michael, 140
Fuller, John, 171
Fuss, Diana, 1

Gallop, Jane, 114
Garvey, Marcus, 36, 46
Gates, Henry Louis, 66
Gender socialization, 40–42
Giarelli, James, 98, 99
Giroux, Henry, 73, 87, 97, 98, 111, 115, 122; and Peter McLaren, 28, 36, 47, 73, 99, 195
Goodlad, John, 54
Greene, Maxine, 72
Grossberg, Lawrence, 122
Gustavo, Gutierrez, xvii, xx

Hanh, Thich Nhat, xvii, xx, 215–216
Hansbery, Lorraine, xvii–xviii
Harris, Kevin, 28, 55, 135, 137, 149
Haywood, Chanta, 66, 67
Hegemony, 18, 86, 91, 119, 122, 123, 164, 213
Herrnstein, Richard. J., and Charles Murray, *The Bell Curve*, 24
Hirsch, Eric Donald, 16, 96, 97, 99, 136
hooks, bell, xv–xxi, 1, 5–6, 158, 161, 163, 164, 166, 167, 169–173, 176, 178, 179, 184–186, 188, 189, 192, 193, 195, 198–202, 204–211, 213–217, 219–226; on feminism, 18–19, 60; on internalized classism, 59–61; on internalized racism, 10, 24, 29, 31–37; on internalized sexism, 47–51; on mass media, 6–11; on materialism, 2, 55–61; on social myths, 21–25, 76; on white supremacy, 5–6, 10–16, 24; writing style, 6, 11, 12. *See also* West, Cornel
Houston, Charles, 66
Hurston, Zora Neale, 25
Huxley, Elspeth, 148, 152, 156, 158–160, 162, 163, 166, 167, 169, 174, 177, 178, 187, 188, 190, 204, 208, 211, 212, 214, 221

Jacobson, Jodi, 177
Jan Mohammed, Abdul, 16, 30, 31, 169

Kallet, Arthur, and F. J. Schlink, 171
Keen, Sam, 128
Kenya, xxv, 9, 64, 88, 105, 143–151, 153, 154, 157–160, 162, 165, 169, 170, 172–174, 182, 185, 186, 188–193, 196–199, 201, 202, 206, 208, 209, 211–216, 219, 222, 224–226; classism, 185–188, 222; colonial era, 148, 152, 156–159, 160, 162–

About the Author

NAMULUNDAH FLORENCE is an adjunct faculty member in Fordham University's Graduate School of Education and College of Business. She was born in Kenya.

ISBN 0-89789-564-9

90000>

EAN

9 780897 895644